Southern Witness

Southern Witness

Unitarians and Universalists in the Civil Rights Era

Gordon D. Gibson

For Jacqui, with appreciation for her great gifts.

Gordon Gibson

3/7/15

Bloody Sunday + 50

Skinner House Books and the
Unitarian Universalist History and Heritage Society
Boston

www.skinnerhouse.org

Printed in the United States

Cover design by Kathryn Sky-Peck
Text design by Suzanne Morgan
Author photo by Karen Krogh

print ISBN: 978-1-55896-750-2
eBook ISBN: 978-1-55896-751-9

6 5 4 3 2 1
17 16 15

Library of Congress Cataloging-in-Publication Data
Gibson, Gordon D. (Gordon Davis), 1939-
  Southern witness : Unitarians and Universalists in the civil rights era / Gordon D. Gibson.
     pages cm
  Includes bibliographical references and index.
  ISBN 978-1-55896-750-2 (pbk. : alk. paper)—ISBN 978-1-55896-751-9 (ebook) 1. Unitarian Universalist churches—Southern States—History—20th century. 2. Civil rights movement—Southern States--History—20th century. I. Title.
  BX9833.43.G53 2015
  289.1'7509046—dc23
                                    2014040347

CONTENTS

A NOTE ON LANGUAGE

The alert reader will note that, although civil rights issues in the South in the 1950s and 1960s primarily pertained to the rights of people of color, a majority of the voices in this narrative belong to people of European ancestry. This reflects the membership of Unitarian Universalist congregations in that era and area. Where racial identity is not noted, you should assume that the person quoted or described is White. However, most of those congregations included a number of people of African ancestry, so the text notes their racial identity along with their important contributions.

Although *race* as generally understood is sometimes challenged academically as a flawed and suspect categorization of people, it persists as a category in non-academic conversation. Perhaps because of its flaws, terminology referencing people of African ancestry has shifted repeatedly over many decades and will undoubtedly continue to shift: *colored, negro, Negro, Black, Afro American, African American*, and so on. In this text, I use the capitalized terms *Black* and *White* because I prefer that labels be equal and clear. It was a major step forward when stylebooks moved from *negro* to *Negro*, and I don't want to step back from that. As you read, please translate my *Black/White* choice into terminology that is appropriate and understandable to you. And know that when I quote others' written statements, I have left their terminology as they wrote it, even if it seems anachronistic or offensive.

I refer to "the civil rights movement" because that is the common term for the Black-led drive that sought to reorder society more justly in the 1950s and 1960s. Many people who were immersed in this effort instead called it, even as it happened, "the freedom movement." Looking back at it now, and talking with other veterans of it, they will simply say "the Movement." This usage reflects the reality that it came to be an effort that went far beyond a cup of coffee, a bus seat, a school assignment, or access to the ballot box. It was a critique of the social order and an attempt at a reordering. "The Movement" continued in various forms long after the 1960s. Many people who had been radicalized and introduced to organizing techniques went on to lead or support anti-war, feminist, environmental, LGBT and other progressive change efforts.

For example, the mid-1960s college student rebellions such as the Free Speech Movement at Berkeley typically involved students who had been volunteers in Mississippi in 1964. More recently, Representative Barney Frank, House sponsor of the Dodd-Frank Act to re-regulate financial institutions, was also a 1964 volunteer in Mississippi. Maybe the "civil rights movement" ended its active phase by the late 1960s, but the larger Movement of which it was a part continues to create ripples. Consider this book as a challenge —not to re-live the civil rights movement of the mid-twentieth century—but to join the larger justice-seeking Movement that it helped to create.

PREFACE

Although Unitarian Universalists constituted a tiny sliver of the population in the South during key years of the civil rights movement, they kept popping up in small but often interesting ways in the story of that movement. The movement was not dominated or directed by Unitarian Universalists—far from it—but this small group appears regularly in various roles in and around the civil rights stage. Their story has not been told and it merits being recorded before all memories fade and other records are lost. It may suggest ways that future generations can be of use in the work of making justice visible.

A note about the author: I am a White southerner of slightly contrarian bent. I was born and raised in Louisville, Kentucky. Louisville is on the southern bank of the Ohio River, a river regarded as the dividing line between North and South. Louisville probably could identify with the Midwest, just across the river, but it doesn't. As a child, I sometimes got to accompany my father on business trips around the state. Later, at Yale, I took Professor David Potter's course, The South in American History, in which he remarked that Kentucky was the only state that seceded from the Union after the Civil War was over. I thought back to the many monuments I had seen around Kentucky dedicated to "the Confederate dead" or to this or that military unit of the Confederate States of America, and could remember no Union counterparts. The presidents on both sides of the war had been born in Kentucky, not far apart. The state remained divided during the war, sending troops to both armies, but after the war it looked south. I, however, identified strongly with the tall, angular Kentuckian who as president preserved the Union and freed the slaves.

After college and seminary, I was called, in September 1964, to the ministry of the Theodore Parker Unitarian Church in West Roxbury, Massachusetts. At that time, the Unitarian Universalist Association (UUA) was asking ministers to volunteer for seven- to ten-day stints with the National Council of Churches' Delta Ministry in Mississippi. With authorization from the church's Standing Committee, I volunteered to go. But a few weeks before leaving, the UUA asked me to shift locations and check out a new project in Alabama that Dr. Martin Luther King's Southern Christian Leadership Conference had initiated in a place I had never heard of: Selma. In February 1965, two days after I was ordained and installed in West Roxbury, I headed with my colleague Ira Blalock to Selma. Six days later, I dropped my observer mentality and took part in a demonstration at the Dallas County Courthouse, which resulted in my serving seven days of a five-day sentence for contempt of court.

The Selma experience radicalized and transformed me, as it did other participants. My radicalization was complete a few weeks later, following the Bloody Sunday attack in Selma on nonviolent marchers. Two days after that event, Orloff Miller, a close friend and the minister who guided my wife and me in writing our marriage ceremony, was attacked by White thugs in Selma, who fatally injured Rev. Jim Reeb as they roughed up Orloff and Rev. Clark Olsen.

In August 1965, my wife, Judy, and I visited my parents in Louisville. Their minister at First Unitarian Church of Louisville phoned with the news that Donald Thompson, a Unitarian Universalist minister in Jackson, Mississippi, had been shot. Judy and I offered to take some of my remaining vacation time to drive down to assist the Jackson congregation, and our offer was accepted. Our first experience of Mississippi was a moving introduction to White people of conscience operating in the Deep South.

In 1969, I was called to serve that Jackson congregation. In the wake of Don Thompson's shooting and exile from Mississippi, the membership had shrunk to about twenty-five, but they had money from the sale of their former property and the hope that, with a minister, they might again grow. I am eternally grateful that they were crazy enough to try it and that I was crazy enough to accept their invitation. I served as full-time minister until 1972, and then worked in Jackson for the Equal Employment Opportunity Commission for seven years as an investigator. From 1978 through 1984, I served the Jackson congregation on a part-time basis, and also served the Our Home Universalist Unitarian Church of Ellisville part-time from 1977 through 1984. We went to Jackson hoping to survive, physically and emotionally, during their three years of funding. We fell in love with the place and the people, and stayed fifteen years.

In Jackson, I came to know and work with many veterans of the civil rights movement. I also began to dig more deeply into Universalist and Unitarian history in the South and to collect some of the stories of Unitarian Universalist work during the civil rights era of the 1950s and 1960s. My first systematic attempt to gather material resulted in a twenty-seven-page paper prepared for a ministerial study group in 1982: "Unitarian Universalists and the Civil Rights Movement—What Did We Do, and What Can We Learn from What We Did?" That paper circulated among congregations, along with the Commission on Appraisal's 1983 report, "Empowerment."

I was called to the Unitarian Universalist Fellowship of Elkhart, Indiana, and began my ministry there in January 1985. This was and remains a warm, energetic, and socially aware community. I spent a three-month sabbatical in 2000 crisscrossing the South, delving into church files, and conducting oral history interviews with people who had been active in the civil rights era. Then, after years of hearing anecdotes and stories about the movement, members of the Elkhart congregation urged me to take them to some of the civil rights sites. Judy and I agreed to put together a tour for spring 2004. It was so enthusiastically received that we were prevailed upon to do another in 2005, just before my retirement. These have now morphed into the Living Legacy Project, with leadership for pilgrimages and other events shared among a team of people who have deepened and expanded the experience. The project, which has touched scores of lives, seeks to reimagine the possibilities for social change in the world today by experiencing the depth of human spirit in the civil rights movement. I believe that the Living Legacy Project has challenged and affected more lives than all of my preaching over the years.

As a White Unitarian Universalist southerner who has been changed by his involvement on the edges of the movement, I have felt a personal need to learn and write about other southerners, White and Black, especially those co-religionists touched and radicalized in some way by the movement. The following pages tell their story, as well as the sadder tale of some who resisted change.

This story is sometimes truncated or minimalist because it describes people who were so busy *doing* that they did not stop to record what was being done. In addition, it could feel dangerous to record too much, because one wouldn't want a diary, journal, or letter used as evidence of "subversive activity." This story may not turn up in congregational records because, often, the actors were not acting officially on behalf of the congregation but on behalf of the ideals expressed and explored in that community. The story would be richer and more detailed if we had begun assembling the record twenty or thirty years earlier, before memories had faded and some key actors had passed from the stage. Even with these limitations, it is an amazing story. I still find myself wondering at the courage it took to "do church" in a way that offered such conscientious witness in the South by people living there.

I must be clear that this is not a complete history of southern Universalism and Unitarianism. That is a different book, one that would emphasize the Universalist part of the story more because, until about 1945, a majority of our southern history was Universalist. This book should not be imagined to include every congregation and individual of Universalist, Unitarian, or Unitarian Universalist identity who interacted with the movement. It should not be read as an assertion that Unitarian Universalism was a vital, central part of the movement, because that's nonsense. But I do assert—and these stories demonstrate—that on our good days, we did our part (and sometimes much more) to offer a southern witness.

GENESIS: THE CONTEXT

The South was not "without form and void" when Unitarians and Universalists brought forth new congregations upon that soil. In fact, southerners had well-defined senses of place and self. Some of that sense was defensive. The South owns a regional sense that it's the only part of the United States to know what losing a war feels like, but of course that's really true only of the White South. The South has been characterized and caricatured as an economic and educational backwater, and southerners know this. Some southerners have used these images to their advantage—think of Senator Sam Ervin of North Carolina claiming to be "just an old southern lawyer" as he skillfully grilled witnesses in the Nixon impeachment process—but the images still fester, creating bitterness and something of an inferiority complex.

It is difficult in the twenty-first century to understand, or remember, the extent and intensity of segregation in mid-twentieth-century southern society. Restaurants served either White or Black patrons, although some White restaurants had a window at the back or side where Black people could order takeout. Some service stations had three restrooms, labeled "men," "women," and "colored," and some only two, with none for Black people. City, county, and state parks in the South were designated for use by White or, more rarely, Black people. Even national park areas in the South were segregated; for example, Shenandoah National Park in northern Virginia set aside Lewis Mountain as an area where Black visitors could stay overnight. In Birmingham, Alabama, and almost certainly other places, it was illegal to play an interracial game of checkers.

Some of this segregation was by law. Some was by custom, and the unwritten de facto rules could be as ferociously enforced as the laws. Conscientious Black parents in the South taught their children, sons in particular, to look down and move aside when approaching White people on a sidewalk. A Black man who looked directly and unabashedly at a White woman could be judged guilty of "eyeball rape" and lynched. The fact that lynchings were sometimes photographed—with spectators clearly shown and the photographs sold as postcards—confirms the widely condoned extrajudicial enforcement of racist customs.

Two societies existed in the South—separate, unequal, but intermingling or at least touching at some points. Churches, schools, and funeral homes were either Black or White. Virtually all maids, janitors, and other service workers were Black, their employers and supervisors almost always White. Black communities afforded funeral directors, doctors (if any), lawyers (if any), preachers, and teachers relatively high status, and churches became oases of self-governance. Schools were subject to fiscal control by White school boards, but some Black schoolteachers and administrators retained a degree of autonomy about how their building or classroom functioned. Although southern Black schools typically received only a fraction of the funds and supplies that White schools did, they often had highly motivated and credentialed teachers who challenged and inspired students. And Whites may not have realized that a maid, cook, or janitor was a preacher, choir director, Sunday school director, or leader in a fraternal order or civic association in the evening or on weekends. White southerners had few reasons to be in Black neighborhoods, but Black southerners often spent their working hours in White neighborhoods and establishments, filling clearly circumscribed roles.

It is hard to change law or custom, much less a combination of both. Following the 1962 enrollment of Black student James Meredith at the University of Mississippi—the first step in desegregating this state symbol, resulting in a White riot that killed two people and required the intervention of US marshals and army troops—

distinguished Ole Miss professor James Silver mused about how southern society reacted to challenge and change. As the retiring president of the Southern Historical Association, Silver shared his observations and experience at the 1963 association meeting in a talk titled "Mississippi: The Closed Society." He subsequently expanded the talk to book length. In the book, published in 1964, Silver describes "the closed society":

> For whatever reason, the community sets up the orthodox view. Its people are constantly indoctrinated—not a difficult task, since they are inclined to the accepted creed by circumstance. When there is no effective challenge to the code, a mild toleration of dissent is evident, provided the non-conformist is tactful and does not go far. But with a substantial challenge from outside—to slavery in the 1850s and to segregation in the 1950s—the society tightly closes its ranks, becomes inflexible and stubborn, and lets no scruple, legal or ethical, stand in the way of the enforcement of the orthodoxy. The voice of reason is stilled and the moderate either goes along or is eliminated. Those in control during such times of crisis are certain to be extremists whose decisions are determined by their conformity to the orthodoxy. The likelihood of intelligent decisions is thus being reduced, and eventual disaster is predictable.

As if to confirm what happens to someone who will not conform to the orthodoxy of a closed society, Silver, who had taught at the University of Mississippi for over a quarter of a century and chaired its History Department, became the target of a campaign by the White Citizens Council to have him fired. He took a leave from his position and never returned. He went on to teach at Notre Dame (1965–69) and then the University of South Florida until his retirement in 1982.

Religious as well as secular institutions were pressured to conform in the South in the quarter century following World War II. Some leading Protestant denominations, including the Baptists and the Presbyterians, were still divided along regional lines that dated back to the pre-Civil War era. From time to time, a minister or layperson might verbalize a moderate or cautionary viewpoint as being more Christian than that of hardcore segregation, but many people did not welcome this stance. For example, in January 1963, twenty-eight Methodist ministers in Mississippi issued a statement quoting the Methodist Discipline: "Our Lord Jesus Christ teaches that all men are brothers. He permits no discrimination because of race, color, or creed. 'In Christ Jesus you are all sons of God, through faith' (Galatians 3:26)." Their statement carefully opposed Communism and supported public education. Read with fifty-plus years of hindsight, it seems extraordinarily, even absurdly mild, but it was not considered so in 1963. Inman Moore Jr., one of the signers, reports, "Within a week, three of the ministers were locked out of their churches. Several others were asked to leave as soon as possible. Within six months of the document's publication, twenty of the twenty-eight had left Mississippi." Moore notes that even his own parents did not understand why he would risk his career by signing such a statement.

In an American society that was slowly and often reluctantly changing—desegregating the armed forces, eroding racial covenants that had kept many northern residential neighborhoods segregated, Jackie Robinson breaking the color line in Major League Baseball, the US Supreme Court ruling positively on challenges to segregation—the South felt challenged, besieged, confused. Black southerners knew that the old, accepted ways were wrong, limiting, and un-American. Many knew of decades of work, beginning even before Emancipation, to win and retain rights, but they also faced daily reminders of the dangers, up to and including death, in undertaking such work. There were no safe or easy ways forward. White southerners knew that former patterns were no longer securely in place, but as Professor Silver noted, the dominant White southern response was fierce resistance to change.

This was not a paradise that new Unitarian and Universalist congregations entered. But it was a land that offered both peril and great opportunity. The disturbance of the old ways made a

place—challenging perhaps—for something new. Some southerners, White and Black, had had opportunities during World War II
to see other parts of the country, other parts of the world, and now
came home with altered understandings. Some other Americans,
seeking fresh job opportunities, moved to the South with a job
offer in hand.

Sources

The quotation by James W. Silver comes from page six of his
book *Mississippi: The Closed Society* (New York: Harcourt, Brace
& World, Inc., 1964). For an example of the impact of dedicated
pedagogy on an impoverished community, see the chapter "My
Teachers" in John Oliver Hodges's *Delta Fragments: The Recollections of a Sharecropper's Son* (Knoxville: University of Tennessee
Press, 2013).

GENESIS: A TYPICAL STORY

In *The Mind of the South*, a classic of southern history, W. J. Cash writes a brief account of the "typical" White southern planter. Cash's method of presenting recurring themes and currents makes individual variations stand out. In similar fashion, I will recount a "typical" story of the founding of an outpost of religious liberalism in a city or town of the Deep South.

In this hypothetical municipality—located somewhere in the sweep from Louisiana to just south of suburban Washington, DC, a swath of country roughly encompassing the states that in 1861 had attempted to secede from the Union—there had never been either a Unitarian or a Universalist church.

A handful of Universalist congregations were scattered around the state. Some dated back to the nineteenth century, as White settlement encroached on Indian lands. Others had sprung up due to missionary efforts in the late nineteenth and early twentieth centuries. Rev. Quillen Shinn had made productive missionary forays into the South. Hardy Universalist circuit riders traveling by foot, horseback, or rail served the scattered congregations and sometimes helped to found new ones. But most of the Universalist congregations were in or near small- to medium-sized towns, not in what would become cities.

No Unitarian churches existed in the state. Unitarians had organized in a few coastal cities in the South in the first half of the nineteenth century, but only New Orleans and Charleston retained congregations when the drumbeat of war fell silent in 1865. The American Unitarian Association (AUA)—reluctantly formed in Boston in 1825 as a private membership group for the cautious and tasteful support of disseminating Unitarian ideas to promising areas—never looked upon the southern states with much favor. Enough New England expatriates had settled to form congregations in a few spots, but none thrived for more than a few years.

In 1945, with World War II over, soldiers returned from military service in the far corners of the country and the world. Many of them took advantage of the GI Bill to attend college. Industry, geared up for war production during the early 1940s, shifted to producing consumer goods. Marriages were made, children born, new housing built and sold. This dynamic took place all over the country, but it had special implications for the South. Southerners may have been more insular than other Americans, but World War II had shipped many southern young adults far beyond the shores of the small island of culture where they had spent their first eighteen years. The new increased accessibility to college for all Americans had special impact in the South, where previously higher education had seemed out of reach for many, especially immediately after the Great Depression. Industrial production had traditionally been secondary to agriculture in the southern economy, but as factories were built and distribution systems grew, even agriculture was mechanizing.

In Boston, the AUA staff developed a way to take advantage of expected new growth opportunities following World War II. Created as an association of New England gentlemen, the organization had by the twentieth century become an association of congregations. In the 1930s the humanist-theist controversy sparked theological ferment, and the 1934–36 Commission of Appraisal caused organizational ferment with its report *Unitarians Face a New Age*, calling for the reinvigoration of the Unitarian movement. After the war, the idea emerged to extend Unitarianism by establishing "lay centers in communities where there is no Unitarian church and where there is a sufficient number of individual Unitarians." By 1948, the terminology had shifted slightly, and the first lay center, now called a fellowship, was born in Boulder, Colorado.

Fellowships permitted denominational extension work without the investment of personnel and finances necessary to set up a full-service church. Initially, chartering a fellowship required a minimum of ten members, although many began with significantly more. An office at the AUA focused on creating and then supporting these congregations. Monthly mailings from the Association provided materials they could use for services. Some groups initially met in homes, but most moved fairly quickly to renting space in a public or commercial facility. With small memberships and no professional staff, the fellowships were radically democratic but were sometimes subject to the influence, good or ill, of one or two strong personalities. Nevertheless, the fellowship format seemed a welcome vehicle for the democratic, egalitarian, rational message of Unitarianism. Some fellowships died after months or years of work, but many persisted and even thrived.

The Universalist Church of America (UCA), also having experienced a period of theological ferment and diversification, was cautiously exploring collaborating with the American Unitarian Association. Universalism also made some efforts toward establishing lay-led beachheads in promising but unchurched spots.

Southern cities and towns quickly began to emerge as promising locations for fellowships. Lay-led congregations often emerged in college towns, sometimes closely associated with a campus. Fellowships were often filled with people moving to a new area for employment opportunities in expanding industries. They were populated by some who had long embraced the Unitarian label, but also by some who had just discovered Unitarianism, perhaps responding to an ad by the Unitarian Laymen's League that asked, "Are you a Unitarian without knowing it?" Such conditions existed in many spots across the postwar South.

If we were to interview a typical charter member from one of these congregations, the member might say something like this:

So there we were, circa 1951. Someone from the AUA, I think it was Fellowship Director Munroe Husbands, noticed that six or seven of us here or nearby were members of the Unitarian Church of the

Larger Fellowship. (AUA started the CLF in 1944 to be a "church by mail" for isolated religious liberals.) Munroe wrote to inquire if we were interested in starting a fellowship and asked what prospects we thought a fellowship might have. Several of us said we were interested. He then placed an ad in our local newspaper describing Unitarianism and asking people to respond if they would like to come to an informational and organizational meeting. He set a date to come to town, asking one of us to book a function room at one of the leading downtown hotels. He submitted a couple of more newspaper ads about the meeting at the hotel and encouraged all of us who'd responded from CLF and from the first ad to talk to our friends about the meeting. He got to town a day early and phoned all of us. The evening of the announced meeting arrived, and we were excited to see the sign outside our meeting room saying, "Unitarian Fellowship." Munroe spoke briefly but clearly about Unitarian beliefs and how a fellowship could be organized, and then he answered questions. Almost all of the eighteen people in attendance seemed very interested. After all, we had been living in a society in which the main religious options had been Baptist or Methodist churches, so with our beliefs and our lack of any like-minded institution, we felt more exotic than Catholics or Jews.

We said that night that we wanted to start a fellowship. We agreed to meet again in a week, and two of us volunteered to begin filling out the necessary paperwork. We needed a written charter with a statement of purpose. Munroe left us a sample charter and a sample set of by-laws. We would need to get at least ten people to sign on as members and vote to adopt the charter and by-laws. A week later, we had most of the work done, but we waited a while before sending it in so that we could get a few more names and begin to make plans for holding our first meetings.

That downtown hotel seemed to be a good place to start meeting. Munroe had told us that some fellowships met in members' living rooms, but that the hotel option would be better. It was centrally located, and everyone in town knew where it was. One of us knew the manager and negotiated a good rate to rent that function room on Sunday mornings, pointing out that there wouldn't be a lot of other use for it at that time and that they could rent it again later in the day. We got our first mailing of information from Boston, which included a couple of sermons by famous Unitarian ministers that we could use for our services, along with suggestions for readings and recorded music.

We announced our first service to all the people who had been at any of the meetings or who had sent in their names in response to the ads. Twenty-two people came. We had a portable record player for music, and from the mailing from Boston we had two readings, a prayer, a sermon, and a benediction. We engaged in a lively discussion after the service, which felt odd because that wasn't what any of us had experienced before at church. Three more people said they wanted to become members, but the person who had the membership list hadn't brought it for them to sign.

We continued in similar fashion for several months, meeting every other week. The first two big changes were to start meeting weekly and adding a children's program. The AUA Fellowship Office had told us that including programs for children would be important as we began to attract families. We rented a slightly bigger function room for the adults, because more and more people attended, and we had the children's program in the small function room where we had started. We also asked the hotel to bring in coffee at the end of the service, and we enjoyed having coffee during our discussion period, which was a real highlight for a number of us.

When our membership rose to around fifty, with more and more children attending, we finally decided that the hotel no longer filled our needs. The school board had rented to some other churches, so we negotiated with them for use of the auditorium and two classrooms in an elementary school in the area of town where most of us lived. That worked out fine—well, not really fine, but okay—for a couple more years.

As we conducted more of our own services, we relied less and less on the materials from Boston. We invited interesting local people to speak, as well as many of our members. When the US Supreme Court handed down its 1954 decision in *Brown v. Board of Education*, striking down school segregation, we knew we should address the issue. One of our members gave a sermon called "Simple Justice," and a new young faculty member from the university's Political Science Department shared his thoughts about how long it would take to desegregate our own schools. We don't know how word of this got to the newspaper, but that Wednesday they ran a story about us. They hadn't talked to any of the officers of the fellowship, but they included a list of who they were. The story included some slanted, prejudicial descriptions of Unitarianism. Three things happened right away. Three members never returned to the fellowship. But five new people appeared at the next Sunday service, excited to learn that we existed. And the next Monday, we received a letter from the school board's attorney, cancelling the rental agreement for the following fall.

We spent that summer looking for a place to meet. The Sunday after Labor Day, we were back at the hotel, but they didn't seem happy to see us, even though we now used three rooms. Two months later, a professor from the Negro college in town came to a service and brought her daughter to Sunday school. By the afternoon of that day, our hotel rental had been cancelled. Fortunately, one of us was on board of the YWCA, so we met in that building the following week. Feeling insecure with that arrangement, however, we established a committee to investigate buying a house, preferably one with a living room or living and dining rooms big enough to hold our services. It took two months and some harried fundraising, but we pulled it off.

That was the hardest year of our existence as a fellowship, but in some ways it was our best. Under pressure from the wider community, we became clearer about who we were and what we needed to be about. We achieved more visibility in the community, and even when some of it was intended to be negative, we achieved some positive results. And having our own meeting place, which we had been thinking we would need "someday," was wonderful. We no longer had to box up and move our stuff every week. We didn't have to hold committee meetings in the homes of members. And we could expand our programming.

The first expansion of our programs involved creating a good preschool. All of the fellowship families worried that if they sent their children to one of the existing preschools, which seemed to be located only in churches, the kids would be exposed to religious fundamentalism. Thoroughly sensitive to issues of racial segregation, we knew that all the existing preschools served only one race. So we opened the town's first nonsectarian, nonsegregated preschool. Some university families were delighted to enroll their kids in our school. A couple of families from the small Reform Jewish congregation sent their kids, relieved to avoid Christian indoctrination. Several faculty members from the Negro college, including our visitor at the hotel, enrolled their children.

With a clearer self-definition, we lost a few members but gained more than we lost. Some people experienced pressure at their jobs because of their membership. I think one or two people quit the fellowship but were still fired or forced out of their jobs. A few felt significant social pressure from family and friends. We were sad to see anyone drop out of the fellowship, but mostly, the pressures just made us close ranks. More than ever, our closest friends were other fellowship members.

We surprised ourselves by finding the resources to buy that big old house, and by realizing how much more we could offer than just our Sunday services once we had it. Our membership had now reached about seventy-five, close to the number the AUA required before according church status. We paid someone to work five hours a week as our director of religious education, although actually she worked more hours than that. To relieve the pressure on volunteers, we tried to have someone work about eight hours a week in the office, running the mimeograph and answering phone calls. And we began to talk about having a minister. The AUA's Atlanta regional director encouraged us to work toward this goal, and soon we called a new seminary graduate as our first minister.

Later on, after we established the preschool and called our minister, sit-ins began here as they did all across the South. By that time, many of us were acquainted with some of the established Negro leaders. The local NAACP president had spoken at a couple of our Sunday services. We had also discovered that we were not totally alone in the White community, finding some quiet allies among the Jews, a socially conscious Methodist Sunday school class, a few Episcopalians and Catholics, and some renegade Baptists. We didn't know any of the students who were sit-in leaders, but through the NAACP, which put up some bail money, and through our contacts at the Negro college, including fellowship members now, we heard about some of the meetings called at Negro churches to support the students. Our most adventurous members were among the few Whites who attended those meetings, although not many of us felt comfortable doing so. Our minister was sometimes invited to participate in the meetings and was asked to join the team trying to negotiate with the store owners and city fathers.

A few years later, after our first minister had moved on, we called a new minister. We changed our name to use the word *church* instead of *fellowship*, and began a building program that would move us out of our beloved but overcrowded house. That was 1965, when Bloody Sunday occurred in Selma, Alabama, and Dr. King called for people to come. The board met by phone, agreeing to support the minister in going. Three of us went with him. While in Selma, we were having dinner just down the street when White thugs fatally injured Jim Reeb, a Unitarian Universalist minister. When we returned home two days later, we received some hate mail but a lot of support from our allies, both White and Black. We knew we had done what we as religious liberals needed to do.

After acquiring our new building, a space designed to serve a congregation, we increased our membership still more and continued many of our programs. The preschool drew support from liberal Whites and from the Black community, who recognized it as a way to prepare some of their children to attend public schools with White kids. Speaking of the public schools reminds me that several of us in the church worked with local Black leaders to try to move school desegregation beyond a token, "freedom of choice" system that placed a huge burden on Black families and students.

That was slow work. Meetings on the White side of town were often held at our building.

Over the next few years, the focus gradually shifted. Some of the younger Black leaders in town started participating in the Black Power movement. Although the people we had worked with through the sit-ins and the school desegregation struggle didn't start shaking their fists in the air and shouting, "Black power," they were no longer eager to include us in their meetings and actions. And many of us in the church were now concentrating our social justice efforts on opposing the war in Vietnam. Some of the women who had been the real backbone of our best social justice work—not necessarily the people who got up and spoke at public meetings, but the ones who raised money, organized events, made phone calls, and so on—wanted their own turn to experience social change. Feminist study groups met, and we soon realized that some of the wording in our nice, new hymnal was not gender inclusive.

Many of us were confused and conflicted about the issue of the Black Affairs Council in the Unitarian Universalist Association (UUA). On one hand, we had been working so hard on integration that hearing calls for Black self-determination, which sounded a lot like separatism, seemed odd. Some of us thought, "That's just what we've been fighting against the last ten or fifteen years." Others thought that when you really got down to it, we had been working all along for Black self-determination. Whatever we had been able to accomplish had involved following and supporting Black leadership. So in 1970, after about a year of this confusion and conflict, the UUA said, "We can't afford to fully fund the Black Affairs Council." They also decided that they couldn't afford district staff and a lot of the support services we had enjoyed. We drifted into being less involved with issues of race, less involved with the UUA, and more focused on just keeping our own church going.

We experienced some tough times. Our religious education enrollment faltered, and in some years membership stagnated. Some marriages in the congregation didn't hold together. Some people blamed that on feminism—if they were complaining about it, they would call it "women's lib"—but I think it was due to the restlessness and experimentation both men and women experienced. Anyway, we seemed to have lost the energy and social focus of our early years. That's the story of how we got started. Those were exciting times. Our congregation sometimes felt like an oasis of freedom in a desert of magnolia-scented repression. That freedom at times felt scary, but mostly it was energizing.

• • •

In reality, across the South no congregational story fully fit the typical pattern. Local conditions and individuals created rich variations.

Sometimes the congregation had clear dedication, strong leadership, and a programmatic commitment to confronting injustice. In many instances, while the congregational context made action possible, it was the ingenuity and energy of individuals that produced change. When researching these stories, often the congregational record formed by board minutes, newsletters, and reports to church headquarters in Boston is muted, and the primary or only voice is that of individual memory.

We will start in Virginia, move down the Atlantic seaboard, and then proceed westward.

Sources

Researching this chapter involved hearing many stories and reading many files. Other important resources include works by Laile Bartlett, especially *Bright Galaxy: Ten Years of Unitarian Fellowships* (Boston: Beacon Press, 1960). In addition, Holley Ulbrich's *The Fellowship Movement: A Growth Strategy and Its Legacy* (Boston: Skinner House Books, 2008) offers perceptive reflections on fellowships in general and the South in particular.

NORFOLK, VIRGINIA

The Universalists had an organized presence in the Norfolk area well before the Unitarians. The Virginia Convention of Universalists met in Portsmouth in 1836, and in 1848 Universalists led by Rev. Hope Bain organized churches in Norfolk and Portsmouth. Between 1848 and the outbreak of the Civil War, these churches were served by Bain, Edwin Lake, and Alden Bosserman. All three ministers were loyal to the Union. None of the churches survived the war.

In 1887, organized Universalism returned to Norfolk with the founding of the First Universalist Church of Norfolk. The founding minister was Joseph Jordan, who in 1889 became the first person of African ancestry to be ordained by the Universalists. The church had an educational outreach and provided schooling to scores of Norfolk's young Black people. It also birthed a satellite congregation in Suffolk. Following Jordan's death in 1901, the Norfolk church and school shrank and finally disappeared, but the Suffolk work continued.

Thomas E. Wise, who had worked with Jordan in Norfolk, was ordained in 1895. With support from Quillen Shinn and other Universalists, money was raised to support the church and school in Suffolk, and Wise also founded a third effort at Ocean View. In 1904, feeling waning Universalist support, Wise resigned, joined the African Methodist Episcopal (AME) Church, and took eight members of the Norfolk church with him.

Joseph Fletcher Jordan (not related to Joseph Jordan) and Mary Jordan were deeply religious. Joseph had served as pastor to AME,

AME Zion, and Presbyterian congregations, but both he and Mary
had struggled with doubts. A friend sent the couple a book by Universalist minister Edwin Lake, who had once served in Norfolk,
and its arguments impressed them. Upon hearing Universalist
missionary Quillen Shinn preach in the Durham, North Carolina,
courthouse in 1902, they enthusiastically embraced Universalism.
During the 1903–04 academic year, Joseph studied Universalism
at St. Lawrence University. In 1904, he and Mary moved to Suffolk
and took up the work Wise had just abandoned. Under their leadership, the church and especially the school flourished. By 1911,
the Jordan-led school had served fourteen hundred pupils (even
those who could not pay the five-cents-per-week tuition), and it
earned praise from both Black and White leaders of the community. Mary Jordan died in 1916, Joseph Fletcher Jordan in 1929.
The Suffolk school continued under the leadership of their daughter, Annie B. Willis. Despite the always-minimal nature of support
from the wider Universalist movement, by the late 1930s, national
Universalists felt free to dictate a shift from schooling to social
services. In 1949, the new Universalist Service Committee facili-
tated a renewed focus on education. But the Unitarian Universalist
merger again shifted priorities, and financial support shrank, ending in 1969. Annie Willis died in 1977, and the last of the school
programs ended in 1984.

Unitarian organizing efforts between 1912 and 1918 failed to
establish a continuing congregation in Norfolk but did provide
a platform for a reorganized congregation in 1930. Robert W.
Sonen's service from 1939 to 1944 is remembered as a high point.
In contrast, Frank Glenn White's brief ministry (September 1945
to January 1946) constituted a low: News stories describe members' objections to White advocating free love; his letter of resignation mentioned differences over "racial and economic issues."
After White moved to New York City, Norfolk area papers carried
notices that he and "Miss Anne Anderson, 23, colored woman,
and a recent USO worker in Norfolk" planned to be married.

In the early 1950s, the life of the congregation took a turn for
the better during the service of Aubrey C. Todd. Long-term mem-

bers recall that some newcomers became members during this period. When Black people started attending services occasionally and even became members, some White members who were "religiously liberal but socially Virginian" departed. But a few like Elise Green (who described her family as "always in Virginia, back to Pocahontas") stayed on, becoming mainstays. Green commented that the exit of racists began before Virginia's school crisis, and that the crisis brought new people in, some of whom became long-term church members and some of whom left when the excitement died down.

The US Supreme Court had in 1954 and 1955 announced its landmark decisions about school desegregation. In Virginia and other southern states, these rulings triggered efforts by the White political and business establishment to prevent, subvert, or circumvent change. For example, Virginia empowered its governor to close any schools that desegregated. James Brewer encountered this situation when he was called to Norfolk in 1956. Long-term member Phil Caminer recalls public opinion initially being about two to one in favor of school closings. With the approval of the church board, Brewer worked with others to organize the Norfolk Committee for Public Schools (NCPS), which engaged business and civic leaders to make the point that public education was essential to maintaining the city's economic well-being. A congregational vote overwhelmingly supported this work. Ultimately, Caminer says, public opinion swung to two to one opposing school closings, with a lot of credit due to Brewer and the NCPS. An out-of-town reporter's question to Elise Green reveals the centrality of the Unitarian Church of Norfolk to the process: "How did you get so interested? Or are you a Unitarian?"

People from the community were attracted to the church, and people in the church felt empowered to act in the community. Bill Price, a high-ranking navy officer in the Norfolk Naval Shipyard, and his wife were attracted to the church. Betty Moore, who had moved with her husband from New England, went from being the local host for the television show *Romper Room* to starting the first integrated nursery school in Norfolk. Dot Attaway, a teacher at

Maury High School, worked with other teachers after school integration to create a special American studies course so Black and White students could learn with each other the parts of history they had each been denied during segregation.

Members of the congregation report that, in the wake of dealing with issues of race in the 1950s and 1960s, during the ministries of James Brewer and James Curtis, the congregation dealt with the wave of issues that followed: women's issues, the Vietnam war, LGBT issues, and so on. Phil Caminer opines, "We became the radical church. If anything was happening in Norfolk, it was happening at the UU church." Ron Buck says, "This church most of the time was ahead of the wave."

Sources

A 1982 congregational history by Willard Frank and his five chapters in *Darkening the Doorways: Black Trailblazers and Missed Opportunities in Unitarian Universalism*, Mark D. Morrison-Reed, ed. (Boston: Skinner House Books, 2011) provided data on the early Universalist and Unitarian efforts in the Norfolk area. Morrison-Reed shared material on Frank Glenn White from Willard Frank. The online *Encyclopedia Virginia* (www.encyclopedia virginia.org) provided some detail on school desegregation. Material from UUA files and from the church and church members proved helpful. Elise Green, Phil Caminer, and Ron Buck gave oral history interviews on March 18, 2000.

LYNCHBURG, VIRGINIA

The First Unitarian Church in Lynchburg, Virginia, dates back to 1913, and so has a longer history than many more southerly congregations that began in the 1940s or later. But by the beginning of the civil rights era, the church had not grown into a large and thriving enterprise. It did have a solid, visible church building in the heart of the downtown area.

Margaretta Harper, the oldest member in the church when she was interviewed in 2000, remembers moving to Lynchburg in the 1930s as a young bride. Because she found some old women "still fighting the Civil War," she didn't feel very welcome in the community. And the Unitarian Church, although counting a prominent family among its founders, had a reputation in the community as "weirdos and Communists." A charming and dignified minister, Edwin Slocum, had achieved for them a degree of acceptance, but it was still very different from her hometown of Weston, Massachusetts, where the Unitarian Church was *the* church, except for the Catholic church attended by the servants.

In the 1950s, without a minister, the congregation turned to a talented and skilled member for leadership. Sidney Freeman, a professor at Sweet Briar College, served for five years as a lightly compensated lay leader. When he announced in 1957 that he was resigning to formally become a Unitarian minister, the congregation entered a period of lay leadership with occasional visiting ministers and many guest speakers from the community and nearby colleges. That year, the congregation reported having eighteen to twenty-five attendees at a 10 a.m. discussion group, and twenty-five to forty-five at the 11 a.m. service, held October through May. The 1956–57 budget was $1,991.50, including $605 for the lay leader and guest speakers.

In September 1958, the Unitarian Church, chaired by the redoubtable Lucy Crawford, a professor of philosophy at Sweet Briar, voted unanimously to make its building available for meetings of the Lynchburg chapter of the Virginia Council on Human Relations. The leader of the council, Ken Morland, a Baptist layperson, remembers being turned down for meeting space in every other White institution in town. When efforts were made to form a local American Civil Liberties Union chapter, the church was available as well. Margaretta Harper recalls that the church also was open to hosting meetings of Planned Parenthood. As she put it, it was "the only place to meet."

But these were not the congregation's first or only steps in matters of race. A congregational history reports that in 1944, a group of students from Randolph-Macon Woman's College used the building as a meeting place to "confer with two Negro leaders." In 1955, Lucy Crawford announced at the church's annual meeting that she had been invited to deliver the baccalaureate address at a Black school in Amherst County. Church members responded very positively. The chair of the meeting then asked whether a Negro could join the church. "The assent was so clearly in the affirmative that no formal vote was taken," according to the minutes of the meeting.

On December 14, 1960, over ten months after the sit-ins began in Greensboro, North Carolina, four White and two Black students sat in at Lynchburg's Patterson's Drug Store. One of the White students was Mary Edith Bentley, a senior music major at Randolph-Macon, who was serving as organist at the Unitarian Church. Twenty-five years later, she reported this in the Alumnae Bulletin:

> How truly naïve we were when we sat down at the lunch counter that day. The newspaper and other people often credited us with deep, profound sorts of planning that we

never participated in. I had gone down that day with Rebecca Owen, my classmate, and our black friends . . . , with the intention of just telling Mr. Patterson that he really was mistaken with the policy of not seating blacks. . . . But he just wouldn't give us an audience. . . . We all said, well, let's just sit down and then see what he does. . . . Mr. Patterson did come, huffing and puffing, and gave us his word . . . if we didn't leave, he was going to have us arrested for trespassing. The police did take us away in the paddy wagon, we did have a trial, and you know the rest.

Part of "the rest" is that she served twenty days of the thirty-day sentence before being released early due to good behavior.

Tom Gilpatrick taught at Sweet Briar, starting in 1959, and both he and his wife, Jean, were involved in academically based efforts at interracial understanding, such as the Four College Student Group and the Danforth Associates. Jean joined the Unitarian Church in 1962, and Tom became a member a few years later. Jean recalls regular lunches with Dr. Clarissa Wimbush, the first Black female dentist in Virginia, during which they checked on the implementation of desegregated service at the Peck's Department Store restaurant. When the Gilpatricks ate there as a family, Black staff members brought four roses to their table and gave their children free ice cream—a thank you for the Gilpatricks' support of desegregation. In 1968, Jean, who later served as a Unitarian Universalist minister, was a White faculty member at Virginia Seminary, a historically Black institution. When Martin Luther King Jr. was assassinated, Jean posted a note of condolence on the bulletin board. She was concerned that she would face some hostility after this event. She was reassured when, at the end of the year, she was given an "Honorary Negro" card.

Greta Worstell Crosby served as part-time minister from 1962 to 1966. She had earned a law degree at Harvard but decided that the ministry better fit her values and interests. After graduating from Meadville Lombard Theological School, she worked briefly for Beacon Press in Boston and then began serving the congregation in Utica, New York. She married Robert Crosby in January 1961, and later that year, he was transferred by General Electric to Lynchburg. She began her service to the congregation in May 1962. Her ministry strengthened the church's programs, but she also challenged both the wider Lynchburg community and the congregation.

On March 10, 1963, the *News* published Greta's lengthy letter addressing issues involved in a high-profile rape case in which a Black man had been convicted and sentenced to die. She expressed her legal training and her religious values well. On advice of the congregation's board, she had signed only her name, but her position with the church was well-enough known that the congregation took some heat from those offended by questions she raised about true equality before the law, capital punishment, and conditions for an insanity defense. At the annual meeting of the congregation on May 26, there was an unavailing motion to dismiss her as minister. The congregational leadership held meetings in the fall to hear complaints and statements of support, and ultimately to bring the minister, complainants, and supporters together. Later accounts suggest that both church and minister emerged wiser and mellowed from dealing with these issues.

Crosby was among the Unitarian Universalists active and holding offices in the Lynchburg chapter of the Virginia Council on Human Relations. At times, she criticized the council for being insufficiently engaged as a change agent. At one point, she called the council "only a tea and cookie outfit." Bernice Hill, a Black teacher, responded, "Where else can we have tea and cookies together?"

Lynchburg was far less threatening than some Deep South cities and towns. And members of the First Unitarian Church did not stake out extreme positions. Yet one member, Faye Bennett, remembers that some of her co-workers at the General Electric facility would mockingly sing "We Shall Overcome" when they saw her at work. She attributed their behavior to her association with the church rather than because of anything she herself had done.

Sources

This congregation published an excellent history in 1990, *Another History of the First Unitarian Church, Unitarian Universalist, Lynchburg, Virginia*, written by Mary Frances Williams. Interviews with Margaretta Harper, Faye and Gene Burnett, Jean and Tom Gilpatrick, Ken Morland, and Bev Cosby on March 20 and 21, 2000, filled in many details.

CHARLOTTE, NORTH CAROLINA

The Charlotte congregation represented an early start in post-war Unitarian growth. In 1946, a small group of religious liberals had coalesced sufficiently to ask the AUA for assistance. With leadership and guidance from Lon Ray Call of the AUA staff, the Unitarian Church of Charlotte was established on November 16, 1947, with eighty-two members. John H. Morgan served as the first minister, from 1948 to 1951. Edward Cahill was called as the second minister, serving from 1951 to 1957, after which he moved to Atlanta.

Ed Cahill found in place at the church a provision requiring a prospective member to make application and be approved by the board, a practice the AUA Extension Department explained was a protection against a church being taken over by "Jehovah's Witnesses or Communists." Ed thought its effect could be racist so launched the congregation into a year's study of the policy and alternatives to it. On Sunday evening, May 16, 1954, the congregation voted, with only four members dissenting, to adopt a membership policy explicitly stating that "the doors of the Charlotte Unitarian Church are open to all men, women and children of this community who wish to enjoy and practice religion dedicated to individual freedom of belief. Neither race nor color of skin nor previous religious affiliation matters at all, for our concern is solely with the individual." Local newspapers the next day reported this vote, and the May 17 afternoon edition also carried the story of the Supreme Court's *Brown v. Board of Education* school desegregation decision. Ed Cahill believed that this decision affected the

Charlotte community by pointing up the segregation of the other churches.

Because of his Unitarian theology, Ed Cahill had been excluded from membership in the all-White Protestant minister's association. At the invitation of the Black Ministerial Alliance, he attended their meetings, participated in their discussions, and was about to join that body when a White Episcopalian colleague reported to him that he had persuaded the White Protestant group to join with the Black group. Ed's prospective membership was the greatest sticking point. So that he would not impede the formation of the first integrated ministers' group in North Carolina, Ed chose not to join the Black group.

In commenting on how work proceeded in that era, Ed Cahill reports,

> Most of the work in a city like Charlotte at that time, the early 50s, had to be done with individuals and with ad hoc groups. I injected myself into as many of the community organizations as I could, and threw my weight around, to the degree that I had any, towards opening up communication with the parallel organizations in the Black community. At that time, the United Nations Association, the National Conference of Christians and Jews, and the Foreign Policy Association were segregated. In order to combat this, we organized a new group called the Joint Council of International Affairs. This group was organized from the outset on an integrated basis, and I was elected its first chairman. We conducted significant public meetings through several years, bringing to Charlotte the most progressive speakers in the field of international affairs to address thoroughly integrated audiences. The highlight of our meetings was when Mrs. Roosevelt came, having previously refused to address the United Nations Association because it was segregated.

Cahill's description of how Charlotte's public library came to be desegregated provides another example of informal and behind-the-scenes work:

> A group of us organized a weekly luncheon meeting in the private room of a restaurant where various individuals came—the librarian, social workers, journalists, labor leaders, progressive liberal businessmen. In an off-the-record way we shared with each other developments that were happening in the city in all areas. This was a White group to be sure, because the restaurant was completely segregated, but all of us had long and intensive communication with the leadership of the Black community. Before and immediately after the Supreme Court school desegregation decision of May, 1954, the library was about to embark on a fundraising drive and a new building program. We met with the librarian, and through him we met with the library board as individuals only. We confronted the board with this kind of proposition, in a sense I suppose you could say it was a kind of blackmail. We told them that we would refrain from any public exposure of the library as a segregated institution *if* they would guarantee that when the new library was built and opened it would be opened on the first day on a completely desegregated basis. We received, after long contemplation on their part, a full statement of cooperation with our purposes and a guarantee that the library would be integrated, which it was, when the new library was built a short time later.

The congregation supported the efforts in which their minister was involved. He exchanged pulpits with Black ministers. He asked professors from historically Black Johnson C. Smith University to speak to the congregation. Black people were invited to and attended services, forums, and discussion groups, but only two or three became members.

Sidney Freeman was called in 1957 to succeed Ed Cahill. Freeman came to the ministry by an unusual path. Holding degrees from the University of Wisconsin, Bowling Green State, and Cornell, he had been teaching speech and drama at Sweet Briar College. While working on his PhD at Cornell, he had become interested and then active in the Unitarian Church in Ithaca. During his time at Sweet Briar, he was asked by the Unitarian Church in Lynchburg to serve as a lay minister. Subsequently, on the basis of his extensive academic work and his six years' experience in Lynchburg, Freeman was granted ministerial fellowship by the AUA. His thirty-one-year service in Charlotte was his only ministerial settlement.

Arriving in Charlotte, Freeman found in place a monthly program called Town Meeting, in which a prominent person would be invited to speak to the church. Rufus Perry, the new president of Johnson C. Smith University, spoke at one of the first meetings after Freeman's arrival. As the two talked after the session, Perry said that he had only one White instructor and was working to further integrate the faculty, perhaps as a prelude to integrating the student body. He then asked Freeman if he might like to teach part-time. The next day, he invited Freeman to the campus to sign a contract. Over the years, Freeman taught English, his undergraduate major, and then speech.

Students at Johnson C. Smith led the sit-ins in Charlotte in 1960. Charles Jones, a student and the key leader, invited Sid Freeman to join them. At first, he was the only White face in the crowd. (The Charlotte police chief, Jesse James, called Freeman in and confided, "I'm totally neutral on this, but you realize that your White face sure sticks out in that crowd." James was unusual in providing considerable security for those sitting in.) Catherine McIntire, a church member and a reference librarian, told Freeman that one of the police officers assigned to escort those sitting in came to the reference desk to learn more about this White guy participating in the sit-ins, who some people said was a minister. She loaded the officer up with Unitarian Universalist information.

Others from the congregation also participated. If some felt distress about the minister and others sitting in, they did not speak up. Once, three women from the church dressed in full southern belle garb, including Jan Karon and Lucy Ross, took part in a sit-in.

After the lunch counters and hotel dining rooms had been desegregated, Dr. Reginald Hawkins, a local Black dentist, raised the issue of Charlotte Memorial Hospital's segregation. Hawkins had fashioned signs and sandwich boards that people carried or wore while picketing outside the hospital. A well-established member of the congregation phoned Freeman and warned, "I will not have my minister picketing as if he were some union organizer trying to change things that don't have to be changed that way." The person left the church. Eventually, behind-the-scenes work, including that of church member Dr. Carlton Watkins, augmented by the picketing and federal laws, brought about desegregation of the hospital.

Not every move to end segregation was large and dramatic. Sid Freeman recalls with some amusement,

The least flap came in integrating the theaters. I had a good close friend, Bob Schrader, who owned the Visulite Theatre, which was the art theater. The film version of "Hamlet" with Lawrence Olivier—no one in town would show it except at the Visulite. The owner told me he'd like to integrate the theater. I said, "Great, man. What do you have in mind?" He said, "Can you get together ten or twelve students from Johnson C. Smith—you know, nice kids. I'll give you comps to come see the show." I said, "That's an offer we can't refuse." So we did. We decided, of course, that we were not going to sit in a group. We came in in twos and threes. Nobody seemed to bat an eye as we were coming in and sitting down. I think Bob Schrader was disappointed. He loved publicity, and it didn't generate much.

Thanks to some Lutherans, Presbyterians, and other mainline ministers, the Charlotte Christian Ministers Association was broadening its scope to be both interfaith and interracial by the time Sid Freeman arrived in Charlotte. Upon reorganization, its first executive committee included two Black ministers, two priests, the rabbi, and Freeman, who was made secretary. When major school desegregation commenced in Charlotte, this clergy group was asked to provide a presence during lunch hour in the high schools.

Carlton and Charlotte Watkins

Dr. Carlton Watkins, a White, North Carolina-born pediatrician, opened his practice in Charlotte in 1946 with an integrated waiting room. He was the only attending pediatrician at Good Samaritan Hospital, the oldest hospital for Black patients in the country. Carlton's wife, Charlotte, was an active volunteer with the YWCA, public schools, and other agencies and institutions. Charlotte and Carlton joined the Unitarian Church of Charlotte two or three years after its founding in 1947.

"YWCA volunteer" doesn't sound tremendously adventurous today, but it could be an adventure in segregated 1940s southern towns. Charlotte reports,

> When we first came here in 1946, before we had any children, I went to the YWCA and volunteered. I started working with Y-Teen clubs in a low-income neighborhood and a low-income high school. I still see some of those girls from time to time; of course they have grey hair and grandchildren now. I was camp nurse for several years and we would take Black and White girls from Virginia, North and South Carolina—believe it or not in 1946—to a camp near Hendersonville. One year a whole group of us set out, I think maybe in a small bus, the Ku Klux Klan in their garb followed us in cars all the way from the YWCA to the county line.

Carlton worked within the hospital system to end segregation. In addition to his work at Good Samaritan Hospital, he was chairman of the Pediatrics Department at Charlotte Memorial, the area's charity hospital. Upon completion of a new addition in the spring of 1964, he set up the four nurseries to receive both Black and White infants as they were born, filling up the first nursery, then the second, and so on, on a nonsegregated basis. Then he took his first-ever vacation, a month away. On his return, he realized that the nurseries were again segregated. He discovered that the head of Obstetrics had ordered re-segregation. Carlton presented the hospital administration with an ultimatum: "You can either accept my resignation, or you can go back to the way it was before I went on vacation." The nurseries desegregated again. He also joined with three or four other physicians to desegregate the county medical society, resulting in its expulsion from the segregated state medical society.

Both Carlton and Charlotte Watkins actively engaged in working to make the schools and PTAs more inclusive, which included ending the practice of Protestant ministers praying and giving sermons at PTA meetings, and, most important, bringing the separate Black and White PTAs together at the local and state levels in 1969. In 1970, as vice president of the Southern Area on the National PTA, Charlotte Watkins ended segregation in the southern region.

Believing that her PTA work gave her credentials to serve on the school board, Charlotte ran in 1962 but lost due to a whispering campaign suggesting that, as a Unitarian, she wasn't a Christian. She says, "They portrayed me as the Antichrist."

Carlton Watkins served six years on the school board, just as the issue of comprehensively desegregating the Charlotte-Mecklenburg schools was coming to a head. Some of his partners in the pediatric clinic were unhappy with his visible and outspoken position on school desegregation. Carlton suffered a heart attack during the time the board was working on planning desegregation; in addition to a full medical practice, he was spending lunch hours and evening time devising his own desegregation plan.

Ultimately, competing plans were presented in federal court. Carlton remembered the chairman of the school board leaning back from the front row to say, "Carlton, you're liable to be run out of the community after you present your plan." Carlton responded, "Well, if the community wants to run me out of town because of presenting a plan that's reasonable, I want to get out of town."

Charlotte Watkins turned down the opportunity to serve as president of the National PTA because Carlton was recovering from his heart attack. She served on President Nixon's cabinet committee on desegregated education, the only woman and the only Democrat on that body. And she did extensive work with the PTA throughout the South. In 1970, she flew to Birmingham to speak to a joint conference between the Black PTA and the White PTA. She was driven from the airport to the City Club, where the mayor of Birmingham met with her. He wanted to know what she was going to say to "his people." She handed him an outline of her opening address about change and why change must come. He said it was okay, "It's time." Then he presented her with the key to Birmingham. She later asked the woman who had driven her from the airport, "Now, what if he hadn't liked what I was going to say?" The driver replied, "I would now be taking you back to the airport."

During this era, Charlotte, through the National PTA, received a $64,000 grant from the US Department of Health, Education, and Welfare to conduct human relations workshops to prepare parents, teachers, and youth representatives for integration. The grant covered North and South Carolina, Georgia, Florida, Tennessee, and Alabama. She was amazed at the number of times she heard White parents say to Black parents as they discussed the issues, "I didn't know you wanted the same thing for your kids as we do."

Even in retirement in 2000, the Watkinses engaged with the broader community and its issues. Charlotte reported that they belonged to a group called Bridge Builders, sponsored by Mecklenberg Ministries. Initially, six teams of Black and White people from a variety of congregations met, but after six years, the team the Watkinses sat on was the only one still meeting. The program involved visiting one another's churches and having dinner together once a month in each other's homes. At the first meeting, as everyone introduced themselves, one Black participant said, "Well, I can tell you one thing. I don't trust any of you White people but Dr. Watkins." Charlotte opines, "I think she trusts the rest of us now."

Although sometimes the breadth and inclusiveness of Unitarian Universalist theology were off-putting to people from other traditions, that theology occasionally created a bridging role. Freeman remembers being invited to Jackson, Mississippi, by Martin Luther King Jr.:

After Martin Luther King delivered the Ware Lecture at the General Assembly he and I spoke. He remembered my name from that, and I got invited to a gathering in Jackson that he called over something, and I can't even remember what the something was. It was a small gathering of clergy, and it was to back up some of the local clergy on some local issue. We were milling and greeting and he said, "Let's all sit down." He leans over to me and says, "Aren't you that Unitarian I met at your General Assembly?" I said, "Yes, I am." He said, "You pray. You won't offend anybody."

In reflecting on his active engagement in the Charlotte community's issues, especially racial justice issues, Sid Freeman in 2000 opined that his activism did not bring in Black members in large numbers, but it did pull in some Whites of conscience. He felt that it helped immensely when the congregation's Open Door School began operation. "We were trusted," he said, so people believed that the school's doors really were open to all.

Founded in 1966 as an integrated preschool, Open Door operated in the congregation's education facilities. It encouraged enrollment of children of all races, religions, economic levels, ethnic origins, and abilities, and supported that aspiration with scholarship funds. According to its website, "Open Door School strives to guard the dignity of each individual so that children feel free to explore, question, experiment and play. The School encourages children to work on resolving conflicts peacefully, to cooperate rather than compete, and to accept and honor the differences among us." A 2000 survey indicated that the Charlotte church was one of only ten Unitarian Universalist congregations in the United States or Canada then sponsoring a school.

Sue Riley and her husband arrived in Charlotte in August 1961, due to her husband's job transfer by Celanese Corporation. She quickly became involved in religious education, and she also joined in the picketing of segregation at Charlotte Memorial Hospital, which she found moving but scary. A few years later, she sparked the creation of the Open Door School as an integrated, creative, nonsectarian preschool. In the early years, she heard that the priest from a nearby Catholic church recommended Open Door School to parents in his parish as a place where their children would not be proselytized. The school also actively recruited in a nearby Black neighborhood. Open Door, which started with thirty-five or forty children, was serving one hundred children thirty-five years later and was even more firmly connected with the church.

MONROE, NORTH CAROLINA

The story of the All Souls Chapel in Monroe, North Carolina, could be told very simply: Aspects of its story are similar to many fellowships across the country, and then, sadly, it closes its doors for good. But a closer look at the history reveals fascinating elements that are utterly unique.

Monroe, south and east of Charlotte, lies in the Carolina piedmont region between the Atlantic coast and the mountains. This small town incorporated in 1843 to serve as the Union County seat. In the 1920s, when the population was only about 6,100, there were, according to one journalist, "five churches, four Republicans, one pool hall, and one whorehouse." Jesse Helms Sr. served as assistant police chief in the 1940s and later as fire chief. Jesse Helms Jr., the late US senator, recalled his first-grade teacher as his "favorite unreconstructed Confederate." But, like many small towns, it boasted prominent families.

J. Ray Shute came from one of these families. He grew up Methodist in one of Monroe's finest White homes, with memories of Black playmates, the sons of the family's cook. His family had not moved more than twenty miles during the past eight generations. With family interests in cotton gins, brickyards, warehouses, and stores, Ray Shute became the central figure in local economic development during and after World War II and served in various offices, including chair of the school board, chair of the county commission, state senator, and mayor.

Shute was elected mayor of Monroe in 1947. At that time, he was part of a discussion group of liberals that met weekly at the local radio station. Twelve members of that group, including Shute, joined the Charlotte Unitarian Church in August 1948, and then formed a fellowship in Monroe and affiliated with the AUA that October.

"All Souls' Chapel in Monroe was the first permanent structure erected to house a Unitarian Fellowship. This was in 1949; and at that time it was the smallest city in the world having such a Fellowship," the *Union Mail* reported in 1956. By the time the article appeared, other facilities had been added: parish hall, children's chapel, museum, swimming pool, and kindergarten. These buildings were erected on Shute family property and remained legally theirs, although unreservedly made available to be "administered by the congregation."

Ray Shute had rapidly become a highly committed Unitarian, devoting resources of money and time to his faith, but he was active not only in Union County. By early 1949, he had become a vocal advocate for the lay-led fellowship idea within Unitarianism and an advocate for Unitarianism in the form of fellowships across the country. UUA files include reports he sent to Munroe Husbands in the Boston Fellowship Office after visiting existing and prospective fellowships in North Carolina, South Carolina, Georgia, Alabama, and Arkansas, and also South Dakota, Utah, California, Oregon, Washington, and Alaska. By early 1956, Shute was serving on the board of the Unitarian Service Committee "to bring about closer relations between it and the denomination."

With Shute's support and guidance, the congregation grew. In April 1952 President Byron Williams could report twenty active local members and an enrollment of fifteen in religious education. All Souls Chapel sponsored the Monroe Association for the UN, which included leadership from a Catholic priest and the choir director of First Baptist Church. Local offices and positions members of the fellowship held then included city clerk, chairman of the county hospital board, and county librarian. Seven members had attended the previous summer's Blue Ridge Institute (now Southeastern Unitarian Universalist Summer Institute), and four, the May Meetings (now General Assembly).

One of the issues eating at J. Ray Shute was segregation. In 1955, Governor Luther Hodges called for "voluntary segregation" as an alternative to following the US Supreme Court's recent ruling to end school segregation. Ray Shute wrote letters to the editors of at least two area newspapers arguing, from the Declaration of Independence and the Constitutions of the United States and of North Carolina, that equality is a cornerstone of democracy. The letter moved to a religious argument and concluded calling for citizens and the governor to "courageously, religiously, democratically confront this problem." Shute worked with several other Whites and a dozen or more Blacks to organize the Union County Council on Human Relations. When the council announced itself to the world during Brotherhood Week of 1956, it projected moderation, saying "no effort will be made to reform society, to radically fight for immediate upheavals and revolutionary changes." Its prime goal was to have "opportunities for discussion and fact-finding" that would involve both racial groups.

One of Ray Shute's important Black co-workers in this matter was Robert F. Williams, who had been away from his hometown for jobs, military service, and college, but who was now back and newly elected to head the local branch of the NAACP. The Union County branch membership had dwindled, and the handful of longtime members let this articulate and opinionated man of about thirty take the reins. Williams already had quite a resume, including early discharge from both the army and the marine corps due to resistance to arbitrary and racist authority. He had published the article "Someday, I'm Going Back South" in the Detroit issue of the Communist Party's *Daily Worker*, and had met Langston Hughes, long one of his heroes. In the Council on Human Relations, a Black physician, Dr. Albert E. Perry, was president, Shute was vice president, and Mabel Williams, Robert Williams's wife, secretary.

A March 20, 1956, All Souls Chapel notice preserved in the J. Ray Shute Papers at the Harvard Divinity School announces:

Sunday morning at eleven our free pulpit will be occupied by Robert F. Williams, local Negro liberal, who will speak on the topic, "Colonel J. C.'s Last Stand." Let's all attend and demonstrate to the community that there is one church in Monroe where the word "brotherhood" has more than a theoretical meaning. Our chapel is "dedicated to Brother-hood and the democratic way of life." Let us demonstrate our belief in "deed, not creed."

Below the announcement of the following Sunday's program is a quotation that someone thought appropriate: "'To live anywhere in the world of A.D. 1955 and be against equality because of race or color is like living in Alaska and being against snow.' —William Faulkner, Nobel Prize-winning Mississippi author."

Robert Williams spoke about the Montgomery bus boycott, then well underway, and celebrated "the patriots of passive revolution."

A few months later, on September 9, 1956, Williams wrote a note:

Dear Mr. Shute:
If you feel that the time is right, I'd like very much to become a member of All Souls. You be the judge, if you feel that my membership will not engender strife, the announcement will be in order Sunday. However, at this time I cannot predict how long I'll be here. The duration of my stay will depend upon the job situation, but as long as I'm here, I'll be with the fellowship.

This too is preserved in the Shute papers at Harvard. And Robert Williams did become the first Black member of All Souls Chapel.

Over the next couple years, several racial issues arose in Monroe, straining efforts, civic or religious, to cross racial lines. In the summer of 1957, Williams and other Black leaders pushed again to get the Monroe public swimming pool, built with federal and local tax funds, desegregated so that Black children would have a safe place to swim.

On October 5, 1957, the Ku Klux Klan sent a motorcade to the home of Dr. Albert Perry, but when the Klan fired their guns at the house, they received answering fire from a group of well-armed, disciplined Black men led by Robert Williams. The Klan left much faster than it had arrived. The next night, Dr. Perry arrived home to find the police with a warrant for "criminal abortion on a white woman." The police agreed to release Dr. Perry on $7,500 bond after the Black community, especially the women, surrounded and invaded the police station; Ray Shute signed the bond for Perry. Dr. Perry's case made its way slowly through the courts, and ultimately he did serve a prison sentence.

In the meantime, the "kissing case" created further havoc in the state. An interracial group of children were playing, and a White girl suggested a game involving kissing. Two Black boys, eight and ten, were jailed and sent to reform school, producing great anguish and anger in the Black community, but eliciting only silence from the White community.

Then on May 5, 1959, two racially charged cases came to trial in Monroe. Charges were dropped against a White man clearly guilty of assaulting a Black female hotel housekeeper, even though the defendant refused to show up for his court appearance. Another White man on trial for aggravated assault with intent to rape was acquitted by a jury after forty-five minutes' deliberation, despite clear testimony from his Black victim and one of her White neighbors who had witnessed the assault. NAACP president Robert Williams, who had been urging calm, due process, and adherence to the rule of law, snapped. To a reporter, he said, "We must be willing to kill if necessary. We cannot take these people who do us injustice to the court and it becomes necessary to punish them ourselves. . . . Since the federal government will not bring a halt to lynching in the South and since the so-called courts lynch our people legally, if it's necessary to stop lynching with lynching, then we must be willing to resort to that method." The statement led, on one hand, to his being suspended by the national NAACP as branch president, but on the other, it propelled him to the forefront of a new Black militancy. Black intellectuals, organizers, and theoreticians now accorded significant attention to Robert Williams as he advocated a blend of Black consciousness and integration.

Williams even used his prominence to leverage world attention to obtain results in Monroe. In his 1962 book *Negroes with Guns*, Williams reports,

> World protest saved two young boys from fourteen-year reformatory sentences in the Monroe "Kissing Case." In 1960, when the Monroe city officials drafted an "urban renewal plan" calling for Federal "slum clearance" funds to condemn and destroy the houses of the colored community, we telegraphed a protest-appeal to honorary NAACP member Jawaharlal Nehru, who at that moment had President Eisenhower as his guest in India. The Federal Housing Administration subsequently refused to approve the Monroe project. In 1961, after the Cuban invasion fiasco, when President Kennedy justified U.S. intervention for "the cause of freedom," we sent an open telegram (read at the United Nations) to the President requesting equivalent U.S. tanks, airplanes, artillery, machine guns, and mercenary troops to fight the Klan in North Carolina.

In the late summer of 1961, tensions mounted further. Freedom Riders, Black and White, who had been released from jail in Mississippi, came to Monroe at Robert Williams's invitation to support local Blacks who were demonstrating about the still-segregated swimming pool and other issues. James Forman of the Student Nonviolent Coordinating Committee (SNCC) paid a return visit to Monroe at Williams's invitation. Area Whites, including Klan members, responded with violence and threats of violence. On Sunday, August 28, the situation got totally out of hand. Apparently because Ray Shute had a reputation as a liberal, fifteen shots were fired into his home. Robert and Mabel Williams, accused of kidnapping a White couple who had taken refuge in their house, fled from their home and from Monroe.

By 1961, the Unitarian congregation known as All Souls Chapel was apparently not functioning. The *Unitarian Yearbook 1959-60* reports only thirteen members, and that number is a repetition of the prior year's report. The *Directory—Unitarian Universalist Association 1961-62* lists no entry for Monroe.

J. Ray Shute had chaired Universalists and Unitarians for Cooperation Without Consolidation, but that effort to derail the consolidation of the two denominations was too little too late. He also was experiencing increasing health problems that may have caused him to draw back from pouring heart and soul into both a local congregation and a continental effort. In January 1965, Munroe Husbands of the Fellowship Office in Boston wrote, "Dear Ray: It has been a long time since I have heard from you although I think of you and Sarah continually. One time your life was so involved with the AUA that I wondered how you had time for other endeavors. You, Ray, gave more time to Unitarianism when you were active than any other layman I know." Ray Shute died at age 84 in 1988. But he was not forgotten; a January 2, 2000, *Charlotte Observer* headline reads, "'Visionary' Ray Shute Named Union County's Person of the Century."

Robert and Mabel Williams escaped to New York, then Canada, then Cuba. Fidel Castro, who had met Robert Williams previously in New York and Havana, welcomed him to Cuba, and soon Robert and Mabel Williams were broadcasting *Radio Free Dixie* from Cuba to most of the eastern United States. The radio broadcasts and Williams's book *Negroes with Guns* influenced from a distance such organizations as Deacons for Defense and the Black Panther Party. As the welcome in Cuba waned, the Williams family moved to North Vietnam and then China. In China, Williams was accorded honors and attention. Robert and Mabel Williams were provided an apartment in a former Italian embassy building, servants and a limousine, and Williams met with Mao, Zhao Enlai, and other leaders. He wrote to a friend in the US, "On October 1, China's National Day, I was allowed to stand beside Chairman Mao on the Tien an Mien, as a representative of oppressed Afro-Americans and deliver an uncensored speech to one and a half million people." While Williams was in exile, Malcolm X referred to him as "a very good friend of mine." Robert Williams returned to the United States on September 12, 1969. He slowly backed away from the eager but doctrinaire embrace of younger Black militants who offered him honorary positions in their organizations: Revolutionary Action Movement and Republic of New Afrika. Gradually, he worked out his legal problems and provided firsthand information to academics (and probably indirectly to Henry Kissinger and Richard Nixon) on conditions and leading personalities in the Chinese government. He died in Michigan on October 15, 1996, of Hodgkin's disease. For his funeral at Central Methodist Church in Monroe, his body was dressed in a gray suit that had been a gift from Chairman Mao. Rosa Parks, in her remarks at the funeral, said that she and others in the movement "always admired Robert Williams for his courage and his commitment to freedom. The work he did should go down in history and never be forgotten."

Sources

The UUA files offer some material on Monroe, and the files in the J. Ray Shute Papers in the Andover-Harvard Theological Library at Harvard Divinity School are helpful. In his book *His Honor the Heretic* (Monroe, NC: Nocalore Press, 1950), Shute offers his take on some elements of this story. Robert Williams's *Negroes with Guns* (Detroit: Wayne State University Press, republished 1998, original publication 1962 by Marzani and Munsell) tells part of his story and includes a vigorous advocacy for armed self-defense. Its one reference to the fellowship relates to the public library desegregation in 1957; it states, "We started a struggle in Monroe and Union County to integrate public facilities and we had the support of a Unitarian group of white people." Timothy B. Tyson tells much of Williams's story and some of Shute's in *Radio Free Dixie: Robert F. Williams & the Roots of Black Power* (Chapel Hill: University of North Carolina Press, 1999), and some of it can be cross-referenced in James Forman, *The Making of Black Revolutionaries* (New York:

The Macmillan Company, 1972). Jeanne Theoharis' *The Rebellious Life of Mrs. Rosa Parks* (Boston: Beacon Press, 2013) discusses the connections between Williams and Parks while they both lived in Michigan. Charles E. Cobb Jr., in *This Nonviolent Stuff'll Get You Killed* (New York: Basic Books, 2014), discusses Willliams at some length. Nancy Proctor, of the Outer Banks of North Carolina, generously shared some of her research into the work of J. Ray Shute and the Monroe congregation.

CHARLESTON, SOUTH CAROLINA

The city of Charleston has a rich, sometimes sad, but interesting history from European settlement to the Civil War and on to the present. During part of that history, Charleston served as a hub where slave ships landed and from which men, women, and children were sold as chattel.

The Independent or Congregational Church of Charleston was begun in the late seventeenth century as an amalgam of French Huguenots, Scots and Irish Presbyterians, New Englanders, and British dissenters. In about a century, it grew to the point of needing a second building and a co-ministry. The new building was dedicated in 1787, construction having been slowed by the American Revolution. In 1815, Anthony Forster became half of the ministerial team. Forster's theology was in transition from the moderate Calvinism he had been taught to the Unitarianism of Joseph Priestley, which he learned from books borrowed from his father-in-law.

In the spring of 1817, the Independent or Congregational Church divided, with slightly over half of the members following Forster in a Unitarian direction. In 1819, following Forster's death, Samuel Gilman, a young Harvard graduate of clear Unitarian leanings, was elected pastor and ordained. Gilman, although very much a New Englander (living for a time in the same house in Gloucester, Massachusetts, that Judith Sargent Murray and Rev. John Murray had previously inhabited) and very much a Harvard man (writing "Fair Harvard" for the school's bicentennial), became a fixture in Charleston until his death. In 1832, the Second Independent or Congregational Church became the Unitarian Church of Charleston. Black attendees, almost certainly maids and coachmen accompanying their masters and mistresses, sat in the balcony.

Following Gilman's death in 1858, three ministers served brief stints at the church before the shots fired at Fort Sumter in Charleston's harbor signaled the beginning of the Civil War. After the war, the congregation and the AUA engaged in a short legal tussle over control of the building and selection of a new minister; the congregation won the tussle and obtained the services of Thomas Hirst Smith of England.

In succeeding years, the church endured a succession of mostly brief ministries, hurricanes (1885 and 1938), and an earthquake (1886). But it retained a building in a highly visible location that was recognized in 1974 as a National Historic Landmark.

Mid-twentieth-century memoranda and letters in UUA files reveal concern about ministry in Charleston. In 1949, after Horace Westwood announced his resignation, effective January 1950, George G. Davis of the AUA wrote, "The placement of the right man in Charleston is to Frederick Eliot and me of the very greatest importance from the larger denominational and regional point of view." He continues, "In selecting the new minister, we ought to look for a man who will not only fill the bill in Charleston, but who will be qualified to act as an Associate Regional Director." In this era, headquarters provided a stronger guiding hand in recommending ministers for settlement. The AUA initially put forth Dan Huntington Fenn and Richard Gibbs as potential ministers, but ultimately the congregation called Alfred Hobart.

Hobart had re-entered active Unitarian ministry in New Orleans. He then served in Charleston from 1950 to 1953. He served as regional director of the Thomas Jefferson Conference in addition to his duties in Charleston. During his regional service, he founded the annual summer conferences now known as the Southeast Unitarian Universalist Summer Institute. In 1953, he resigned to organize a church in Birmingham, Alabama.

Charleston posed challenges to anyone concerned with racial justice. Hobart's answers to a questionnaire, circa 1953, from the

Commission on Unitarian Intergroup Relations reflected this. Question 9b read, "To what extent do you believe it advisable to take the initiative in bringing Negroes and other non-whites (specify) into your church?" Hobart responded,

> Speaking for the Charleston church, this is a very explosive matter, not only in the church itself (with some, but not all people in the congregation) but in the community. I would hesitate to institute the initiative in asking negroes to attend this church without very careful preparation, and even then am not sure that the members would be willing to withstand community pressures. Charleston is a state of mind. It is also essentially a small town. And it is the most southern of southern cities. There is not even a race relations group active here. Negroes would be very hesitant about overstepping the community mores even if they were assured of a welcome—which I certainly could not guarantee.

The chair of the 1953 search committee believed that "a dynamic speaker with a fresh story to stir active minds can certainly swell Sunday attendance from the usual plus or minus 30." He added, "[W]e would not choose a man with stereotyped ideas other than on the ubiquitous race subject—and on this question we would need a man who has experience enough to know that lasting gains in our civilization come through evolution rather than revolution." All this for a salary of $5,000, which would increase only if congregational numbers increased.

Successive ministers included Rhys Williams (1953–60), H. Paul Osborne (1960–62), Spencer Lavan (1962–64), and George ("Pete") Tolleson (1964–69).

Spencer Lavan, who later became a noted scholar and an effective president of Meadville Lombard Theological School, endured one of the most tumultuous ministries the Charleston congregation had known. He was called to Charleston in the summer of 1962, following his graduation from Harvard Divinity School. During the 1962–63 church year, Spencer and his wife, Susan, were

Interview—Dottie Klintworth: One Layperson's Experiences

I was born and raised in a Presbyterian family in Charlotte, North Carolina. My mother taught me that if there is a God, all are equal in God's sight. That's the way I grew up. I met and married Otto, and he was a Southern Baptist here in the South Carolina Low Country. We and our two little boys were attending a Baptist Church.

We had a Jewish neighbor, a lovely older woman, who had been born in the Ukraine and was taken to England by a brother-in-law after her parents were killed in front of her, and their dairy farm confiscated. In England, she married a rabbinical student, and he moved the family to the United States. Then he died very young and left her with four children to raise, and she had had no chance for any formal education. She raised those children. One of them was a doctor. She became a very good friend.

One day in church, the minister of that Southern Baptist Church sent that woman's soul to hell because she did not accept Christ as Savior. I just knew that I could not keep going to that church, and Otto agreed with me. There were two Unitarian families on our street, and one of them brought me some brochures. I knew immediately when I read it that this is the way I thought about life. In 1949–50, Otto was called back to service in the naval reserve, but when we got back here in 1950, we started attending the Unitarian Church. The Baptist minister came to see me, and he said that he was gravely concerned for my salvation. I said, "Well, Reverend, the way I see it, you have to be concerned for yours, and I have to be concerned for mine." We started attending in 1950 and signed the book in 1954. I wanted to be sure.

I remember that one Sunday night, we had a big meeting in Gage Hall, and it was to do with race. There were a lot of community leaders in the hall that night. The speaker was a very well-known Catholic sister, Sister Anthony. Lo and behold, she was from Charlotte, and her family and my family were real close. I knew her as Margaret Monahan when I was growing up. She looked at me, and she knew who I was, and she asked me, "If you have any time I could sure use some help." I went over to the worst part of this town. She was at a Catholic Church there, and I went to work with these Black children who had never seen the ocean. I mean, here we are right on the beach practically, and these children had never seen the ocean. I arranged a lot of cars to take all these children to the beach on a picnic. One of my sons, John, was home from college, and he helped, and a young fellow studying for the priesthood helped. When we got back to our cars, none of them would start. Somebody resented our taking all those Black children to the beach and had tampered with our cars.

Guy Carawan was doing a lot of work out on the Sea Islands. Spencer and Susan Lavan invited Otto and me out to Johns Island on a Sunday night to hear this group of Black singers. Later, this lovely lady in our church who started this program in Gage Hall called Gage Hall Saturday Night—it was kind of an arty thing, plays and poetry and music—she invited that group to sing. We had two men in our church. One of them told me that blood would flow in the streets if we had that group in Gage Hall. We didn't know what was going to happen that night, but we had that concert. And nothing happened. We didn't know if they were going to drop a bomb on us or what.

You would have had to have been here and lived through it to feel how it was. In this town, there were a lot of fine people that did not think that way. But you know what Edmund Burke said: "All it takes for evil to triumph is for good people to remain silent." But you see the fear. Many of the good people were afraid.

active in the community in such organizations as the Charleston Symphony, the Charleston County Mental Health Association, and the Association of University Women. Susan gave birth to their first child. Spencer, like many other young, new ministers, discovered the challenge of producing a variety of good sermons week in and week out. Also typically, he discovered that organizational and administrative responsibilities consumed vast amounts of time and energy. But at the congregation's annual meeting on May 17, 1963, after a "lengthy review" of his first year's service, Spencer received a formal vote of confidence.

In June 1963, Spencer wrote a letter on church letterhead to the Fort Sumter Hotel in Charleston, protesting its "calling in the police to arrest Negroes" who sought to use its dining room. The letter notes that other local hotels were not doing this, and announced that the Thomas Jefferson Unitarian Universalist Ministers Association would be moving its meetings to one of those other hotels.

The manager of the hotel replied, "I would not dignify your letter with an answer." However, two church members responded with blistering letters. Unbeknownst to Lavan when he wrote the initial letter, these church members were two of the hotel's stockholders.

On October 2, 1963, a letter from the vestry of the church reported to the membership about the July and September vestry meetings. In July, the vestry had supported freedom of the pulpit but noted that church stationery should not be used for contents not sanctioned by the church, and that the minister, when communicating on controversial issues, should speak in a personal capacity rather than as minister of the church. Many of the vestry members spoke supportively of Spencer and Susan's work in the community.

The September 1963 vestry meeting was attended by four members who "raised issues which touched upon the honesty and integrity of the Minister, his activities with respect to integration," and his letter to the Fort Sumter Hotel. Letters from some church members reducing their pledges were read, but in counterpoint, several vestry members announced increases in their pledges. A motion (not seconded) from one vestry member called for a special meeting of the congregation to consider dismissing the minister and withdrawing the congregation from the UUA. Clifton Hoffman, executive secretary of the Thomas Jefferson Unitarian Universalist Conference, attended the vestry meeting and spoke in support of Lavan's conduct. The vestry ultimately voted, with one dissent, to affirm the honesty and integrity of the minister.

In a January 26, 1964, letter to the vestry, Lavan submitted his resignation, effective early June. He detailed "almost nine months of serious reflection and soul searching," leading to a decision to return to graduate school in July 1964. This letter was shared with the congregation in a February 3 letter.

In a February 7 story covering Lavan's resignation, the *Charleston News and Courier* notes that the resignation followed an announcement in the church newsletter "that folklorist and singer Guy Carawan will perform a program of folk music in the church's Gage Hall on Feb. 15." While acknowledging that the concert was not sponsored by the church and that Gage Hall was being rented, the story also relates the objections of some church members. The story later reports that Carawan "who has identified himself with civil rights movements, worked last summer with Esau Jenkins at the South Carolina Sea School for Negroes on John's Island. He and some 40 other individuals made headlines in 1957 when they toured Communist China after the U. S. State Department had forbidden them to do so."

The February 19, 1964, issue of *The Hanahan News* carried a signed column discussing the Lavan resignation and the Carawan concert. While again raising the specter of Communism, the column introduces another scare factor:

> It is a matter of public knowledge that Carawan went to Red China in 1957 against State Department orders, has been listed in Communist publications as an entertainer at functions sponsored by organizations cited as subversive by the House Committee on Un-American Activities, collaborated with Pete Seeger (an "identified Communist" according to Congressman Gordon Scherer) and two other white civil-rightists in arranging the new words and music of "We Shall Overcome," the battle hymn of the integration movement.

During the summer of 1964, after Spencer Lavan's ministry had concluded, M. P. Lelong, the vestry member who had called for a congregational meeting to consider Spencer's dismissal, wrote a twenty-nine-page "Dear Fellow Churchmember" letter detailing his disagreements and conflicts with H. Paul Osborne and Spencer Lavan. The nature of much of his argument can be conveyed with a single sentence: "For nine years I have been a member of this Church and for three years I have been a member of the John Birch Society."

The congregation should not be considered totally averse to expending money or energy on programs that addressed social issues. In 1957, during the ministry of Rhys Williams, it borrowed money to purchase and level a nearby slum dwelling. Williams

Candie and Guy Carawan: White Workers for Civil Rights

Candie and Guy Carawan are both from Southern California, but they met at the Highlander Folk School in Monteagle, Tennessee, while Candie was spending a year as an exchange student at Fisk University, a historically Black college in Nashville. During this time, Guy was on the staff of Highlander, helping to spread the music of the expanding civil rights movement between different campuses and cities. Candie had grown up in a Southern California Unitarian fellowship. Guy had attended a Christian Science Church with his mother until he turned eighteen and had then gotten close to the First Unitarian Church of Los Angeles. They were married in 1961 in Claremont, California, with Steve Fritchman of First Unitarian Church, Los Angeles, officiating.

In 1960, Guy was not invited to perform at the Newport Folk Festival, but Ewan MacColl and Peggy Seeger, who had been invited, brought him up on stage to close one night. He sang "We Shall Overcome," a song that was beginning to be widely used in the movement, thanks in large part to Carawan. Part-way through his singing of the song, the lights were turned out, but he kept on singing. The recording of that rendition is on a Smithsonian/Folkways CD of music for social change.

After Highlander Folk School at Monteagle was raided and closed down by the state of Tennessee, it reopened in Knoxville as Highlander Research and Education Center. Guy and Candie were on the staff from fall 1961 until April 1962, working to bring together students from the University of Tennessee and Knoxville College (a historically Black campus). Candie remembers Rev. Bob West of the Tennessee Valley Unitarian Church as being very good on the Knoxville sit-ins but a little cautious about embracing Highlander, which had been widely red-baited. She remembers Knoxville church members, such as Harry Wiersema Sr., who were very much involved in the sit-ins.

The Carawan family lived on Johns Island, South Carolina, 1963–65. Guy worked in a supportive role with the citizenship schools that Esau Jenkins and Septima Clark had set up there, learning a great deal about the traditional songs of that community. During that time, the Carawans faithfully attended the Unitarian Church in Charleston and became close friends of Spencer and Susan Lavan during the year that both families were there. Candie recalls a few wonderful progressive members of the congregation, but some who were very conservative and resistant to accepting change. When the Carawans arranged for Jenkins and Clark to speak at a forum at church about their work, they got a call from "the Klan" (but they were sure it was from a church member), predicting that "blood would flow in the streets."

was quoted in a newspaper story as believing in a "working, not just talking, religion." For a number of years, starting at least in the 1950s, women of the church conducted rummage sales of clothing and household goods, partly to raise funds for the church or for the Women's Alliance, but also to provide a low-cost venue through which many poor people, Black and White, could clothe themselves and obtain household goods. (By the 1990s, the sales had moved from a marketplace to the church's Gage Hall, and the clientele included college students, downtown residents, and dealers.)

With the advent of the War on Poverty, the church agreed to house a Head Start program. Billie Hall, who had started attending the church in 1926 when she was eight years old, reports, "Head Start didn't have to pay rent here. We got something out of it, because they paid about $10,000 to get the kitchen done over. It cost us some money too I think. They had mostly Black children but some White." Dottie Klintworth, a church member since the 1950s, worked in that Head Start program and remembers, "Here I was working with those little three year-olds. One of the little White boys would come over and kiss my cheek, and then a little Black boy would come over and kiss my cheek, and I said to myself, 'Please, God, I've never been kissed by a Black. Don't let this child see any thing [any shocked reaction] in me.' I learned a lot."

During Pete Tolleson's ministry, in addition to the congregation initiating the integrated Head Start program, he asked Dottie and Otto Klintworth to start a program on Friday nights for Black youth in the community who lived near the church. Dottie recalls, "They had no social thing to go to. A lot of White children had things to go to. We had a program in Gage Hall on Friday nights for the Black children—the teens. We had that for at least a year or two. I got some of the parents to be the chaperones at that."

Tolleson observes that, having grown up in South Carolina, he may have had or found more latitude to address issues than a minister who had grown up outside the region. He also notes that his wife, Mary Leta, probably took on more issues than he did. Mary Leta was also a southerner, who had grown up in western North Carolina. When she encountered problems with the Whites-only YWCA, she quit and became the first White member of the Cummins Street YWCA. She was the first White teacher in a Charleston school with an all-Black student body. She won over her colleagues by not claiming to be the great White expert but instead frankly telling them that she needed their advice and guidance.

Coda

In late 2013, *UU World* reported that the Charleston church had used bricks removed while building a handicap-accessible ramp to create an appropriate monument to the people who had dug clay, fired bricks, and constructed their church building. The inscription on the monument base reads, "In memory of those enslaved workers who made these bricks and helped build our church." The front of the monument displays a wrought-iron sculpture of a sankofa bird, a West African symbol of looking back in order to move forward.

Sources

Spencer Lavan generously shared several file folders of his personal records from Charleston. The records of the UUA cast some light on the Charleston history, while records of the congregation itself told much of the early history.

Interviews with Dottie Klintworth, Billie Hall, Rosemary Hutto, and Jacqueline Collins were conducted in March 2000. Candie and Guy Carawan were interviewed on March 2, 2013. I am also grateful that James Hobart sent a series of emails in 2000 about the ministries of his father, Alfred Hobart, including the

Charleston period. George "Pete" Tolleson was interviewed on February 17, 2014.

The Winter 2013 issue of *UU World* carried the report of the Charleston sankofa monument.

COLUMBIA, SOUTH CAROLINA

Columbia is the state capital and the seat of the University of South Carolina (which began as South Carolina College). For more than a century, there were people in Columbia who identified as Unitarians, and there were sporadic thoughts of starting a Unitarian congregation.

One of the earliest of these was Thomas Cooper, who had been an associate of Joseph Priestley in England and who had come with Priestley to America. Cooper was a lawyer, scientist, and physician. Thomas Jefferson recruited him for a faculty position at the University of Virginia, but he did not take up that post, partly because of clerical opposition to his religious views. In 1820, he was hired for the faculty of South Carolina College, where he was soon elected president.

James Silk Buckingham, an English writer, traveler, and reformer, published an 1842 account of his visit to Columbia, in which he mentions a Unitarian church as among the six in the town, but there is no other record of such a church.

Correspondence in the files of the UUA show individual inquiries and occasional meetings from 1926 to 1943 about starting a congregation, but there is no evidence of one being organized until 1950.

The Unitarian Fellowship of Columbia was founded in 1950 through the work of AUA Fellowship Director Munroe Husbands. It began meeting twice a month in the homes of members. By 1954, it was meeting weekly in free or low-cost space, public or private, sometimes finding that its religious views or its openness

Interview—Helen Rader

My Lutheran father-in-law called my attention to a very small paragraph way down in one corner of an inner page of the newspaper to the effect that there would be a meeting for anybody interested in Unitarianism at the old Jefferson Hotel. That was the second meeting in the process of starting our fellowship.

We met in people's houses for a couple of years, then we looked for a place to meet that would be free. We found an "upper room" at the telephone company. It was a horrid little building, and the chairs were hard, and you could count on snagging your hose (because we all wore hose). We would have about six or nine people there, and we would have a regular service, dutifully singing two hymns. Of course, our Unitarian hymn singing is kind of feeble anyway, so you can imagine what it was like with no accompaniment. I think we could just have the service there once a month.

At the height of the civil rights movement, as a group we didn't do much, although we always made people welcome at our services when they came. Several of our members worked for a company that cautioned —literally to the point of sending around memos—implying that if they knew what was good for them, they wouldn't get involved with civil rights. What we did on the whole, we did by ourselves, but we did quite a bit. One of our ladies was very active in the Council on Human Relations, which was a biracial group. Several others of us were too; I was an officer for several years. We worked with what they then called the "colored" section of one of the state convalescent centers.

I very well remember one time when we were still meeting at the Masonic Temple. We had an African-American visitor. I think it was Easter Sunday or Father's Day—something a little special. I was tidying up the kitchen after most members had left, and two members of the Masonic Temple walked in, and they looked around everywhere—closets and cupboards and everywhere. At first it seemed like a weird coincidence, and then I remembered that there was a White Baptist church just a block away, and they undoubtedly had seen our guest. The next month or so, when we tried to see if we could continue to meet at the Temple the following year, they said no, because we left the kitchen a mess, which we did not. We generally left it a whole lot neater than we found it.

> Once we had our own place, we posted "Wayside Pulpit" signs. I was the one who changed the Wayside Pulpit. Anytime there was anything the least controversial religiously, it would get taken off. I remember one Christmas that the saying Boston sent was, "Any night a child is born is a holy night." I put it up Saturday, and by Tuesday it was torn down.
>
> One of the last years we were in the former Episcopalian church, we got a huge "KKK" spray painted on the building because we had Black members in the congregation.

to all races shortened its residency. For example, after Rev. A. Powell Davies visited and spoke in favor of integration, the YWCA where the fellowship rented space asked it to move. In 1960, after several African Americans attended a service, the Shandon Masonic Lodge declined to continue renting to the fellowship. At that point, the Aurora Club for the Blind took them in and had no problem with Black attendees. Fellowship president Theodore Lafferty commented, "In our relief, it occurred to us that, being blind, they could see some things better than others could." In 1962, the fellowship purchased a house, affording much friendlier space for a religious education program, but even that purchase had to surmount opposition, including a city council decree that all churches must have one acre of land.

Giana Wayman remembers that the typical membership of a Unitarian fellowship in the late 1950s consisted of mostly university-related people and businesspeople. But she also noted a contingent of people who came from a Universalist heritage. Her own grandmother sometimes took Giana to the Universalist church in Newberry, South Carolina. Homer H. B. Mask was a distinguished older member in Columbia who had grown up in an Alabama Universalist congregation before working in the New Deal, and his middle initials, which he always used, stood for Hosea Ballou.

The first minister, Roger Sizemore, was called in 1972, spurring growth from a membership of forty-five to one hundred. The congregation purchased a former Episcopal church building in 1975.

Interview—Giana Wayman

I was a member in the Columbia Fellowship 1957–59 while I was in high school, and I have visited there while I was in college and since.

While I was active in the fellowship, we were meeting in the Masonic Temple. It was a fairly new building and a perfect size for our group. In general, attendance at services was about twenty to twenty-five, sometimes less, and on a really good Sunday, there might be thirty-five people.

In about 1958, a Black army officer, a doctor who had a really distinguished appearance, attended services. After the service, some of the leaders of the fellowship took him aside and explained "the facts of life": that they could not use the building if they were an integrated group, and that there were some members who would have to resign from membership, or they would lose their jobs if he continued to attend. He never returned. I heard this from a couple of the leaders who talked with him.

Sources

Congregational history materials collected and/or written by Patrick Price provided considerable assistance. Material from the files of the UUA was useful. An oral history interview with Helen Rader on March 12, 2000, helped greatly. Alfred Hobart's manuscript, "The Unitarian Universalist Witness in the Southeast 1950–1966," proved to be a substantial resource. I am grateful for a telephone interview with Giana Wayman on September 9, 2013.

ATLANTA, GEORGIA

According to a 1982 centennial history assembled by Atlanta's Unitarian Universalist congregations, both the Universalists and the Unitarians began to make efforts to establish congregations in Atlanta in the late nineteenth century.

W. C. Bowman led the first Universalist effort in 1879–80. The second, involving notable evangelist Quillen Shinn, began in 1893, and on February 24, 1895, resulted in the organization of First Universalist Church. Membership rose as high as 170 in 1910.

Unitarian efforts in Atlanta began with the January 1882 arrival of George Leonard Chaney. Chaney, who had served Boston's Hollis Street Church 1862–77, was of independent means and socially improving impulses. He served for twenty-five years on the board of the Tuskegee Institute and was also a trustee of the Hampton Institute and Atlanta University, all of which were devoted to the education of Blacks. While he lived in Atlanta, Chaney and members of his church helped found the Artisans Institute in Atlanta, a forerunner of Georgia Tech. In addition, after discovering in Atlanta a library that charged fees and loaned only to White males, he established a free lending library open to all, regardless of gender, race, or economic situation. In 1895, the Carnegie Foundation bought the church building and accepted the donation of this book collection to found the Atlanta Public Library. But by his departure from Atlanta in 1890, there were, despite his best efforts, fewer than sixty-five members.

Both the Unitarian and the Universalist congregations struggled, waxing and waning. In 1908, at a point of Unitarian decline,

the two congregations considered merging but that plan was narrowly voted down by the Unitarians. The Unitarians rebounded, and
in 1915, the AUA financed construction of a new 240-seat church
on Peachtree Street. Just three years later, following the death of the
Universalists' minister while he was in France, the congregations
voted to merge, taking the name Liberal Christian Church.

Life as a merged congregation did not lead to great growth,
solid financial strength, or enduring harmony. The most successful ministry was probably Clinton Lee Scott's (1926–29). Later
one of the leaders in reshaping and re-energizing twentieth-
century Universalism, Scott manifested a clear vision of the congregation's growth and great energy in helping it fulfill that vision. In his
memoir *Some Things Remembered*, he recalls that Atlanta's Southern
Methodist bishop of that day did not like liberals and took particular offense at the Unitarians and Universalists. One of his tactics
included sending "theological students from Emory University to
picket our services. We invited them in and some continued to come
to church. One went to Meadville to prepare for the Unitarian ministry." The bishop wrote a more direct attack in a pamphlet called
"The Menace of Unitarianism." Scott thought that the bishop "gave
us credit for influence far beyond anything we could have claimed
for ourselves," so they bought the pamphlet in quantity and used it
for publicity purposes. After Scott's ministry, the progression was
mostly downward. For example, during the ministry of Aubrey Hess
(1930–35), members cast ballots in 1934 whether he should remain
or resign; forty-seven people supported the minister, twenty-three
opposed, and seven claimed to be "indifferent."

In 1945, Isaiah J. Domas was urged to candidate for the pulpit. He declined for various reasons, including lack of sympathy
for segregationist views of the board. In 1947 the pulpit was again
vacant and Domas again was urged to candidate, and this time he
did. His racial views were probably a factor in eleven no votes, but
he accepted on the basis of thirty-six yes votes. Even as he was preparing to move from Springfield, Vermont, there was controversy
over the call and over paying his moving expenses. He arrived with
his wife and child in early September 1947.

Almost immediately, Domas was contacted by Thomas Baker Jones, who had been a member of the Unitarian Church in Columbus, Ohio, while earning his PhD. Jones, who was Black, was now professor of social administration at Atlanta University (a historically Black institution). Domas and Jones met at the parsonage—the kind of radical move Domas had warned the congregation he would do—and Domas, by his own later report, urged Jones not to attend a church service just yet—a cautious move, but also reportedly in line with what he had told the congregation. In October 1947, Jones's minister in Columbus, Frank Ricker, sent a letter endorsing Jones's eligibility for church membership; Mrs. Domas was made instructor in group work skills at Atlanta University; and Domas himself became part-time director of social research at the school. Domas was also asked to co-chair an appearance by Henry Wallace sponsored by the Southern Conference for Human Welfare, a progressive interracial activist group that was often red-baited. Wallace, who had served as vice president of the United States from 1940 to 1944, was preparing to run for president on the Progressive ticket.

In November 1947, Thomas Baker Jones attended a service and was seated in the congregation without a fuss, according to Domas. But later some members of the congregation raised a fuss, including making motions at congregational meetings to maintain segregation and to oust Domas. By May, Domas had resigned. Most, but not all, of the pro-segregation members in the congregation identified as Universalist, although there were some outspokenly progressive voices in that camp as well. More of those who identified as Unitarian at least tolerated Domas. Domas had complicated the picture greatly through his activity in the Wallace presidential effort and by some perhaps inept interaction with an already factionalized and highly stressed congregation. In a letter to members and friends, Domas wrote, "There are seventeen churches in this community which maintain policies, on the race and kindred issues, far more liberal than those which have characterized this church." Domas reported in letters to Unitarian headquarters a number of new members attracted to the church during his brief tenure, but the congregation voted thirty-three to thirty-two to accept his resignation.

In May and June, the Unitarian Ministers Association voiced its support of Domas and urged members of its organization not to accept a call to the Atlanta congregation until it had changed its stance on race.

By August 1948, a new minister, neither Universalist nor Unitarian, had been called. Dr. Earle LeBaron, an ex-Catholic, was described by some as Methodist and others as Christian. In November, the congregation passed a vote repudiating "all Communistic, Fascistic, totalitarian, and authoritarian forces and stating that those sympathetic with Communism or fellow-travelers were no longer actively connected with the church," tacitly agreeing with the red-baiting of Domas and his supporters. In a more positive vein, in October 1949, the congregation voted to "repeal the resolution barring Negroes from the worship services of their church," although they stopped short of opening membership to Blacks. At the same church business meeting, the congregation voted to inquire of the AUA about selling either the entire property or "the parcel on which the remains of the parrish [sic] house stands." The parish house having recently been seriously damaged in a fire, they wanted assurance that the proceeds would be available for their use.

The UUA files contain a copy of a February 9, 1951, letter that may or may not have been sent. Directed to Waldo Rasnake, the clerk of the United Liberal Church of Atlanta, it includes spaces for the signatures of both the president of the AUA and the superintendent of the UCA. It reads, "In spite of the loyalty and devotion of many Unitarians and Universalists, problems have arisen in recent years which have led both denominations to believe that the time has come for the dissolution of the present church and the establishment of a new venture which shall not only conserve all the values of the past but also present a new program for vigorous liberal advance." It continues, "The new church, by vote of the Board of Directors of both denominations, shall be under the auspices of the Universalist Church of America and the American Unitarian Association."

Interview—Jean Levine

Ray and I came down to Atlanta in 1958. I have to admit I was kicking and screaming every inch of the way, to leave the North to come to the segregated South. After my second child was born and was old enough to be left with someone else, I decided I would go back to work. But I would only work with the civil rights movement. I went to work with the Southern Regional Council, and shortly after that, they had an offshoot, the Voter Education Project. Wiley Branton was the first executive. I was the executive assistant.

The Voter Education Project got money from foundations in the northeast—the Taconic and other foundations. We would get applications from Black groups, usually young, all over the South, that were trying to do voter education. We used to meet with Dr. King and Ralph Abernathy almost every Wednesday. These people were doing tremendous amounts of work, but they were not businesspeople, and keeping records, which we needed, was like pulling teeth. So we would meet almost every Wednesday and go over the records that we needed so that we could account back to the foundations for the money that we were dispensing on their behalf.

When the Bloody Sunday attack occurred in Selma, I found out that there were a bunch of Unitarian ministers, some from here and others coming down from Boston, and they were going to meet at the Atlanta airport and then drive to Selma. I took my car out there, and we all drove over to Selma. One of them was James Reeb. We were there all day. Getting ready to come back about five o'clock, we were going to drive some of the ministers to the airport in Montgomery. James Reeb put his suitcase in the trunk of my car. At the last minute, he decided he was going to stay one more night to see if there was anything he could do to help.

Yes, issues around race contributed to the dissolution of the original Unitarian/Universalist congregation. Other factors included inadequate support by the membership, extreme factionalism, persistent dysfunction, high ministerial turnover, and probably some episodes of ministerial ineptitude. The national offices of both the Unitarians and the Universalists offered support over the years but apparently did not always understand or respect the local dynamics. Both the AUA and the UCA dropped the congregation from membership sometime between 1949 and 1951, but possibly neither body notified the congregation of their action.

In February and March of 1951, Lon Ray Call, fellowshipped in both traditions, surveyed the situation in Atlanta. He found many Universalists and Unitarians who felt bruised by over thirty years of fractious congregational life. He found considerable resentment of "Boston," the headquarters for both groups. People told him that Boston was not fully aware of what was going on and was only intermittently in communication with the Atlanta congregation, and that the communication they sent often felt as though they were dictating. He found these assets: a Unitarian-owned church property to be used or sold, a fund of over $20,000 from the sale of the Universalist building decades earlier, and some Universalists and Unitarians willing to try again.

In a pulpit address on February 25, 1951, in Atlanta, Call announced that both the Universalist and the Unitarian headquarters would support a new congregation and would not attempt to dictate its by-laws. However, he continued,

> When application is made for recognition there must be an expression that the congregation approves of and is in general sympathy with the purposes of the denominational bodies. Perhaps the best illustration of this is the principle of race segregation. . . . We recall a strong resolution of the American Unitarian Association at its Annual Meeting May 22, 1947, that renounced the principle of segregation as "unnecessary, undesirable, and a denial of the concept of God and of the brotherhood of man."

By early 1952, Glenn O. Canfield had been sent to Atlanta by the AUA and the UCA to start a new congregation. The first service was held on February 24. In his April 1952 report, attendance at church services ranged from forty-one to fifty-five; church school had begun with six to eight teachers and fourteen to eighteen pupils under the supervision of former State Child Welfare Director Loretto Chappell. Canfield was working with a mailing list of 183 families or individuals. Canfield notes,

> General conclusion: The fact that many of the better people who were formerly active in the old church and left when the "red scare" was on and the charges were leveled against Miss Chappell (which have since been withdrawn and Miss Chappell given a clean bill of health by the legislature) are not active in our new church, together with the fact that a new family who had been very active in Knoxville until the husband lost his job with the City, and took a similar job here in Atlanta recently, told me that they had decided not to join our church but were going to join a Methodist or Presbyterian church "for personal reasons," and another family from New Orleans seems to be wavering, points up the fact that it seems to take more than the usual courage to affiliate with a liberal church in Atlanta. In several discussions in the church service as well as with several individuals, we have discovered a subdued fear in several people that something might happen, especially on the race issue, which would get them into trouble like Miss Chappell. I have assured them that whatever happens on any matter that we shall not make an issue of it and make a sensational fight about it, but will follow our carefully considered educational procedure.

The following month's report conveyed positive public relations news. On May 4, the fellowship had invited members of the Greenville (South Carolina) and Birmingham (Alabama) fellowships to attend, and six from Greenville had come for the weekend. The religious news editor of the *Atlanta Constitution* serendipitously attended that service and took pictures, which led to a positive story with a two-column picture the next day.

But soon thereafter race became an awkward and inescapable issue. On May 11, "a young Negro woman"—a graduate student in social work at Atlanta University whom Canfield and his wife had known in Syracuse, where she was part of the Unitarian congregation's Channing Club—attended the service. Soon after that another "young Negro woman, a teacher at Atlanta U.," inquired about bringing her five-year-old daughter and a niece to church school. At that time, the Unitarian Universalist services were being held at the Briarcliff Hotel. Adults attending the service entered directly from the street, but children going to church school entered through the main lobby and used the elevators. Canfield wrote,

> I felt it proper to consult the hotel manager with whom I have developed a good friendship. He was quite sympathetic to our cause and to our ideal of establishing an unsegregated church, and maintained that all churches should be that way. . . . And he said that he wished it were possible for us to develop an unsegregated group in his hotel, as the Quaker meeting downtown at the YMCA is unsegregated, but he quite honestly and fairly explained that a hotel is a public place, and that although there is no law forbidding it, that social and political pressures are so great that a hotel is particularly vulnerable to the attack of the prejudiced people who are determined to preserve segregation and to "keep the nigger in his place," and are willing to go to almost any extreme, either physical damage or reprisals against church members, to preserve white supremacy. After a one-hour conversation in which he also explained that if the hotel owner, one of the Coca Cola Candlers, ever found out that we were having Negroes, that we would be ordered out immediately, that very likely he would be fired and would never again get a job in a hotel, and that the hotel would get a bad reputation. I then said, "Well, then, it looks like we just can't have them." He replied, "I would not put it as blunt as that. I will say that I would rather they would not come." This seems fair considering everything. I explained that since we cannot conceive of a truly liberal church which would exclude intelligent

Negroes, even in the face of the strong feeling against it, it would be necessary for us to find another place to meet. He hoped that we would stay, and promised to do everything to make us comfortable.

Canfield hoped to accomplish a shift of location, which he believed to be imperative, before services started again on September 7. Options included "the Jewish Education building, the YMCA, the YWCA, and the Academy of Medicine building, in all of which unsegregated meetings are held." He comments of the congregation, "There are of course a few who would rather go along as we are and compromise on one of humanity's gravest problems. The majority, however, are following me sincerely in my slowly moving, calm, patient but determined effort to establish a church on the highest levels that we know."

In June, Canfield reported spending many hours and many miles searching for an alternative rental that would permit non-segregated functioning. He wrote, "We may have to stay at the Hotel until we can buy a place, and make our own rules." In September 1952, he presented a disappointing report on a large old house that had looked promising; it had severe termite problems and issues with plumbing, wiring, and the removal of load-bearing interior walls.

Then in October, the Unitarians and Universalists began negotiating with the Mormons for a church building and parsonage that the Mormons would vacate in a little over a year. Negotiations became frenetic after a January 1953 notice from the Briarcliff Hotel that the meeting space the church had been using had been leased to a business after February 2. By January 25, Canfield wrote, "The Liberals and the Mormons have reached complete and amicable agreement! At least on some things!" The liberals would sign a purchase agreement and make a down payment, and they would begin using their building-to-be on Sunday afternoons and Wednesdays.

Fifty-eight people attended the church service, and five teachers and thirty pupils attended church school the last Sunday in the hotel, according to the February 1953 report. The first three Sundays meeting in the afternoon in their new space produced attendance ranging from 109 to 125.

Once the congregation, with the aid of the UCA and the AUA, owned a meeting place and could function as an integrated congregation, the final steps were taken to organize formally. On January 20, 1954, they organized with 127 members and pledges of $5,000.

While the US Supreme Court was hearing suits on school segregation, legislators in Georgia passed an amendment to the state constitution permitting the legislature to close the public schools and provide tuition grants to send children to private schools. This amendment was on the November 1954 state ballot for ratification. On October 24, the United Liberal Church passed a resolution advocating defeat of the amendment and sent copies to area news media.

By October 1956, when Glenn Canfield resigned, membership in the church had doubled.

The installation service for Ed Cahill in early 1957 included opening sentences read by Rufus Clement, the Black president of Atlanta University and a church member. Atlanta mayor William Hartsfield brought greetings to the installation.

Following Cahill's installation service, a reception was held for distinguished guests at the home of Coe and Betty Hamling in the suburban community of Avondale. No one thought much about the fact that a few of the guests were Black—not until they heard a commotion outside caused by the arrival of Avondale police and a fire truck. Guests left quickly. Within twenty-four hours, church member Morgan Stanford lost his job as city attorney for Avondale. Betty Hamling lost her job as a librarian in an Avondale school and was asked to resign as PTA president. Coe Hamling, who worked across the southeast selling home furnishings, received some pressure from his employer and found that all his customers had been told about the incident, but he held on to his job.

Another church member during this time was Whitney Young, dean of the Atlanta University School of Social Work. Later, as

Interview—Bill Cherry

Amy and Phil Stasch—he was an engineer for Lockheed. They had a daughter and maybe another child in the youth group in the church. At that time we had some Black students in the youth group. Their daughter had become very good friends with one of these Black kids. He had started to go to school out of town, but one weekend or sometime when he was back, he phoned and wanted to see her. He went up to where they lived. When he arrived, she ran out of the house and gave him a hug. First thing they knew, the neighbors had called the police, and there were police officers out on the lawn. The police escorted the young man away "for his safety."

Phil Stasch shortly thereafter lost his job with Lockheed, although he had just been commended for his work. He was an expert on helicopters. His boss was a friend of his and said, in essence, "I hate to tell you this. It breaks my heart, but I have my orders. You are to pick up your paycheck on Friday." He went out to the West Coast and got another good job out there with somebody else.

head of the National Urban League, Young would be one of the major Black civil rights leaders who sponsored the 1963 March on Washington.

Cahill recalled two instances in his four-year ministry when the congregation responded to a challenge in ways he found especially gratifying:

Atlanta University students had organized a sit-in at the segregated lunch counter in Rich's [Department Store]. Several hundred were arrested for trespassing, and jailed. On Sunday morning during the talkback, the chairman of the Public Affairs Committee asked how many members would be willing to return their Rich's charge cards in protest. Over a hundred hands went up, and over a hundred cards were in the mail that afternoon.

Interview—Elizabeth Reed

My husband, Jerry, was a dentist. We had moved to Atlanta from New York.

Jerry advertised for someone to clean office and learn dental assistant. He had about three hundred replies, and he selected a Black woman. That got him started working on Black employment. About the same time, we found the Unitarian Universalist church. I call our church an oasis. I had been living here for about two years, and for the first time I was in a place with Black people.

A group of Black college students published a full-page manifesto against segregation. We Unitarians were very sympathetic. We called a meeting, which was at my house, with Helen Bullitt, an assistant to the mayor. Finally, the students show up, late. This was the Christmas holidays, and I had a nice decoration on the door, and I had the floodlights. (I belonged to the garden club.) Lonnie King, one of the leaders of that group, said, "I can't believe you let us come in the front door with these lights on. What are your neighbors going to say?" And he said, "Do you think we can live in a neighborhood like this someday?"

My husband ran for the school board. Of course this "New York Jewish boy" got written up in the papers—you wouldn't believe—because he reported that in the Black schools, the books were falling apart. They had a typewriter; the typewriter didn't work. Of course, he got every Black vote, a couple of White votes.

He integrated the opera. The Metropolitan used to come down here every single year. He got tickets for Coretta Scott King. Isn't that appalling? That that had to be done behind the scenes?

Not only was he fighting this battle, he was fighting anti-Semitism at the Emory School of Dentistry.

He dropped dead at fifty-one.

There was one Black child in the schools. An organization was formed, a handful of people, not Unitarians but we were part of it, and they called themselves HOPE, Help Our Public Education. We had these little stickers on our cars. All we did, we had little coffee klatches to discuss what would Atlanta be like if they shut down every single school. How could we go on? That's what they threatened to do. One Black child, we close all the schools. And that's how it started. Very gradually, the power structure came on board like we had never started it. They took all the credit. And then the ministers and rabbis got together and said, We can't let this happen. When HOPE started, we were getting racist calls at night because we had this sticker on our car. I mean real hateful calls, and that was kind of scary.

One time, I had Ed Cahill, Dr. King, and a rabbi who taught at the Jewish Community Center over. To this day, I grieve that I didn't have a tape recorder. Can you imagine the three of them talking about religious issues?

The second illustration involved the Ebenezer Baptist Church, where Coretta Scott King was leader of the Youth Group. Our church arranged joint Sunday evening programs, alternating between the two churches, so black and white young people could get to know one another. The Klan called Mrs. Cahill, in my absence, and threatened violence at the next Sunday evening meeting at the United Liberal Church. Coretta King was consulted; she said to go ahead. All the parents were called to give them the option of keeping their children home. Not one parent held back. In fact, all the fathers came that evening and ringed the church outside to form a visible wall of protection.

Cahill in late 1958 was one of a group of 311 area clergy amplifying and reissuing an Atlanta manifesto that supported public education, free and rational discussion of issues, and formation of a citizens committee to preserve harmony. In the same era, members of the congregation played roles in the formation of HOPE, Inc. (Help Our Public Education). Gerald and Elizabeth Reed helped generate an attendance of thirteen hundred at the first public meeting. Eliza Paschall and Gerald Reed served on the HOPE Executive Board. In October 1960, the congregation voted unanimously to endorse the goals of the sit-in movement.

Eugene Pickett was the final minister to serve this congregation during the civil rights era of the 1950s and 1960s. By the time he left in 1974 to join the UUA staff, church membership had surpassed a

Letter from Coretta Scott King

On October 31, 1968, Coretta Scott King wrote Eugene Pickett a letter stating, in part,

Please convey to the members of your congregation my deepest appreciation for their help at the time of my husband's death. Their concern and sympathy were demonstrated in many ways, and made a tragic and confusing period less trying for my family and me.

It would have been impossible to provide for the many visitors to my home without the generosity of the members of the Atlanta Unitarian Church. The food, transportation and lodging which they provided will be remembered as a tangible demonstration of the brotherhood-in-action which the Unitarian Church has always stressed. Opening, sorting, and handling the tremendous amount of mail sent to my children and me would truly have been an insurmountable task without the help of the people who responded to the Unitarian Church's appeal.

Through the years, the Unitarian Universalist Congregation of Atlanta has been a leader in bridging the gap between the white and black communities. My family and I will always remember how warmly and willingly you extended friendship and love during our most difficult hour. Please know that we will always be grateful.

thousand, a new and much larger building had been constructed, the name had been changed to the Unitarian Universalist Congregation of Atlanta, and the Northwest Unitarian Congregation had spun off. Despite these successes, the growth of the congregation was not unimpeded. In 1962–63, Atlanta politicians covertly voiced objections by warning of "potential traffic congestion" to block the church from at least one building site. Church member and lawyer Morgan Stanford recalls hearing the city attorney say, when opposing the church building on that site, "We've got to consider the morals of our community. This church is integrated."

Interview—Boyd McKeown

We actually came here to UUCA for the theology. And finding it to be integrated was a plus, because we were up there in Marietta, Georgia. I was a schoolteacher, and we were going through this business, "one Black child enrolled and we'll shut down the school system." To express some concern about that stance at the faculty lunch table was to cause forks to drop to the plate and jaws to hang open. No one expressed those sentiments, even though I think more people had those ideas than we knew about at the time.

The father of one of my students was on the Board of Stewards at First Methodist Church, where we were members at that time. Of course, you take a vow not to use alcohol or tobacco when you're on the Board of Stewards, but after the Board of Stewards meeting one Sunday night, he dropped by our house for a drink. He was all upset because the youth group that Sunday night had had a Black man come to address them. "Maybe that was all right, but he went right up in the sanctuary and sat down and stayed for Sunday night church." This was the kind of thing we were exposed to up there. So when we joined the church down here, we were glad to see that we were in an integrated congregation.

I come by that naturally. My father was instrumental in getting Race Relations Sunday started in the Methodist Church. It's now called something else. He started that back in the 1930s.

Gays and lesbians are undergoing a lot of the same discrimination now that we've been talking about. It's a matter of degree, but they're still being very discriminated against. While we were still living in Marietta, the County Commission passed an anti-gay resolution. You couldn't appeal it because it didn't have the force of law; it was just a resolution. But it was very anti-gay. We went to the meeting. My wife, Edna, had signed up to speak at the meeting. We got a call the night before that we'd better get there early because the Baptist churches and some of the Methodists were busing people in. They had bused people in to fill that county commission chamber, and they had their colors to wear, and we had our signs, "Hate is not a family value" and that sort of thing. I have never felt such hostility. You could cut it with a knife. I thought, "What happened to Christian love?"

Sources

The Atlanta congregations collectively produced *Unitarian Universalists in Atlanta: 100 Years* in 1982, and it provides a wealth of information. The UUA files were also a rich resource. The ministry file on I. J. Domas held at the Andover-Harvard Theological Library of the Harvard Divinity School generally conformed to other material in UUA files. The Church of the Larger Fellowship published Clinton Lee Scott's *Some Things Remembered* in 1976. Jeffrey Jones's paper "Prophets of the Southern Kingdom: Unitarian Universalist Contributions to Race Relations in Atlanta" (1997) added significant detail. Historic papers of the congregation now known as the Unitarian Universalist Congregation of Atlanta are held in the Robert W. Woodruff Library of Emory University and were consulted. A 1982 letter from Ed Cahill was also of use. There was a wide-ranging group interview on February 10, 2000, which included Coe and Betty Hamling, Bill Cherry, Boyd McKeown, Jean Levine, Elizabeth Reed, Ned Cartledge, Peggy Beard, and Morgan Stanford.

Cahill's report of a Klan threat on a joint youth group meeting with Ebenezer Baptist Church was not recalled by Coretta Scott King when I asked her about it in 2000, but the memory may have faded among the multitude of threats she had heard over the years. During a visit to Atlanta in 1962, I attended one of the joint youth group meetings.

ELSEWHERE IN GEORGIA:
SAVANNAH, AUGUSTA, ATHENS

As the 1950s began, apart from Atlanta, the state of Georgia had no Unitarian congregations, and there were only a handful of Universalist congregations in rural small towns: Canon, Senoia, Winder, and Windsor.

Universalists had over many decades been far more energetic than Unitarians in propagating congregations across the Southeast. The 1893 *Universalist Register* listed eighteen Georgia congregations. Some lay dormant and others conducted only monthly or occasional services, but they were recognizable sites of Universalist belief. Dates of organization ranged back to 1843 in Senoia. In all, these eighteen congregations reported serving two hundred families and having wood or log buildings worth $4,900. The *Year-Book of the Unitarian Congregational Churches for 1894* listed only an Atlanta congregation. In that era, a similar pattern persisted throughout the states of the Deep South: a scattering of small Universalist congregations, virtually all in small towns, and only occasionally a Unitarian church in a major city.

Savannah

Savannah bucked the trend a bit in the South. A Unitarian congregation had existed in Savannah from 1831 to 1859, served by at least four ministers. During the pastorate of John Pierpont Jr. in the 1850s, his younger brother James directed the music of the church. (Notably, James Pierpont wrote "Jingle Bells"—historians still dispute whether he wrote it nostalgically while in Savannah, or earlier while he lived in Medford, Massachusetts.) But the congregation did not survive the growing conflict between North and South. By 1859, the church property was sold and the congregation dissolved. AUA Administrative Vice-President Charles R. Joy was present on January 19, 1931, when again, Unitarians organized. This iteration was short-lived, as was a fellowship that sprouted after that. The current congregation was founded in 1958.

On Saturday and Sunday, March 13 and 14, 1965, UUA Department of Education Consultant Eugene Navias visited Savannah to conduct an area religious education conference. His report on the weekend includes these passages:

> The conference was greeted with enthusiasm, but the terrible events of the week in Selma were first on everyone's minds, and they rightfully demanded expression.
>
> • • •
>
> The original plan for Sunday was a service and sermon, led by the Consultant, on religious education. When I arrived at the hotel Friday evening, I found many urgent phone messages waiting for me, and on calling Fellowship President, Milton Rahn, learned that he and all those of the Fellowship that he had talked with wanted some kind of memorial service for James Reeb on Sunday. We spent all of Friday evening hurriedly arranging the service. Before my coming, the Fellowship had put an "In Memoriam" ad on the church page of the newspaper, a similar sign in the Wayside Pulpit and had draped this in black.
>
> • • •
>
> The Sunday service was arranged to have a representative of the Negro community who attends the group, the President, and a splendid professional folk singer (Tamson Duffil) and myself taking part. And as it happened, the service was overwhelmingly moving and meaningful. Mr. W.

W. Law, one of the leaders of the Negro community and President of the NAACP, attended, along with several other Negro visitors.

· · ·

During the Coffee Hour, Mr. Law invited the Consultant to give the principal address at the NAACP Mass Meeting that afternoon and asked Fellowship members to attend. I extended my stay to include the meeting, hastily wrote an address and went with John Ralston. The location was the Zion Fair Baptist Church, a poor old wooden structure in one of the worst Negro suburban neighborhoods. I doubt that the church had ever seen such a congregation— with a dozen white members of the Fellowship conspicuous among the crowd. The Mass Meeting is of the revival meeting kind with much spirited singing of spirituals and freedom songs, addresses, a collection for the NAACP and impassioned encouragements for recruiting new members, for using voting rights, for applying for children to attend integrated schools and the many causes still to be worked on in that community. I shared the platform with an impressive array of Negro ministers, and with one other white minister, Father Bagley of St. Anthony's.

· · ·

I do not believe I was ever more moved, stimulated and exhilerated [sic] than when my address was continually punctuated by choruses shouting "AMEN!" "You said it!" "Un-huh!" and applause. Nor was I ever more amused than when Mr. Law asked Fellowship members Milton Rahn and Captain Spencer to raise the collection. This literally meant holding up each bill as the donor gave it and encouraging more and larger bills to follow. It further meant counting the money on the spot and urging the group to make up the difference between the total and the next big round number. Be it said, that this memorial was as moving in its way (and it lasted two hours) as the one in the morning, and that by the time we intellectual Unitarians were through with the two services, we were gratified, warmed beyond measure, but depleted.

. . .

The gratitude expressed by the Negroes to the Fellowship people, their warmth of welcome, was truly impressive.

. . .

From another standpoint, the two events carried the Fellowship further into declaring that it is integrated and that it stands behind the human rights cause, than it had ever gone before. The group has been very quiet about its status until that day, although some of the Negro community knew of it. Now the group seemed to forget the risks, the business reprisals, etc. They were invited to take part in a NAACP march on the coming Sunday, a march to commemorate local events and to urge the Negroes in their own community to register, etc. Fellowship members will be making a big decision this week on whether to participate, as they would probably be the only members of the white community to do so.

Augusta

Augusta came closer than Savannah to the usual pattern. An antebellum congregation in Augusta started in 1827 with the construction and dedication of a church building. Daniel Whitaker first served there followed by Stephen Greenleaf Bulfinch, son of noted architect Charles Bulfinch. After eight or nine years of service by these two men, the congregation continued for another twenty years or so without a settled minister. By 1850, the building was occupied by a Jewish congregation, and by 1856, the congregation was no longer listed by the AUA.

The current congregation in Augusta organized as a fellowship in 1954. Perceiving a need in the community, the Unitarian Fellowship of Augusta started a preschool. The school's brochure offered this description:

> The Augusta Open Door Kindergarten, Inc., founded in the spring of 1964, provides a non-sectarian kindergarten open to children of all races. The founders felt Augusta needed a kindergarten which would reflect the continuing advances in education while building upon the heritage of the past.
>
> A unique aspect of this Kindergarten is its multi-racial structure. In our rapidly shrinking world, the child who has experiences in working on a give and take basis with persons from backgrounds other than his own has distinct advantages. The Augusta Open Door Kindergarten, Inc. provides this opportunity.

Funds from the fellowship and from the UUA's Freedom Fund helped the school get started. Fellowship members were part of the early staffing.

A Concerned Augusta Citizens Committee grew out of a Sunday service at the fellowship and focused on housing issues. Ultimately, it merged with and rejuvenated the Augusta Council on Human Relations.

In 1968, on the Sunday following the assassination of Martin Luther King Jr., the fellowship held a memorial service and gave this report in the next week's newsletter:

> Sunday morning we planted a tree. We planted a tree on the front lawn of the Fellowship House, near the James Reeb tree, as a living memorial to Dr. Martin Luther King. As this tree flourishes and grows, may the ideals and hopes that he lived and died for also flourish within us and throughout the land. During our memorial service, members and friends shared their sadness and were comforted by reflecting on Dr. King's courage and his abiding faith in the great-

Horace Montgomery

In January 1961, Charlayne Hunter (later Charlayne Hunter Gault of PBS, NPR, and CNN) and Hamilton Holmes were admitted to the University of Georgia under federal court order. On January 11, following a riot on campus, Hunter and Holmes were suspended "for their own safety."

By mid-afternoon of January 12, Horace Montgomery and several other faculty members were drafting a statement to be presented for faculty signatures. The draft concludes, "[W]e insist that the two suspended students be returned to their classes and that all measures necessary to the protection of students and faculty and to the preservation of orderly education be taken by appropriate state authorities." Ultimately, about 80 percent of the resident faculty signed the statement, giving support to the university president in readmitting Holmes and Hunter and demanding that state authorities enforce the law. The University of Georgia's desegregation was thereby made less fractious than its counterparts in Alabama, where Gov. Wallace stood in the schoolhouse door, or in Mississippi, where Gov. Barnett incited a riot.

Decades later, Horace Montgomery proudly displayed in his home a framed envelope and note. The envelope arrived, postmarked Seattle, January 30, 1961, with three cents postage due. The typed, unsigned message inside read, "Horace, Judas received 30 pieces of silver for Betraying only one Man. HOW MUCH DID THE N.A.A.C.P. PAY YOU FOR BETRAYING YOUR RACE? PLEASE BE THE MAN THAT JUDAS WAS."

Horace Montgomery and his wife had married before the formation of the Athens Fellowship, and thus had had to use someone other than Universalist or Unitarian clergy. Ironically, they found out years later that the minister who had officiated at their wedding was a Ku Klux Klan Cyclops.

ness of America and her people. Mrs. Eliza Paschall, Unitarian and civil rights worker from Atlanta who gave the memorial address, spoke of her personal friendship with the Kings, and stressed the point that even seemingly small acts (such as paying your maid a living wage, writing your congressman to urge civil rights legislation, using Mr. and Mrs. in addressing all adults, etc.) can be very important. Many came away with the realization that all of us can be a living memorial by the way we live our lives.

Athens

The fellowship born in Athens, Georgia, gestated for over a year. One reason for its delayed birth was anxiety about its parentage. Some members of the initial core group identified themselves as Universalists and had made contact with the UCA. Others thought of themselves as Unitarians and so had contacted the AUA. They all thought it would be fine to be recognized by both the UCA and the AUA, which were in the process of discussing merger or consolidation.

In Boston, officials of the Universalist Church were willing to work with such a joint approach, but Munroe Husbands, fellowship director of the Unitarian Association, said "[Y]our members must choose to affiliate with either the Universalists or the Unitarians." The Universalist Unitarian Community Church of Athens officially organized on November 14, 1954, with UCA affiliation but both Universalist and Unitarian in the local name. It thus became one of only a handful of fellowships formed by and affiliated with the Universalist Church.

The Athens congregation had a typical childhood, using borrowed or rented quarters for over ten years, and then reaching sufficient maturity to incorporate and purchase a building. In 1970, a financial crisis within the UUA created the opportunity for the Unitarian Universalist Fellowship of Athens to take the next step in growth and obtain ministerial services. Clifton Hoffman, like district executives across the association, was terminated by the

UUA in early 1970 in a cost-cutting move. With the cushion of UUA severance pay, he could afford to take on a less-than-full-time ministry in Athens. Predictably, ministerial services led to further growth and the 1972 purchase of a church building.

Horace Montgomery, a University of Georgia professor of history and the fellowship's first president, wrote a history of the fellowship's first twenty-five years. He noted that in 1955, a mimeographed questionnaire indicated that all the members approved of the US Supreme Court's school desegregation decisions, which encouraged them in addressing issues of segregation and having Black speakers.

That history also notes that in 1968, the fellowship's Social Responsibility Committee sparked the formation of a credit union to offer low-cost loans to borrowers, Black and White, who might otherwise be at the mercy of finance companies.

Sources

For Savannah, the UUA files provided the data, and additional information about James Pierpont came from other sources. On Augusta, UUA files and a 1968 history of the congregation constituted the sources. Regarding Athens, the UUA files provided a large amount of material, including the twenty-five-year history written by Horace Montgomery. Montgomery also provided an interview on February 13, 2000.

JACKSONVILLE, FLORIDA

Materials in the UUA files tell small fragments of the story of a less-than-successful Jacksonville congregation begun in 1906. For at least part of its history, it had both Universalist and Unitarian backing, and letters suggest that the death knell was sounded by a mutual decision of both Boston headquarters in 1931 to discontinue $300 each in annual support. According to one document, the AUA bought a building lot for the congregation for $6,500 in 1907, almost succeeded in selling the lot and building for $125,000 in 1925, and ultimately sold it to the Nazarenes for $12,000 in 1943.

In 1944, scouting possible church starts or restarts for the AUA, Lon Ray Call visited San Antonio, Texas, and Jacksonville. He reported, "I entered San Antonio with the names of 17 people, all alive. Soon the list grew to over 50. I entered Jacksonville with 26 names, all dead or gone but 5." A San Antonio congregation was organized in 1945. In April 1950, a fellowship was finally formed in Jacksonville.

Life at the Unitarian Fellowship of Jacksonville proceeded for several years in fairly typical fellowship fashion, with services held in various rented spaces. Between 1953 and 1957, tensions increased. Papers filed by the fellowship in 1957 tell the story: They requested a $6,000 loan from an AUA fund set up specifically to aid Unitarian congregations in the South experiencing housing difficulties due to racial issues. Their loan application included this explanation:

In 1953, the Fellowship church school was begun, and immediately greater housing needs began to be felt. These were solved for a time when the Fellowship was allowed to meet at the YWCA. However, after almost a year of meeting there, tensions began to build up. Our presence was not apparently offensive when we did not advertise, but when our publicity program (consisting principally of AUA-supplied mats) got under way, it became evident that we were gradually becoming less welcome. Finally, after a sociology professor from the University of Florida spoke to us on some aspects of the Kinsey Reports, we were told that there was no longer any available space for our meetings.

Since our removal from the YWCA we have met in various meeting halls, but our tenure has become increasingly precarious in all of them because the Fellowship has gradually gained a reputation in the community as a group with liberal racial ideas.

The attitude of the community began to crystallize in the fall of 1956 when John B. Orr, Jr., a Unitarian member of the State House of Representatives, was invited to speak. He had gained a state-wide reputation for his lone vote against the measures then recently adopted by the Legislature to preserve segregation in the public schools. His visit was publicized in advance and was well attended by hecklers, apparently from the Ku Klux Klan, and sedate observers from the DAR [Daughters of the American Revolution] and UDC [United Daughters of the Confederacy]. There were also a few Negroes in attendance.

Following that meeting, which was held in the auditorium of the Independent Life Building, a local newspaper described the service as "radically integrated" and a telephone campaign was conducted by the UDC and DAR protesting our use of these facilities. The campaign was effective and we are no longer welcome at Independent.

In early spring of this year, Dr. A. Powell Davies was scheduled to speak to the Fellowship. Arrangements were made with the Prudential Insurance Company to use its auditorium. When Dr. Davies' address was announced to the public, a rumor was spread that he was a colored man, and the day before he was scheduled to appear, the official in charge of the auditorium called to cancel the engagement. We satisfied him that Dr. Davies was not a Negro, but he again threatened to cancel when we could not guarantee him that the meeting would not be integrated. The meeting was allowed to go on only because the official was convinced that cancellation would bring more unfavorable publicity than unpublicized integration. Needless to say we are no longer welcome at Prudential.

For two years prior to October of this year, we met regularly in the Jacksonville College of Music. The two meetings described above were held in special places because larger crowds than usual were expected. While the facilities at the College were not entirely adequate, there were rooms to house both children and adults. Moreover, inasmuch as one of our own members was its president we felt relatively secure in our tenure there. This situation changed suddenly in October of this year.

The changed situation arose from a change in attendance. Instead of occasional Black visitors, at least one Black man attended regularly. Neighbors phoned the college to protest. The college, worried about finances, told the president that if he wanted to keep his job, the congregation had to segregate or leave before the next Sunday.

Under that pressure, the fellowship found marginally acceptable temporary space and located a large house to purchase. The living room offered over 650 square feet that could be used for adult services, and there were many potential classrooms. With the assistance of the AUA loan, a contract to purchase the house was closed on December 29, 1957. But that was not the end of the story. Neighbors pressed the seller to cancel the sale on the grounds that the Unitarians solicited "colored people" as members. The seller, a Catholic layman, was not only persuaded to resist these pressures, but he arranged for his bank to finance the purchase and moved up the closing date. Then neighbors raised issues about the lack of off-street parking and questioned whether the fellowship was really a church. On February 12, 1958, the board of directors of the AUA welcomed the Unitarian Church of Jacksonville as a member congregation.

In early November 1959, Grant Butler began his service in Jacksonville as minister-at-large. The AUA used at least two ministers as "ministers-at-large" who could be placed by the AUA with a new congregation to grow it rapidly to the point of calling a settled minister. Attendance of adults and children quickly grew to require double sessions on Sunday mornings. By late January 1960, twenty-six families had joined the church during the minister-at-large program.

Charles White McGehee candidated February 7–14, 1960, to become the church's first minister and was called. A White man, McGehee was born in Summit, Mississippi, to a Baptist mother and an agnostic father. He did not attend college, at least in part due to an arthritic condition that forced him to rely on crutches. At age twenty-two, he became editor of the town weekly, as perhaps the youngest editor in the nation, and went on to other print journalism and radio work in McComb, Mississippi, and Birmingham, Alabama. In Birmingham he was a member of the Unitarian Church of the Larger Fellowship and then a charter member of the Unitarian Universalist congregation there. At forty-two, McGehee decided to enter theological school. He served in Upton, Massachusetts, before serving in Jacksonville, 1960–76. He had a part-time ministry in Chattanooga, 1976–81.

McGehee and several other individuals helped to shape and maintain the congregation's response to issues involving race. Isaiah Williams was one of the Black members whose presence made the purchase of a meeting place unavoidable. He was active in the NAACP branch and advised the NAACP youth. He kept others in the congregation informed and was often involved in interracial meetings at the church and elsewhere. When he left town to attend Florida A&M Law School, his advisor's role with NAACP youth was taken over by Quillie Jones, another Unitarian Universalist. In

1963, the Unitarian Universalist Service Committee provided the services of Ernest Lent as director of the Human Relations Council. In Jacksonville, as in other southern cities, the Human Relations Council filled a void. There was no other purposefully bi-racial organization, no other group doing strategic planning and communication aimed at ending racial exclusion. Human Relations Councils did not often undertake desegregation campaigns, but they certainly sparked those that were led by other groups.

In September 1963, in the immediate aftermath of the fatal bombing at the Sixteenth Street Baptist Church in Birmingham, Alabama, Gov. George Wallace was scheduled to speak in Jacksonville at the Civic Auditorium. The NAACP announced its intention to picket the event. The Ku Klux Klan announced its intention to disrupt the NAACP picketing. Ernie Lent of the Human Relations Council arranged for a group of White women to picket the event, which gave the NAACP the opportunity not to picket and denied the Klan an attractive target. Most of the picketing women came from the Unitarian Church.

After desegregation of the schools had been ordered by federal courts, the Duval County Federation for Constitutional Government persuaded the county commission to include a straw ballot on desegregation of public facilities with the primary vote. The Human Relations Council sued to prevent the straw vote. An injunction against it was granted, provided that a $25,000 cash bond was posted within three days. The Unitarian Universalist Commission on Religion and Race loaned $1,000, and much of the rest was raised through the Unitarian Church.

The NAACP conducted a March for Jobs and Freedom in September 1963, ending with a rally at City Hall, at which Charles McGehee was the only White minister among the speakers. In March 1965, St. Stephen AME Church hosted a bi-racial memorial service for James Reeb. McGehee was among ten White ministers who spoke to the sixteen hundred attendees. McGehee traveled to Montgomery, Alabama, for the final leg of the Selma-to-Montgomery march.

Charles McGehee and his family received threats. In November 1963, officers of the NAACP learned from an informant in the

Klan that there were threats from that quarter to "get" McGehee. Phone calls brought other threats. None were ever acted upon, and after a year or two, they subsided.

Although the congregation relied on ministerial leadership and on information and suggestions given to individuals by the Community Affairs Committee, there were clearly occasions on which the congregation acted as a whole. In 1972, this culminated in what McGehee called the "supreme accomplishment" of the congregation during his time in Jacksonville. Several members of the congregation had been active in Community Action District Six, referring to the most impoverished area of the city, plagued by pollution and dilapidated housing. Working with the Black and White residents of District Six, the church members and residents incorporated as Unicity and set about establishing facilities and programs to "promote, encourage, and improve the lives and conditions of the residents."

Notes

The Kinsey Reports mentioned in the fellowship's 1957 loan application refer to two controversial books based on surveys of male and female sexuality.

A. Powell Davies, the Welsh-born minister of All Souls Unitarian Church in Washington, DC, was one of the leaders of the post–World War II surge of Unitarian numerical growth and a much-coveted guest preacher.

Sources

Information for this chapter came, in part, from the files of the UUA and the deceased minister file on Charles McGehee at Andover-Harvard Theological Library at the Harvard Divinity School. An August 9, 1982, letter from Charles McGehee was also extremely helpful. A document compiled by Alfred W. Hobart in early 1966, "The Unitarian Universalist Witness in the Southeast 1950–1966," provided valuable data as well.

MIAMI AND OTHER CITIES IN FLORIDA

The Unitarian Universalist Congregation of Miami organized in 1939 as First Unitarian Church. By June 1942, Joseph Barth, who served as the first minister, finally felt that a real year-round church with effective lay leadership was underway. The tone of some of his reports suggests that at the beginning this was far from a foregone conclusion. The onset of World War II in late 1941 limited tourism, long the major local industry; it brought some people into the area, while others moved away for war-related jobs.

In an unusual development, a nascent sister congregation formed in Miami's Black community. A fundamentalist minister named William H. Floyd had moved in a liberal direction. He began gathering people to listen to Joe Barth's Sunday afternoon radio broadcasts and went on to organize a congregation. Floyd and Barth developed a working relationship. Records suggest that the AUA contributed some hymnals and at least $500 in supporting funds, but they leave unrecorded the fate of Floyd's efforts.

Barth served as minister until December 1955, when he accepted a call to King's Chapel in Boston. A few months before his departure, a church history notes that "two Negro members joined."

Glenn Canfield, who had served as the founding minister of the new Unitarian restart in Atlanta, was called in 1956 to follow Barth. Canfield spoke strongly from the pulpit in favor of "calm and orderly desegregation" in the schools. In the state legislature, John B. Orr, a member of the Miami congregation, raised his voice and cast a lonely vote on the same issue. In a special session of the state legislature, a Pupil Assignment Law was passed 89–1 to assign pupils on the basis of "intelligence, background, previous training, compatibility with other students in a particular school and various socio-economic factors." Orr cast the one dissenting vote, causing another politician to predict, "He won't get enough votes at the next election to serve as pallbearers at his political funeral." Orr was later defeated for re-election to the legislature, but the US Supreme Court ultimately invalidated the law, and in 1972 (when he was no longer a church member), he was elected mayor of Miami.

Robert Sonen served Miami 1959–63, John Papandrew served 1964–67, and Fred LeShane 1967–77. Papandrew in particular threw himself into civil rights issues and brought some members of the church with him. Even before coming to Miami, Papandrew had taken part in demonstrations in Albany, Georgia, and had been jailed there for a day and a half. During his first summer in Florida, he and some church members traveled with a Miami delegation to St. Augustine, where the Southern Christian Leadership Conference was leading demonstrations and often facing White mobs. In March 1965, John Papandrew and congregational president Bob Ross were among the Unitarian Universalists who responded to Martin Luther King Jr.'s call to come to Selma.

Tampa

Munroe Husbands of the AUA Fellowship Office writes in his report of a 1955 trip to Tampa, Florida:

> In my opinion this is the only *truly* interracial Fellowship in the South. The President, Charles B. Varney . . . is a professor in the segregated all-white Tampa University. (The dean of the school has informed the faculty that if he learns of any professors sitting down to a meal with colored people, they will probably be looking for new jobs.) The Vice-President of the congregation is a Negro gentleman, the Secretary a young white woman, and the Treasurer is also a Negro man.

Membership is about 5/8 white and 3/8 Negro, with one Japanese-American member. The group is well aware of the fact that it will have tough sledding—few meeting places are available to it. At the evening meeting held at the Negro Y.W.C.A., about twenty-five were in attendance, five or six who were new to the group and apparently interested. It is my recommendation that the Association lean over backwards in assisting this Fellowship since, being integrated in Florida, it has one if not two strikes against it.

Tallahassee

In Tallahassee, Unitarian Universalist students were among key campus leaders at Florida State University who initiated a program of negotiation and, ultimately, picketing and brief sit-ins in 1963 to desegregate restaurants near the campus. (The university itself had cautiously begun to desegregate in 1962, with perhaps a dozen Black students in a student body of eleven thousand.) When funds were needed after a few people were arrested in a sit-in, local and national Unitarian Universalist bodies helped out. Count Basie, in town to play at a fraternity-sponsored concert on December 3, 1963, was asked to join the effort; he sought entrance to one of the restaurants and, when denied, briefly joined the picket line. After several months of almost constant work by organizers, the restaurants ultimately desegregated.

Sources

UUA files, including a Miami church history sent to the UUA in 1987, provided the material on Miami and Tampa. The story of the Tallahassee student efforts was told by Alfred Hobart in his 1966 summation of Unitarian Universalist work in the Southeast. This valuable record has recently been made more broadly available through the work of Prof. Thomas Kersen on the Hobart papers.

KNOXVILLE, TENNESSEE

Next to the front entrance to the Tennessee Valley Unitarian Universalist Church in Knoxville is a plaque that reads, "Everyone Welcome." It continues:

> On February 12, 1950, when Jim Person, an African American, arrived at this church, he asked a greeter if the door sign, "Everyone Welcome," included him. In a highly segregated Knoxville community, Mr. Person was welcomed and eventually joined the church, making TVUC one of the first integrated congregations in Knoxville. Today's sign includes only two changes: the word Universalist, added in 1991, and the rainbow flag designating this church as a welcoming congregation, added in 1993. In the original spirit of inclusion, we open our arms to all who worship with us.

At the time of Jim Person's first visit, this congregation was only a year old, having formally organized on February 6, 1949. Although new, it was not without some pre-existing building blocks. A short-lived Universalist congregation was started in 1895 with twenty members. Unitarian congregations had been started three times—in 1869, 1895, and 1923 (among the members of the 1895 iteration was Mrs. J. C. Tyler, grandmother of author James Agee). These earlier congregations had lasted only one to eight years, but they had left a few people in Knoxville who still thought of themselves as Unitarians. Added to these were people drawn to the area by the University of Tennessee, the Tennessee

Valley Authority (one of the largest New Deal programs), and the
nearby town of Oak Ridge, built in secrecy during World War II as
part of the effort to develop an atomic bomb.

In 1948, a handful of Knoxville Unitarians asked for AUA assistance in starting a congregation. The AUA sent church planter Lon
Ray Call, and a congregation was formally organized with 112 persons from Knoxville and Oak Ridge signing the original statement
of purpose in 1949. Both the Oak Ridge and Knoxville congregations trace their founding to this date. Call was replaced briefly by
Grant Butler and then by Daniel Welch, who had served as minister for a time in the 1920s. The AUA assisted with the ministerial
salary, hymnals, and other resources, which continued with the
settlement of the first called minister, Richard Henry, in October
1949. By 1950, Oak Ridge became a separate congregation and
called its own minister.

For the first year or more of its existence, the Tennessee Valley
Unitarian Church rented space in the Christenberry Junior High
School for its services and Sunday school. Details differ in local
tellings of the story, but some time after Jim Person's visit, the con-
gregation entered a period they call "wandering in the wilderness."
Henry recalls,

> We met in six different locations in seven weeks: the An-
> drew Johnson Hotel, the Seventh Day Adventist Church, a
> private school, a theatre. Each Monday following Sunday
> services, I would receive a phone call: "We're terribly sor-
> ry, you'll have to move. We've received complaints," etc. I'll
> never forget the manager of the Booth Theatre's telling me:
> "Mr. Henry, I fought in Korea for our Bill of Rights and it
> makes me feel terrible to tell you this, but my owner called
> and told me, 'Get those Unitarians out or resign,' and Mr.
> Henry, I've got a wife and two little kids."

In July 1950, the congregation bought 3.7 somewhat hilly acres
along Kingston Pike, the main east-west thoroughfare of the community. In November of that year, as a temporary meeting place

until a church edifice could be erected on the Kingston Pike lot, they bought a former rooming house near the University of Tennessee campus and dubbed it Unitarian House.

Henry recalls, "When we began, we were a lily-white congregation, but a pretty radically-oriented one—at least the community thought as much." One local newspaper ran a story about the church renting space from a school with the headline, "Red Question Raised About Unitarians." Henry continues, "There was a liberal sprinkling of labor leaders among us. . . . There were a healthy number of East Tennessee accents among us and, contrary to, I suspect, a majority of UU congregations then as now, a substantial number of folks who were in socio-economically somewhat marginal circumstances."

As if simply being an interracial congregation were not enough, in 1950, several TVUC members were instrumental in starting Fellowship House Camps, a two-week summer day camp experience that was intentionally interracial. Before the US Supreme Court rendered its *Brown v. Board of Education* school desegregation decision, these camps provided a space in which children, youth counselors, and adult leaders met and collaborated across lines of race and religion. Nikki Giovanni, now a noted Black poet and teacher, but then a youngster who spent summers with her Knoxville grandparents, was one of the participants. Jews, Episcopalians, Presbyterians, and others joined Unitarians in supporting the camp sessions that continued until 1974. There was never a formal connection between TVUC and Fellowship House, but of the fifteen people who served as director of Fellowship House, at least ten were TVUC members.

Unitarian House, while not spacious, was a center of welcome in Knoxville. A wide variety of community organizations, some of which may not have had many other options, met there. In 1952, the Ohio State Symphonic Choir, scheduled to perform at the University of Tennessee, was not permitted to eat on campus because not all of its members were White. Unitarian House welcomed the choir. Thanks to a subsequent donation of cots by the American Friends Service Committee, Unitarian House then became something of a hostel for groups with slim budgets or interracial composition. One Japanese visitor wrote, "When we arrived in Knoxville, the group assembled at Unitarian House, where an impressive scene awaited us. We saw a Negro conducting a chorus of white people—a scene I did not expect to see in the South." The TVUC choir director at that time was Calvin Dash, assistant professor of vocal music at historically Black Knoxville College.

Clinton, Tennessee, just north of Knoxville, was the first community in the country to begin court-ordered school desegregation. A group of African-American parents had brought suit to end the practice of busing children at the parents' expense to Vine Middle School and Austin High School in Knoxville, rather than admitting them to secondary schools in Clinton. Initially, a federal judge found against the parents, but after the Supreme Court's *Brown* decision, he reversed himself and ordered desegregation in Clinton at the start of the next school year. For a short time in the fall of 1956, things went moderately well, but then White racist outside agitators generated threatening mobs. In response to that situation, Richard Henry and TVUC members authored a "Declaration of Conscience," urging obedience to the law. A local newspaper ran it on the front page for three days. The declaration attracted over two thousand signatures.

When Henry left Knoxville in 1957 to become minister of First Unitarian Society of Denver, work was underway on the congregation's new building, and there was a strong legacy of work in the community by both minister and members and friends of the congregation. Bob West, a native of Virginia, had just graduated from Starr King School for the Ministry and accepted the call to settle in Knoxville. In October 1957, he was ordained and installed in a service at Temple Beth El, since the TVUC building was still under construction.

Even as Henry left and West arrived in Knoxville, the Unitarian Service Committee (USC) was making a quiet but well-considered entrance to "assist representative local organizations in meeting problems in human relations, particularly those related to the desegregation of schools and other community facilities and services." Galen Martin, formerly executive director of the Kentucky Council on Human Relations, was the USC staff person in Knoxville, and soon assisted in the founding of the Knoxville Area Human Relations Council. This added another to the long roster of groups through which members of TVUC worked: National Conference of Christians and Jews, Knoxville Ministerial Alliance, Fellowship House, AFL-CIO, and more.

Bob West and the congregation were often in the news across a wide range of issues: advocating for legalizing the sale of liquor, opposing censorship, and opposing religious teaching in public schools, while advocating teaching evolution.

The largest-scale events involving issues of race during the years of West's ministry were the sit-ins of 1960, in which he was centrally involved. He writes,

> Beginning in early February, I was one of a group of some six-to-eight persons that coordinated efforts and developed strategy to accomplish desegregation of lunch counters without violence. Leaders of the group were three black ministers. A Knoxville College student body representative was a member. We met frequently, often daily and sometimes twice a day. That group determined day-to-day strategy and conducted training for the sit-ins, created the Associated Council for Full Citizenship, was the nucleus of the Council's executive committee, and called and conducted the mass meetings.
>
> During the three months or so following the initial consideration of sit-ins in early February, I was not in favor of conducting sit-ins in Knoxville and neither was the overwhelming majority of authentic black adult and student leadership.

But, he noted, when negotiations proved unproductive, "continuing organized sit-ins began on June 9. I participated in all of those sit-ins from the first day." West was pushed to this point by what felt like bad-faith negotiation on the part of the merchants.

Peggy and Bob Rainey

The Raineys were active and vocal but not in the same way as some church members who took part in demonstrations. Bob Rainey was a chemist in Oak Ridge at the Oak Ridge National Laboratories, and part of his activism included being a good supervisor and co-worker as ORNL began to employ Black workers in non-menial positions.

Bob recalls the advent of those early Black co-workers at the Oak Ridge Labs:

> I had the only Black technician, and they assigned him to me because they knew that I would take care of this fellow. For years, I had the only Black technician out there. Later we got a Black PhD chemist. He was Catholic. When he was coming, some of the other chemists who were Catholic called the priest and said, "There's no Black Catholic church in the area. What should he do?" The priest said, "You say he's a Catholic? He should come to Mass." Someone talked him into running for city council, and I was his campaign manager. Every day in the newspaper, there was some endorsement from someone or some organization to support him for city council. I told him I knew almost no one in the Black area, and Oak Ridge was segregated. He said, "Don't worry about the Black area, I can take care of the Black area; I need someone in the White area." That's why I got the various endorsements for him. He came in a close second, which was good because if he had come in first, he would have had to serve as mayor.

Although the Raineys describe themselves as working more behind the scenes than in overt demonstrations, they did act in ways that were publicly visible. Peggy remembers writing letters to the department stores about opening their lunch counters. After the era of sit-ins, she and the children would consciously choose seats near Black patrons.

When Bob Rainey was on the Knoxville ministerial search committee seeking a successor to Richard Henry, the committee used the Oak Ridge congregation as a "neutral pulpit" in which to hear potential candidates. Because of his employment in Oak Ridge, he knew the community and made a reservation for the search committee to have lunch after Bob West's sermon in Oak Ridge. He recalls,

Then it occurred to me a week or so before we were supposed to be out there that we had a committee member who was Black. These restaurants were having a lot of trouble integrating, and I called this restaurant and said, "Of course, this is not going to interfere with anything because we will be in a room by ourselves, but I don't want any trouble when we show up, and one of our members is Black. He said, "The time I have to feed a Black in my restaurant, I'll close my doors." I said, "I'll help you." And so I told everyone I knew, I'll never eat in that restaurant again. I didn't tell them why. I have no idea whether he was already on the verge of going out, but within just a couple or three months he was out of business.

The Rainey children picked up on the quietly principled behavior of their parents. Peggy remembers,

When our daughter, Janice, was in ninth grade, the English teacher asked who was in favor of integration, and she and one other person raised their hands. The other gal was Lutheran and some time later was taken out and got into the Lutheran school. Janice was not elected to Beta Club although she was certainly qualified— four years later.

Bob Rainey did not come to issues of race from an academic or "Yankee" perspective. He was a White Mississippian by origin:

I was born in Mississippi, in Charleston, and my mother was from Kosciusko. My father was a southern White gentleman. He was just vigorously opposed to integration. I didn't get along well with him, but when we got married, one of Peggy's things was that she was going to see to it that we got back together. And so he came and visited us in Oak Ridge a number of times. When he was there, we never invited any Blacks to come and have dinner or anything with us because he would have been uncomfortable with that. But if we met one of them on the street, we certainly couldn't pass them up or not speak to them. And we did this one day. We got home that evening, and Daddy just worked it into the conversation: "You know I didn't raise my children to be like me. I expect them to think for themselves."

I had a cousin who was a truck driver, and we had family reunions and all. He was talking to me one time, and he said, "If I ever meet one of those integrationists, I'll kill him on the spot." I looked at him and said, "Terrell, you'll have to kill me."

We did not march, but we lived the integration, and it wasn't easy.

In evaluating the sit-ins and the eventual desegregation of downtown lunch counters, West cites four factors as being "most critical" in the success of the sit-ins:

- the maturity and ability of Knoxville College students and adult black leaders
- the leadership and unstinting efforts of the mayor and police chief
- the quiet but effective work over several years by Galen Martin and the Knoxville Area Human Relations Council
- the active involvement of such a large number of people from the Unitarian congregation, which accounted for nearly all of the white demonstrators.

West writes, "[W]e could count on 30–35 members of our congregation as active participants in the June sit-ins and demonstrations." He continues,

In addition to our members who were active participants in the sit-ins and public demonstrations, there were different types of actions in which other members of our congregation engaged, such as talking with their non-Unitarian neighbors and acquaintances in support of the sit-ins, ceasing to patronize merchants who discriminated, canceling charge accounts, attending the mass meetings, and demonstrating their willingness to eat lunch while blacks were at the lunch counters.

In the course of the sit-ins downtown, TVUC member Jack LeFlore had gone to University Hospital to visit his mother. (University was the only one of Knoxville's four general hospitals at that time that would admit Black patients.) LeFlore had gone to the hospital lunchroom, was denied service, and started a sit-in. The details vary in the telling of the story but all versions of the story agree that through LeFlore's persistence, the facility was desegregated. In one version, LeFlore said to a hospital official, "The taxes I paid probably bought the bricks under the stool I'm sitting on, and I want to use my bricks."

TVUC-affiliated White students at the University of Tennessee got involved in efforts to desegregate movie theaters, including the large downtown Tennessee Theatre, a movie palace opened in 1928. Harry Wiersema Jr., a college student, and Lucille Thornburgh, a union activist, would buy multiple tickets and provide them to Blacks seeking to enter. College student Pete Benson recalls another technique to dramatize the irrationality of segregation:

> Before we went up to the window, we would arrange ourselves in order of skin tone. We would start with the completely white Anglo-Saxon types like myself, and then we'd pick some of us who were maybe just a little bit swarthy or dark-skinned, maybe somebody of Mediterranean extraction, and then some people of mixed white and black ancestry who had kind of a tan coloration . . . and so on to the completely black, purely African people. . . . It would be impossible for the ticket sellers to determine just where the line was between white and black, which was, of course, entirely our point—that there is no sharp distinction. People are people.

One of the Black student leaders of the sit-ins in Knoxville was Robert Booker, a veteran of military service and a few years older than other undergraduates. Booker remembers visiting TVUC during the sit-ins, recalling vividly that, in addition to recognizing some of the members who were involved in the protests, he could tell this church was different. There were ashtrays on all the chairs, and the minister announced that the next Saturday there would be a clean-up party for which the church would supply coolers, but you had to bring your own beer. Booker did not actually sign the membership book at TVUC until he was graduating and got a job offer to teach French and literature in Sitka, Alaska. The Sitka school, operated by the Presbyterian Church, found his academic credentials in order but said it could not hire him until he affiliated with a Presbyterian congregation. His reaction was to think, "Like hell I will," and to join TVUC.

The next ministerial transition sent Bob West to Rochester, New York, in 1963, and brought Kenneth Torquil MacLean to Knoxville in early 1964.

MacLean came to Knoxville with a concern for the civil rights struggle and for other social justice issues. In 1965, he joined other Unitarian Universalists in going to Selma, Alabama, after law officers beat and tear-gassed nonviolent marchers there on Bloody Sunday.

Three years later, the Poor People's Campaign that Martin Luther King Jr. had started, but did not live to lead, came through Knoxville in May 1968. Ken served as local coordinator, with many church members providing crucial leadership in arranging financing, food, and overnight shelter for the Poor People's Campaign caravan of five hundred to eight hundred people. Among the stories still alive in the memory of the congregation is one that people heard from both Ken MacLean and Janet Porter: Ken phoned Janet with the question, "Can you feed a thousand people tomorrow?" The people were fed, so apparently she could.

During MacLean's ministry, a separate Social Action Committee was established and led the congregation in advocating for equality of opportunity in employment and housing. TVUC's board joined three other organizations in sponsoring a meeting, "Free Speech in Knoxville and the Highlander Center." Highlander was and remains a research, education, and organizing center seeking to empower people in Appalachia and the Deep South who have been disadvantaged by the status quo. Founded in 1932 in Monteagle, Tennessee, it initially focused on helping people of the mountains resist exploitation, whether by organizing their communities or by energizing unions. It worked from the outset at being racially inclusive, and by the 1950s, more and more of Highlander's work focused on issues of race. Rosa Parks attended a workshop at Highlander the summer before she refused to give up her seat on a Montgomery bus. She later recalled,

> At Highlander, I found out for the first time in my adult life that this could be a unified society, that there was such a thing as people of different races and backgrounds meeting together in workshops and living together in peace and harmony. It was a place I was very reluctant to leave. I gained there strength to persevere in my work for freedom, not just for blacks but for all oppressed people.

When Martin Luther King Jr. spoke at Highlander's twenty-fifth anniversary, he heard Pete Seeger lead the song that Zilphia Horton of Highlander had brought back from a labor picket line: "We Shall Overcome." In 1960, the state revoked the charter of Highlander Folk School on trumped-up charges, but Highlander Research and Education Center immediately sprang into being in Knoxville and carried on the same work. The institution and the work continue, as do the longstanding ties between the church and Highlander.

A set of issues that began to emerge during Bob West's ministry, and that continued and grew during Ken MacLean's, involved equality of access to services. The Greater Knoxville Council on Human Relations, created with Unitarian Service Committee support, documented unequal distribution of services and programs. In particular, it devoted a multi-year effort of research, education, and advocacy to park areas and recreational programs. Unitarian Universalists allied with neighborhood representatives and advocated over a period of years for providing parks, pools, and programs that could be accessed by lower-income and minority

Wade and Becky Till

Becky Till grew up in Africa, where her parents were part of the United Presbyterian mission. Her childhood playmates were African. Living in Knoxville as an adult, she joined the Cedar Springs Presbyterian Church.

She recalls that a very nice, well-educated, middle-aged Black businessman who lived in that area came and asked to join Cedar Springs Presbyterian. When he was turned down, she left the church and didn't go to any church for a while. Later she joined Tennessee Valley Unitarian Church.

Becky says that she didn't do much in the sit-ins because there were six children at home, and one of them was a baby. She recalls doing some sit-ins at Kresge's and says that it seemed like a third of those sitting in at that time were White. She recalls the church having things pretty well organized.

Wade Till grew up in Mississippi. He recalls noticing and reacting against the mistreatment of Blacks: "When I was in high school, I was beginning to get pissed off about this thing that was going on. Hell, I was raised with Blacks. I knew they were people. I went in the service and wound up playing football and working with Blacks in the air force. We played football together and lived together and worked together. I just didn't go back to Mississippi."

Wade was a salesman for Rawlings Sporting Goods. Given his job, he didn't picket stores or take much overt action in support of desegregation; instead he worked more behind the scenes. Still, his employer heard about his opinions and associations, and did make some remarks to him.

He thought he could act safely by talking out at the golf course to the editor of the newspaper and pushing for more coverage of demonstrations. More overtly, Wade wrote a letter to the editor about the existence in Knoxville of essentially two fire departments. The Black fire department had old beat-up trucks and no extra personnel to substitute if someone got sick, and they had to cover parts of the city where fires were more likely to occur. Some of his Black friends urged him to write the letter. He asked in the letter why there wasn't just one fire department serving the whole city. He received hostile responses to his letter: harassing and threatening phone calls, the delivery of funeral flowers, and more. In the end, his letter did play a role in ending the practice of separate and unequal fire departments. In a later interview, Wade said that he felt that his membership in the Unitarian Church made a difference in his being involved in issues of racial justice in Knoxville.

Jack LeFlore was a friend of Wade and Becky's. Becky recalls Jack LeFlore as "tall, distinguished, good looking, smart" and observes, "He had great presence." Wade says of him:

Jack LeFlore came from Greenwood, Mississippi, in Leflore County. His daddy was a White LeFlore—a very prominent family —and his daddy took Jack's Black momma to his farm out in the country, and told everybody in Greenwood to kiss his ass. He raised about six kids there in Greenwood. One of Jack's brothers stayed there until he died. One of the brothers moved to Chicago. Jack and two sisters and a brother came to Knoxville College. By then, the parents had divorced. Jack's daddy was an alcoholic. His daddy went and lived with Jack's older brother in Chicago. Lived with him until he died. The people in Greenwood wouldn't let him [the son] bring the body down and bury it. They wouldn't do it at the funeral home. After the brother died, Jack had the body exhumed and got the White kinfolk in Greenwood to bury him there.

Jack was a school ring salesman, I think for Balfour. Jack finally got to be vice president of the company nationally. Made good money. Their momma made them all have a trade. Jack's was house decorating. They all had a trade. The one that stayed in Mississippi was a tailor. At least two of them were tailors.

Jack went out to the hospital to see his sister. He went in and bought a cup of coffee, and they handed it to him. And he sat down at the counter with his back to the counter, and they made a remark to him, something about you can't drink this in here. And Jack said something like, "I'll just prove you're wrong," and turned around and stayed. And he'd go home about 5 o'clock, and get up the next morning at 8 o'clock and stay there. They kind of closed while he was there because nobody would come in. He did it all by himself. I think he finally had a couple of people go with him, but mostly he was by himself. He just sat there and looked at them. He said he got bored as hell.

neighborhoods as well as by upper- and middle-income and White neighborhoods. They also challenged racial segregation in the juvenile detention facility.

Coda

On July 27, 2008, a month after the plaque permanently proclaiming "Everyone Welcome" was unveiled next to the front door of the church, a gunman entered the building during the Sunday service, killing two people and injuring at least seven others because he "hated liberals." Both the plaque and the spirit it enunciates remain in place. Just as Jim Person, a Black man, found a welcome in 1950, now it is made clear that LGBTQI persons will also be welcomed. Now, as in 1950, the congregation stands by its principles even in the face of hostility.

Sources

Much of the general material in this account is taken from some well-done local histories, especially, "A History: Tennessee Valley Unitarian Church, 20th Anniversary, 1949–1969" and "Fifty Years of Social Activism at the Tennessee Valley Unitarian Universalist Church."

The quotations from Richard Henry are from postings May 20 and May 25, 2003, to the Unitarian Universalist history email list. An April 27, 2000, letter from Robert Nelson West provided a great deal of material.

Unitarian Service Committee memos of May 22 and September 23, 1957, and other material were drawn either from information in the church files or from file material of the UUA.

Books contributing to this account include *Diary of a Sit-in*, by Merrill Proudfoot (Urbana and Chicago: Illini Books Edition, University of Illinois Press, 1990) and *Unearthing Seeds of Fire: The Idea of Highlander*, by Frank Adams with Myles Horton (Winston-Salem, North Carolina: John F. Blair, 1975). The note on the 1895 Universalist congregation in Knoxville is from the second volume of Russell Miller's *The Larger Hope* (Boston: Unitarian Universalist Association, 1985).

For information on the 2008 shooting, see Olivia Spooner's "Tomorrow: The Tragedy and Healing in Knoxville" on the Unitarian Universalist History and Heritage Society website: www.uuhhs.org. It was the winning essay in the 2009 Youth History Essay contest.

Bob and Peggy Rainey gave a March 7, 2000, tape-recorded interview. Wade and Becky Till gave an oral history interview on March 31, 2003. Note that Wade Till's telling of Jack LeFlore's sit-in differs from the account derived from *Diary of a Sit-in* and from "Fifty Years of Social Activism at the Tennessee Valley Unitarian Universalist Church," which illustrates the joys and hazards of using oral history sources. Bob Booker was interviewed on June 10, 2013.

OAK RIDGE, TENNESSEE

Oak Ridge was and continues to be a unique community, built from scratch in secrecy by the United States government. In 1942, as the super-secret Manhattan Project launched US efforts to devise and build a nuclear weapon, the scientists needed a site to purify uranium. The ideal site would be accessible yet somewhat remote and would have access to water and electric power. They selected an unincorporated and lightly settled area west of Knoxville, Tennessee. The scattered rural population of early 1942 increased to about seventy-five thousand in 1945, with housing built in a city laid out by government authority. Thus, Oak Ridge started with no crinoline and hoopskirt local aristocracy, no Confederate monument on the town square, no facilities that had "always" been used by people of only one race.

However, looking back, we have to remember (or learn) that a community built to 1942 government specifications, especially in the South, would be utterly, totally segregated. Housing was completely segregated and significantly unequal. Employment was absolutely segregated. Education was initially provided only for White children. All public accommodations—restaurants, hotels, buses, barbershops and beauty salons, movies, parks and playgrounds—were segregated.

This project, like the secret laboratories at Los Alamos that fabricated the first weapons, attracted a large number of highly educated scientists and engineers, the sort of population subset that, like a university community, had long been thought to be ideal for the establishment of a Unitarian congregation. By 1949, when the "secret city" was no longer a secret and could actually formally adopt the name Oak Ridge, Unitarians began to organize, acting in coordination with Unitarians in Knoxville.

Even before a Unitarian congregation had begun, some of those who would form it began work against racial disparities. In 1946, Dr. and Mrs. Jean Felton offered vaccinations and health information in the isolated and second-class Scarboro Village, the Black residential area.

In February 1949, Oak Ridge Unitarians joined the Knoxvillians in chartering as a congregation, but the Oak Ridge branch quickly established an independent identity and existence. By 1950, Paul Bliss was serving as the Oak Ridge minister, and by 1951, the congregation was evaluating site options and considering building plans.

By October 1951, some members pressured Bliss because they thought that he was insufficiently dedicated to pursuing issues of brotherhood and interculturalism. In 1954, he was succeeded in the Oak Ridge ministry by Arthur Graham, who served until his retirement in 1975.

Elizabeth Peele remembers moving to Oak Ridge in 1954 and finding "a segregated Army camp." Graham preached a sermon about local segregation, saying it was cruel and dehumanizing. With the support of the congregation, his sermon was printed in the local paper, leading to the formation of the Community Relations Council in 1956. Elizabeth and Robert Peele remember about eight Black members of the congregation at that time, and they note that the Black members were vital in educating the rest of the congregation about Oak Ridge's segregated reality. The Community Relations Council had active Unitarian involvement but also received support from members of Presbyterian, Baptist, Methodist, and other churches. In contrast to older southern cities, issues of desegregation and providing services to Black residents were addressed by these congregations, plus the Episcopalians, Lutherans, Jews, Friends, and others.

Elizabeth Peele admits to naïveté on the part of the Community Relations Council. They thought that if they investigated and documented the segregated conditions, and showed how unfair they were, the conditions would be changed. Although Oak Ridge acted earlier than most communities to end total segregation of its schools, it was not ready to race far ahead. For example, although Black students were permitted and encouraged to participate in varsity athletics, if an opposing team objected to being on the field or floor with them, the Black athletes would be withheld from that particular contest. And most public accommodations remained totally or partially segregated until passage of the 1964 Civil Rights Act.

Ultimately, the Community Relations Council undertook selected actions to dismantle the segregation of public facilities. At a laundromat the council held an anti-segregation picket line while the Ku Klux Klan held a pro-segregation picket line across the street. The council tested segregation in barber shops, sometimes by just asking at the shop whether they would serve Black men, but often by sending two men, one Black and one White, to walk in and seek service. When no barber shop could be persuaded to serve Black customers, the council ultimately brought to town and actively supported a barber who welcomed all customers. Robert Peele served as one of the testers, and Elizabeth Peele reports that half of the barbershop committee was Unitarian.

The 1964 annual meeting of the congregation included a report from the Public Affairs Committee noting that an overwhelming number of church households said that they would welcome Black residents in their neighborhoods but hesitated to sign a pledge committing themselves to sell or rent property on an "open occupancy" basis.

During the summer of 1964, Ronald Meservey of Oak Ridge was one of the student volunteers in the Mississippi Summer Project. He worked in Greenwood, Mississippi, where Stokely Carmichael was the project director. Carmichael, a Black Student Nonviolent Coordinating Committee leader, later became famous (to some, infamous) for promoting the slogan "Black Power." Meservey recalls that in 1964, Carmichael discussed personally canvassing door-to-door in White neighborhoods of Greenwood to ask Whites to join the Mississippi Freedom Democratic Party; he dropped the idea only after being convinced that he might be shot if he tried it.

Sources

UUA files provided some material. Elizabeth and Bob Peele spoke at the 2012 Gathering of Unitarian Universalist Civil Rights Veterans about their experience of living in Oak Ridge, and shared a copy of "A History of Segregation in Oak Ridge 1943–1960," which Elizabeth prepared for the Oak Ridge Community Relations Council. Ron Meservey was also interviewed at the Veterans Gathering.

CHATTANOOGA, TENNESSEE

Both Universalists and Unitarians had congregations in Chattanooga starting in the nineteenth century. Universalist congregations appear to have existed 1860–61, 1897–1907, and 1907–50.
A Unitarian congregation founded in 1889 functioned until about
1934, producing one significant minister. Marion Franklin Ham,
originally a lay leader in the congregation, was, with no theological
education, ordained and installed as their minister in 1898. As the
author of the hymn "As Tranquil Streams," his influence among
Unitarian Universalists continues today.

Beginning in 1951, work began to form a Unitarian fellowship.
Initially, confusion reigned, both in Chattanooga and in Universalist and Unitarian headquarters offices in Boston, regarding
whether this would be a joint Unitarian and Universalist effort and
whether it would attempt to use the facilities of the Shinn Memorial Universalist Church building. The AUA ultimately decided
that the Universalist building was neither well located nor in good
repair, and the Universalist congregation had a history of internal
factionalism and splits; in consequence, a congregation would do
better to make a fresh start in a different facility. The fresh start
occurred in November 1951, with services initially held in the
county court building.

Growth was slow at first. Over the first six months, the congregation grew from sixteen to twenty members, while attendance
increased from ten or fifteen to more than twenty. A fellowship
member invited the whole group to attend a Great Books Club she
belonged to, which she thought was very liberal (with "a Negro

member"). Subsequently, two members of the Great Books group joined the fellowship, and two couples from it attended services.

In July 1952, the Unitarian Service Committee held a youth camp at Highlander Folk School near Monteagle, Tennessee, led by Alfred Hobart, the AUA regional director. Hobart, at the invitation of the Chattanooga Fellowship, preached for them in mid-July, generating a turnout of twenty-five people. He observed, "It is the first time I have preached in a court room and an air-conditioned one, at that. If we could get air conditioning in our churches, we might keep them open all summer."

In 1955, Munroe Husbands, fellowship director for the AUA, went on a month-long field trip into the Southeast with a final stop in Chattanooga. In his report, he grumped about the lack of advance preparation for his visit and a lack of warmth within the fellowship. On a positive note, he observed that the congregation had signed a contract on a church building costing $23,000, a step, he said, "that will make them or break them."

During a two-day field trip to the Chattanooga Fellowship in 1956, religious educator Frances Wood noted conversation about two different social issues. The area schools permitted outside instructors to come in to the schools and teach a hellfire and damnation version of religion. Some fellowship members were concerned but not ready to address the issue head-on. On issues of race, they seemed more deeply and personally engaged. One woman said, "I feel that we are people without a country."

A 1962 religious education field trip by Edna Bruner produced a suggestion from Charles Moore, minister in Chattanooga, 1959–62, for Unitarian Universalist curriculum development:

The Rev. Charles Moore . . . expressed the wish that there might be a unit for high schoolers, tracing the present sit-in movement not only back to Gandhi but back to Tolstoi and Thoreau and Adin Ballou. He was asking something of a sociologist's reporting. This is a live subject down here in which a goodly number of our people have been involved positively in a variety of ways. The next day, in consultation with the Reverend and Mrs. Clifton Hoffman, Mr. Hoffman suggested "case studies in liberal religion at the social action level." Mr. Hoffman was underscoring the case study approach through more than one aspect of current social issues. I had asked him about the persons in this conference who had been most creative and Mr. Hoffman's suggestion that Dr. Sidney L. Freeman of Charlotte might be the person who could do the job. He also suggested Dr. Charles Jones of the Community Church in Chapel Hill, or collaboration between the two.

Ernest Howard succeeded Charles Moore and served 1963–67. He and a number of members of the congregation joined a Black-led march to the Hamilton County courthouse in memory of Jim Reeb in 1965. Some members of the congregation subsequently received harassing calls from segregationists.

Robert Booker, who had been a leader in the Knoxville sit-ins and briefly a member of Tennessee Valley Unitarian Church, moved to Chattanooga in 1962 for a teaching job and joined the Chattanooga congregation. He was the only Black member for the two years he was there. He edited the church newsletter and was part of the church's Way Off Broadway Players acting group and the congregation's active social life. Through church members and their involvement in the broader community, he was on the cutting edge of Blacks being "allowed" to do certain things. For example, a civic group held an annual presentation of readings from Abraham Lincoln's writings, and one year Booker was one of the four readers (and heard that there had been an audible gasp in the audience when he stepped out on stage). Chattanooga had never had a Black person do a television commercial, and Bob Booker was approached about doing the first but moved back to Knoxville before it could be filmed.

For its justice-seeking efforts, the church received an unwelcome form of attention: two Molotov cocktails. In 1965, a basement church school room was burned. In 1967, a bomb was tossed into the sanctuary, scorching some carpet, some hymnals, and the side of a Steinway upright piano. In 2000, the piano, restored to full musical standards and with its civil rights battle scars preserved under Plexiglas, was rededicated in a concert at the church.

Jack Wilkinson was called by the congregation to succeed Ernest Howard. Wilkinson was used in efforts to break the last vestiges of segregated public facilities. At least one nightspot in town was open to Whites only on the pretext that it was a private club. Those seeking to break this barrier had Wilkinson buy a "membership" (readily available to any White with cash in hand) and go by to have a beer and shoot some pool until he became a familiar face there and began to bring "guests" who were readily accepted, even without a membership. Then he brought a Black guest. As it happened, when the resulting case was heard in court, the presiding judge was Black, and the owner abolished the members-only, Whites-only policy on the spot in the courtroom.

A 2002 *Chattanooga Times Free Press* story reported that when suit was filed seeking an end to Bible teaching in the public schools, all the plaintiffs were members of the Chattanooga congregation.

Sources

The prime source for this chapter was the material in the UUA files. Jack Wilkinson recounted his story of nightspot desegregation at the Gathering of Unitarian Universalist Civil Rights Veterans in Asheville, North Carolina, March 30–April 1, 2012. Robert Booker was interviewed on June 10, 2013.

NASHVILLE, TENNESSEE

Nashville, the capital of Tennessee, was the site of two attempts at Unitarian churches and one Universalist church before enduring success was achieved. The 1851–53 Unitarian effort, led by Charles Manson Taggert, reportedly achieved average service attendance of about twenty. Few if any ripples marked its disappearance. Historian Charles Howe notes that Quillen Shinn's Universalist missionary efforts between 1891 and 1907 included Nashville, but Howe does not report on how far toward establishing even a transient congregation those efforts proceeded.

The 1916–34 effort achieved more and left some positive traces behind it. This congregation purchased property but apparently never fulfilled plans to build a more suitable structure on it. Five different ministers served brief ministries of one to four years each. In March 1934, the congregation formally disbanded, with some members joining Collegeside Congregational Church.

In about 1946, some Vanderbilt University students began to meet, thanks in part to the leadership of Frank Schulman—who would later become a distinguished Unitarian Universalist minister. They met in the library and at the Student Christian Association until a dean objected to their self-description as "liberal" and forced them off campus. They then began to meet at Collegeside Congregational Church.

In May 1950, a Unitarian fellowship was formally organized, starting with eleven members and twenty dollars. After meeting in four different locations, the fellowship purchased a house and grounds on Fairfax Street in 1953. Each member family was asked

Will Campbell on Bob Palmer and the Nashville congregation

Will Campbell was a Mississippi-born, Yale-educated renegade Baptist minister who served as the National Council of Churches' chaplain to the civil rights movement. His memoir, Brother to a Dragonfly, *is a notable reflection on race, class, religion, and much else. In an August 25, 1982, letter from his home in Mount Juliet, Tennessee, he writes,*

I do recall most vividly that during the fifties and early sixties there were two places we could meet regularly in the white community. One was the Unitarian Church. The other was the Jewish Community Center. It stuck in my memory because as a deep water Trinitarian I always resented it. Robert Palmer was the Unitarian minister during most of that time in Nashville and it became standard procedure to call on Bob for the invocation. That was for two reasons. One, he was always there. And two, we didn't want to take a chance on the other Christian preachers who were apt to end with, "In the name of the only true civil rightist, even Jesus Christ our Lord and Savior. Amen." Bob was a tough and noble soul (still is) and came in for a lot of harassment. I do not recall any physical abuse he suffered but when the Jewish Community Center was bombed he was in the forefront of protest and reconciliation. Since none of us whites made an A I suppose we'll have to give Bob Palmer a B+ and his congregation a C. That, of course, is looking back from the security of the present. At the time the marks would have been much higher.

to purchase the chairs they would need in the house at the rate of five dollars per chair.

Issues of race had been present almost from the beginning of this congregation. Excerpts from correspondence found in the UUA files illustrate the ways these issues played out. The following excerpt is from an October 5, 1951, letter from Munroe Husbands, AUA fellowship director, to C. Vernon Hines, president of the Nashville fellowship:

A few weeks ago Frank Schulman dropped into my office. We have been good friends for several years and it was a pleasure to see him again. We talked about a number of churches and Fellowships, among them Nashville. One statement he made has caused me a great deal of concern ever since. This was that a verbal agreement has been made among the members (or Executive Committee) of Nashville that if a Negro should wish to become a member, or worship with you, he (the non-white) would be informed that his presence was not wanted. Immediately I checked your by-laws and found that "brotherhood undivided by nation, race or creed" is one of your purposes and that membership is open to anyone who is in sympathy with your "Purpose and program." Therefore, I was inclined to think that Frank had misunderstood. On the other hand, I know him well enough to realize he is not the kind of young man who enjoys "telling tales out of school." Having committed himself to the Unitarian ministry (without his family's approval), I know he is dedicating his ability and talent to the Unitarian ideal.

Hines responded to Munroe Husbands on October 11, 1951:

With all due respect to Mr. Schulman, he either misunderstood our attitude here in Nashville or he did not convey it correctly to you. We have not agreed that if a negro wished to become a member of the Fellowship or worship with us that he would be informed that his presence was not wanted.

When we formed this Fellowship at one of our meetings this question came up and someone had said there were several Unitarians connected with Fisk University and they might offer to attend our Fellowship services. We discussed the matter pro and con and finally decided that if we allowed negroes to become a member [sic] of our Fellowship that we might as well stop where we were. You might break the laws of a country and get by with it but you can't violate its customs without paying the penalty.

We, therefore, agreed that if negroes did offer to affiliate with us that we would explain to them how their con-

Interview—Ralph and Jean Cazort, early Black members of the Nashville Church

We became involved with the Nashville Unitarian Church through our very close friends, Nancy and Tony Eaton. Nancy was Rev. Charles Joy's daughter. The church had just started. They came back and said, "You really ought to go." Tony at that time was working at Fisk University. I [Ralph] was at Meharry Medical School.

We had bought a large house. We were a young family on a professorial stipend. It was a two-family dwelling. Tony and Nancy lived in the upstairs apartment. Our children were about the same age. It worked out quite well. The entire time they were there, we never needed a babysitter because one of us was always going to be home. At that time, there was a law or a tradition or custom that the races didn't mix, didn't stay together in the same dwelling. But we did. I don't recall having any problems, partly because maybe people never knew. We lived in a transitional neighborhood.

It was about 1953 or 1954, we became involved. Once we went, it was Bob Palmer. We were so taken by Bob that we stayed. We were meeting in a large house on Fairfax. It was two stories with a full attic where we had some classes. As things began to grow, we even had classes in the basement, and they referred to that area as "the coal bin."

Bob Palmer was very active in the whole civil rights movement. He invited meetings to the church. The congregation as a whole was not as involved as Bob was.

When we joined this church, some people quit. We were not the first African-American members, but there were times in the 1950s when we were the only active members.

The movement in the South in the 1950s followed the movement up north in the 1940s and early 1950s. I had been involved in a sit-in and jailed in Detroit before I came to Meharry.

Many members of the Unitarian congregation were sympathetic to the movement and played background or supporting roles. They would go to a rally but might not want to be photographed there. Avery Leiserson and Stan Erickson were Vanderbilt faculty members who made a public statement regarding the urgency of equal opportunity. Joe Moore was always eager to discuss issues.

This was the only predominantly White congregation in town, with the possible exception of the Reform Jewish congregation, that made any effort in civil rights. The mainline Protestant denominations didn't do anything. Of course, the Black churches were very active, especially First Baptist [Capitol Hill] with Kelly Miller Smith.

Bob Palmer was the conduit for a lot of information about what was going on in the community. He talked to us about what was going on. After church in Bob's time, there was a meeting of those who cared to attend and discuss that morning's sermon, and that could turn in any direction.

This congregation was thought of around Nashville as a bunch of radicals, not a cult, but also not thought of as a serious religion—a bunch of intellectuals.

nection with us would probably jeopardize our growth and they would be far more advantageous to the Unitarian movement for them to form their own group and allow us to try to grow to the point where we could establish a church on a solid footing. That while it might not stop our growth yet it would certainly make the job difficult. We felt that any colored person who was a Unitarian could understand our position and would not become offended.

Last year a Mr. Parker who was teaching at the School of Theology at Fisk University was asked by one of our members to speak to us. The day he came there two negroes from Fisk came with him. As a result of this visit one of our most ardent members, a woman who had been a Unitarian for thirty years and who had been a regular attendant at First Church in Boston where she lived for a number of years, resigned from our group.

Husbands responded to Hines on December 19, 1951:

First, I wish to state that I believe the liberals in the South, particularly the religious liberals, are doing far more to al-

Interview—Virginia Price

Virginia Price became a member of the Nashville Fellowship early in its history, while it was still meeting on the Vanderbilt campus. She described herself and her husband as the first non-academic people in the fellowship. She tells part of her story:

The main thing that I did [in civil rights] was drink enough coffee to float a battleship. I went to the little lunch bar at Harvey's and the ten-cent stores. We would go to the lunch counter and find a place by a Black person and sit down. And what could you do but order a cup of coffee, and do that several times and then go to another place. So I kept on the run for several days. I forget exactly how long we did it.

One time, we were in McClellan's, and some bottle throwing started going on. In just a few minutes, there were a lot of policemen there, and there was havoc. That was the only time that I ever really felt any danger. I knew everybody was disapproving of what I was doing, but I didn't feel any danger, but this time there were Coke bottles thrown, and it was kind of a dangerous situation there for a while.

The hardest thing I had to contend with was my own family, because nobody understood how I felt about it. It's hard to go against your neighborhood and your friends, but it's even harder to go against your own family.

We lived in a very conservative East Nashville White neighborhood. We lived within hearing distance of Hattie Cotton School. [This school was all White until one Black child had been enrolled there as school desegregation began in Nashville in 1957.] My husband and I were sound asleep when we heard the bomb go off. When it happened, we both jumped up in bed, and I said to David immediately, "That was a bomb," and it was Hattie Cotton. I don't know how I came to . . . I guess we were just expecting it. The next day, I did go over there, and of course, all the people in the neighborhood were there. And the thing that was being said by so many people was, "I don't want integration, but I don't want this." I think that the bombing of Hattie Cotton did more to bring about school integration than any other one thing.

There were separate White and Black PTAs. When I was so active in PTA, I tried to get cooperation between the two groups as much as I could, not making much progress in it. I went out to Pearl High School, a Black high school, to a meeting, and the PTA president was talking about how many people she had invited from the White PTA, and she said, "None of them would come." The person sitting next to me I could see peripherally pointing to me to remind the president that I was sitting there. She said, "Oh, Mrs. Price. She's just one of us." It's one of the nicest things I've ever had said about me.

leviate discrimination than are those of us who live in the North. I hold no brief for Boston, Chicago or Salt Lake City (really my native state). For the most part, many of us talk a good brotherhood program, but in practice ignore it. In Austin, Texas (as in many another southern Fellowship), the question of Negro membership has arisen and been settled, albeit without a 100% endorsement. Several Negroes meet regularly with the group. Austin is the "growingest" Fellowship in the Southwestern Conference. Little Rock has gone through the same experience and, although several members declared that Negro attendance would "kill the Fellowship," it didn't. Others stated that Mr. Peck, owner of the Sam Peck Hotel, at which the Little Rock Fellowship meets, would refuse the group a meeting place; he didn't. You no doubt know that Dallas, New Orleans and Knoxville have Negro members; that at least one Negro attended the Thomas Jefferson Institute at Blue Ridge last summer; and I could add a number of other Unitarian societies in the South which, in their own small way, are not dodging the brotherhood issue.

In the spring of 1954, the congregation had grown to sixty-five member families, the number at which the AUA would agree to change the organization's status from fellowship to church. They had seventy-nine members, forty-three children enrolled in religious education, and a budget of $9,475. Soon thereafter, the church called Robert C. Palmer as its first minister and formally installed him on February 22, 1955. By April 1961, membership had reached 150, and religious education enrollment about 100,

Interview—Ray Norris

I interviewed for the job at Peabody [George Peabody College for Teachers, in the 1950s a separate institution adjacent to Vanderbilt University, and now a part of Vanderbilt]. I interviewed with the president of Peabody in a hotel room in New York City. I didn't want to come down to Nashville to live, but I was persuaded. One of the things he made clear to me in the interview was that everyone down here was aware of the problems they had with segregation, and that they didn't need any Yankee coming down from Columbia University or Pennsylvania and telling them that they needed to do something about desegregating the schools and the society.

One of the first jobs that I inherited—this was in the fall of 1953—was that of giving a series of examinations, the doctoral aptitude battery of tests, to all the aspirants for doctoral degrees at Peabody. I went over on the day I was to give the tests, and they were to be given in two rooms, one on the first floor and one in the basement. I just had two lists of names and didn't know who the people were. It turned out that all the people on the first floor were White. All the people in the basement were Black. I didn't even know we were going to have any Black graduate students in the program. It was the first group of twelve Black graduate students that Peabody College had gotten. They were mature educators on a grant from the General Education Board. They were allowed to attend classes and work on advanced graduate degrees, but they were not allowed to live on campus. They were not allowed to eat on campus. They also were not allowed to walk across the Vanderbilt campus. At the end of the first examination, one of the White students came up to me and said, "I understand that there's another group of people taking this same test today. Is that right?" I said yes. "Why aren't we together?" I said, "I think the dean's office made a mistake and scheduled some people for one room and some people for the other room, but after this hour we'll combine the groups, and we'll all be in the same room."

For a period, I served as acting dean at Peabody. It was a time when the graduate school was desegregated, but the undergraduate school and the Peabody demonstration school were not. President Felix Robb wanted to continue the push and desegregate both the undergraduate school and the demonstration school. In order to get an affirmative vote from the board of trustees, we had to agree that we would desegregate the undergraduate college one year and the demonstration school the next year. The newspapers reported that the board had voted to desegregate both, but they didn't talk about the timing. As soon as the board meeting was over, President Robb took leave and went to Germany for the summer. The board elected me as acting president for that summer. The first day of summer school, I had a call from the principal of the demonstration school. He said, "Ray, I have a man in the office, a Black man, who is trying to register his son. I explained to him what the board has done, but he wants to talk to someone with more authority than I have." So I said, "Okay, send him up." He walked into my office, and it was Kelly Miller Smith, minister of First Baptist [Capitol Hill] and just a marvelous citizen of Nashville. I said, "Rev. Smith, before you say anything, let me tell you how embarrassed I am having to tell you, although you have made a totally legitimate request that I would like very much to be able to comply with, I can't do it. And let me explain why." I explained the board action and why we had needed to compromise. He said, "Where do you go to church?" I said that I was a member of First Unitarian Church. He said, "You're one of Bob Palmer's boys." I said that was right. He said, "Okay, then I believe you. Now, would it help or hurt if I put some demonstrators in front of that school down there?" I told him it would hurt. He said, "All right, I believe you." It was on the strength of that association with Bob Palmer and his reputation that we were able to do that.

Interview—Jane Norris

Ray and I taught a class of sixth graders—maybe seventh graders. We were learning about other religions, and we visited the Baptist church down the street, the Woodmont Baptist Church. When we arrived, we had several Black children in that class, and they really didn't quite know what to do with us. They finally set up a special section, which they roped off with tape so that we wouldn't contaminate anybody.

and the first services were held on newly purchased property that offered the opportunity to construct a building designed for the congregation.

Issues of race had been dealt with in multiple ways by the mid-1950s. A local church history asserts, "As early as 1952, the Fellowship had a stated open membership policy." Constance Burgess, national executive director of the General Alliance of Unitarian Women, visited in the spring of 1953 and noted the genuine concern of the Nashville Unitarian Women's Group for "better inter-racial understanding, and the need in Nashville for a 'Mayor's Committee' or something of that sort." And no later than 1954, Ralph and Jean Cazort had joined, along with at least one other Black member.

In the summer of 1961, one of the summer speakers they invited was James Lawson, minister of Scott Memorial Methodist Church in Shelbyville, Tennessee. In Nashville in that era, Lawson was better known as the person expelled from Vanderbilt for teaching the techniques and philosophy of nonviolent direct action to scores of students who would lead sit-ins in Nashville and become the early leaders of the Student Nonviolent Coordinating Committee. Other civil rights notables who spoke to the congregation included John Lewis and Septima Clark.

A number of members were active in the community in ways small and large that reflected their religious values but weren't connected to the church. T. J. Anderson, professor of music at historically Black Tennessee State University, 1963–69 (and later a member of the commission that created the *Singing the Living Tradition* hymnal), and his wife, Lois, were good church friends of a White couple, the Terwilligers. The two couples chose to be arrested together in interracial protest of segregation at Morrison's Cafeteria.

A church Social Responsibility Committee established in 1964 contacted the governor about voting rights violations in Fayette County near Memphis. In 1965–66, the committee urged members to support the establishment of the Metro Commission on Human Relations. In 1966, the committee led the congregation to establish the Co-op Nursery as a "day care center for culturally disadvantaged and advantaged children." Called "the first racially and economically integrated school in the city," it operated until 1978.

In 1968, as Unitarian Universalists across the continent debated whether the UUA should fund a Black Affairs Council, Nashville Unitarian Universalists supported the idea. Subsequently, members, including T. J. Anderson and Ralph Cazort, formed a Black caucus within the congregation and obtained funding from the Black Affairs Council to combat steering, redlining, and other racial discrimination in the Nashville real estate market.

Sources

The Nashville file at the UUA provided helpful information. Also helpful were the thorough records maintained by the First Unitarian Universalist Church of Nashville, and a tape-recorded discussion that took place on November 19, 1997, with longtime members Virginia Price, Ray Norris, John Norris, Joe Moore, Anna Belle Leiserson, Jane Norris, Virginia Grantham, and Alan Leiserson. Additional interviews were conducted with Virginia Price, Ray Norris, and Ralph and Jean Cazort on January 27, 2000, and with Avery Leiserson and Joan Moore on January 28, 2000. Charles Howe's essay, "'Cousins Twice Removed': Unitarians and Universalists in the South," appears in the Unitarian Universalist Ministers Association's *Unitarian Universalism—Selected Essays, 1996.*

MEMPHIS, TENNESSEE

Unitarianism in Memphis dates back to 1893, according to local church histories. That year, five residents wrote to Rev. Edward Everett Hale, asking his assistance in starting a Unitarian congregation. Hale passed the request on to the AUA, which dispatched Frederick Preston, newly minted minister from the Harvard Divinity School. Preston grew the congregation to around forty people but left about a year later. Several other short ministries followed, with lay member Lida Merriweather often filling in as lay leader and speaker when there was no minister. After about 1900, she was forced by illness in her family to give up such efforts, and the group became dormant until 1908.

In 1908, inspired by a sermon by Harry Elmer Gilchrist, the Unitarian minister in New Orleans, Alvin Ward and Lavinia Selden started services again and reconnected with the AUA. The ministry of John Rowlett began in 1911, and the group was officially chartered in 1912 as the First Unitarian Church of Memphis. The charter reads:

> The purpose of this Church shall be to promote the high ideals of a rational, progressive and exalting religion, in the love of God and service to our fellow man, and to hold regular services in the community. To this end all activities of the Church shall be conducted without distinction related to race, color, or previous religious affiliations; and the right of private judgement and the sacredness of individual conviction shall be recognized in all things.

In this period, Arthur E. Morgan and his wife became active members; he went on to serve as president of Antioch College, and in 1933, became the first chairman of the Tennessee Valley Authority.

Several ministries, some with greater success and some lesser, followed. John Petrie (1929–38) was allowed to join the Protestant Pastors Association and wrote that this was a first in the South as far as he could tell. Richard Gibbs (1945–54) left Memphis to become director of the AUA's Department of Unitarian Extension and Church Maintenance.

Paul Carnes (1955–57) had a brief but important ministry. He was in Memphis when the public struggled to absorb the US Supreme Court's school desegregation decision. Carnes appealed to both the church and the wider community for a full embrace of desegregation. He exchanged pulpits with Black ministers. A 1983 church history reports both numerical and program growth during the Carnes ministry, but also some controversy about the church and the minister engaging the school desegregation issue. Some members thought the church was moving too rapidly, others thought it too slow.

Carnes, in a 1957 letter to Ray Johnson at the AUA, reports that when he arrived in Memphis, he found two areas in which the congregation's constitution required revision. One involved the assumption that the church should be segregated. Both the board (five to two) and the congregation (seventy to twenty) voted for a change. The other problem was a by-law that specified that the minister was called for only one year and must be re-elected sixty days prior to the end of the year, after approval by the board of trustees. Carnes notes that this provision "is . . . an invitation for the disaffected to create a certain amount of stress" and "creates an atmosphere which makes me less enthusiastic than I would like to be about the church."

Eugene Luening followed Paul Carnes and suffered through a controversy-plagued ministry. The church history reports that the vote to call him had not been robust so that he had begun on a weak footing. Some critiqued his Sunday services. "His handling of race relations within the church community and with the media caused such misunderstanding and dissension that there were factions working against each other," reports the history of the congregation, written in 1983. Settled in 1958, Luening was voted out on February 24, 1961.

The Unitarian Ministers Association sent Robert T. Weston to observe at the meeting called to vote on Luening's termination. Weston's long report on the process and the background is worth quoting at some length:

> It was charged that he was inadequate and incompetent as a minister. . . . A chart was presented showing membership, financial and attendance figures from 1956 to 1961, and the presentation purported to explain this as a rapid improvement until he began and an abrupt decline in all three factors from the time of his settlement as minister until the present.
>
> Study of the chart showed this charge to be patently false. There had been a sharp decline in the three factors beginning during the previous minister's ministry. It had continued at the same rate of decline until 1960, a year and a half, about, after Mr. Luening began, and then the figures in all three lines began to improve and are still improving.
>
> Of a voting attendance of 113 people, sixty-one voted to dismiss, fifty-two voted to retain the minister. Careful observation and listening convinced me that this was not a representation of repudiation of Mr. Luening; it was the expression of a sad conclusion that the situation had become impossible. I believe that many voted for dismissal who were very unhappy in doing so, and would have voted otherwise if they had felt that the opposition was not as strong and determined as they felt it to be. They voted to end dissension rather than against the minister. They were also influenced greatly by the charge that statistics proved that the minister's continuation was inadvisable. This is not to say that there was not a large minority who voted as a

repudiation of Mr. Luening. There was. I am convinced it was a minority. The tone of the meeting after the vote was one of deep sorrow.

It appears very probable to me that Mr. Luening inherited a resentment created by his predecessor in two matters: the elimination of annual election of the minister from the church by-laws, and the adoption of an item to the by-laws declaring the church open to all races, as well as the attitude arising from the invitation of a colored minister to occupy the pulpit one Sunday while the minister (Mr. Carnes) was away candidating. This latent resentment could probably have been overcome in time, but it would have required at the beginning some evidence of indifference to these items or else repudiation of them.

Luening himself, in a form letter sent out to friends and colleagues telling them of his termination, writes, "a large part of the opposition . . . came from remnants of segregationism and moderate stand-pat-ism in the congregation." But he admitted, "They could not have done it alone, and my own errors in judgment helped."

James Madison Barr was the successor minister, called in 1962. His ministry was notably successful and lasted until his retirement in 1982. It included purchasing land cleared by urban renewal on the banks of the Mississippi River and building a spectacular new facility, which is still in use. Although a vibrant presence and a strong spokesperson for liberal religion, Barr embraced a relatively conservative set of social ideals. He expressed admiration for "Mr. Jefferson," author of the Declaration of Independence and founder of the University of Virginia, from which Barr had earned his law degree; but he expressed greater admiration for the thinking of another southern Unitarian, John C. Calhoun of South Carolina, a nineteenth-century defender of states' rights and slavery.

As early as 1963, a few members objected to Barr's positions on social and political issues, so in 1964, the Unitarian Universalist Fellowship of Memphis was organized with twenty-two members, mostly former members of First Unitarian Church. This was, not coincidentally, the year of a polarizing presidential contest between relatively liberal Lyndon Johnson and very conservative Barry Goldwater. Neither Barr nor the First Unitarian Church board objected to the formation of the fellowship, because as Barr writes, "a community the size of Memphis ought to have several kinds of emphasis in our liberal religious faith."

The March 15, 1965, Memphis *Commercial Appeal* quotes Barr as charging the congregation to "remove every trace of racial prejudice from the marrow of our bones. There is no place for this in our midst." But in the same article he reportedly said, when reflecting on the death of Unitarian Universalist ministerial colleague James Reeb, "Jim Reeb died because he went to Selma, Ala. And the City of Selma would not have been visited by Jim Reeb save for the demonstrations set up and planned there by Martin Luther King and COFO [Council of Federated Organizations]." Barr implied that responsibility for Reeb's death rested with both King and the men who administered the fatal beating. The article also reports that Barr declined to take part in the Memphis NAACP's march honoring Reeb.

A March 16, 1965, letter to the editor from the fellowship board reads,

> We respect Mr. Barr's right to object to demonstrations, but it must be pointed out that his objections are not consistent. Last May at the General Assembly of the Unitarian Universalist Association in San Francisco he received nation-wide publicity for his one-man demonstration in support of California Proposition 14, while other Unitarian ministers were protesting it. Last winter, he participated in a save-the-park demonstration here in Memphis.

Proposition 14 was a proposal to amend the California Constitution to permit real estate owners to discriminate in renting or selling their property. The referendum on Proposition 14 passed, but the measure was later ruled unconstitutional by both the California Supreme Court and the Supreme Court of the United States.

Barr understood that his stances were controversial, both in Memphis and within Unitarian Universalism. On April 23, 1964, he sent the *Register-Leader*, the UUA's monthly magazine, a clipping from the Memphis *Commercial Appeal*. The clipping describes a free accounting course that had been recently offered under the auspices of the Urban League and taught by Mr. Barr, a director of that body. It reports that before entering the ministry, Barr had taught for five years at the University of Virginia Business School. In the note accompanying the clipping, Barr acknowledges, "[M]y name is bantered [sic] around so by many of the brethren—lay and ministerial—as one who opposes all that is decent and right." He suggests that the magazine carry a story about him to "help those who—with me—abhor the Civil Rights bill—these extremist [sic] demonstrations—and the all too overpowering conformity in such things in the denomination."

Sources

UUA files on both the First Unitarian Church and the Unitarian Universalist Fellowship of Memphis provided material. The references to "Mr. Jefferson" and John C. Calhoun are drawn from my conversations with James Madison Barr. The files on deceased Unitarian Universalist ministers maintained at the Andover-Harvard Theological Library of the Harvard Divinity School contain useful materials on Paul Carnes, Eugene Luening, and James Madison Barr. Talking and sharing resources with Edith Love, a Starr King School for the Ministry student studying Memphis history, also helped.

HUNTSVILLE, ALABAMA

The Unitarian Fellowship of Huntsville began in 1958. Huntsville at that time hummed with scientific and technical activity. The US Army's Redstone Arsenal had become a center of guided missile research after World War II, and in 1960, many of its civilian employees, facilities, and programs were transferred to create NASA's George C. Marshall Space Flight Center.

Some of the early leadership of the fellowship—but not all—were eager to address social issues, especially regarding race. In a December 1958 letter to Munroe Husbands of the AUA, early fellowship president Evelyn Falkowski writes, "I must confess that I sometimes get a little impatient with people who are content to have a small, pleasant group for themselves. I could enjoy a small group as much from the personal standpoint as a large but frankly I would like to see us trying to change the world and growing large enough to do it." A few months later, in a letter to Husbands and Regional Director Clif Hoffman, she writes, "Gentlemen I most passionately believe that this is our hour and this is our time in the South. That we must be intelligent about the race problem but not completely duck it. This is our time while other denominations are split wide open."

Falkowski and a handful of others in the fellowship involved themselves in the Council on Human Relations. In a May 1961 letter to Husbands, she comments,

> It was especially nice to hear from you today. In the past two days I have received about twenty phone calls, including several insults and last night a bomb threat. This be-

cause the Huntsville Council of Human Relations decided,
unanimously, Tuesday night, to publicize its existence and
purpose, solicit members, and deplore the violence that had
just occurred. They threatened to kill Dr. Howie, our pediatrician (Methodist) whose name also appeared in the article. They asked the Presbyterian minister's wife if she was
sleeping with Martin Luther King. (His church might not
back him and it could be pretty hot for them.)

The "violence that had just occurred" refers to the beatings
and fire-bombing of freedom riders in Anniston, Birmingham, and Montgomery. In a later passage, the letter conveys the
push and pull of attitudes and emotions on race (plus some of
the gendered assignment of roles) within this and many other
southern fellowships of the era. Falkowski writes,

The new fellowship bulletin editor brought the fellowship
bulletin over for me to type last night. His views are repug-
nant to me in some ways. Also, I'm getting tired of being
a sort of invisible executive secretary while others say the
word, and the wrong word at that. I told him that he better not hang around as the house was in danger of being
bombed. He said that would indeed be ironic, since he
didn't agree with me. He thought the whole situation would
take care of itself by evolution, and that the freedom riders
were just trying to stir up trouble or be martyrs. However,
when he got home he called and suggested I lock all my
doors and said he wouldn't want anything to happen to me.
Wasn't that touching.

Such tensions could emerge even within a family. A June 1961
letter from Falkowski to Husbands reads,

My husband was very difficult about the notoriety and danger I got us into, but he got over it. I hope. He had asked me
not to be chairman of the Human Relations group. After I

turned it down two months went by and nobody took it, so I decided to take it anyway, and I told him I didn't think he'd mind since my term was ending as Fellowship chairman. His brother visited us and told me that somebody might run our children down on the street, etc. etc. and this sort of thing makes one uneasy, even though its [sic] pretty far fetched.

A month later, she writes more positively, noting that thirty people had turned out for a Human Relations meeting, and eight of the thirty were Unitarians. In August 1961, as she handed off some regional extension responsibilities, Evelyn Falkowski could report of her home congregation:

The pattern thus far is that the group makes a net gain of about twenty members every other year. Membership is now over sixty. The group is well organized and has a building fund of $1600 and a lot. They are looking for a two acre building site and will possibly sell the lot. Local lenders have specifically stated they would be afraid to lend to them due to racial attitudes. Meeting at the Seventh Day Adventist church, but advised not to count on it until after new SDA minister comes in and is consulted. There are some differences in degree as to attitude on race. However, Negro speakers the past two years have brought out about the highest attendance. Apparently, if the situation arose, the group could integrate without shaking more than two members. The entire group wants a building of its own. Also, the whole group seems to be working toward church status. Leadership ability has increased among all the members. Minister-a-month and speaker exchange now fully used, also consultants. 65 in Sunday School.

By November 1961, the fellowship was negotiating the purchase of a large house that could function as meeting space. That process produced anxious questions to regional and national staff about whether the seller and prospective insurers must be told that the group was integrated, and whether insurance could be obtained. Although slim on specific answers, the reply from Munroe Husbands encouraged the fellowship to move ahead. Move ahead it did, acquiring the large house for a meeting place in 1962, achieving church status in 1964, and calling its first minister that same year.

Becky Holm tells the story of how the fellowship connected in the early 1960s with its first Black members, John and Joan Cashin. Becky and her husband, Frank, had moved to Huntsville from Memphis, and they had heard that the best dentist in town was John Cashin. A White woman born in Mississippi, Becky had never before gone to a Black dentist, but she sought out the Cashins. One day when she was in the dentist's chair and John Cashin was working on a tooth, he said he thought she might have to pray over the tooth to save it. She said that she didn't know that her prayers would do any good. Dr. Cashin asked what church she went to, and she said, "Unitarian." John and Joan Cashin began attending services and became active members.

Holm herself had had an unusual introduction to Unitarianism. While living in Memphis between 1949 and 1952, she heard co-workers discuss the Unitarian church and it sounded interesting. However, Holm was working in the FBI office, and the co-workers were agents discussing people under surveillance as suspected subversives.

Just as Holm had recruited John Cashin to the fellowship, he recruited her to be the first White teacher in a formerly all-Black school in the Madison County schools in 1967–68.

Frank Holm observed that Evelyn Falkowski and John Cashin were the two people in the fellowship most crucial to initiating civil rights work. And that work did get going. The Cashins, White allies from the fellowship, and others from the Huntsville community conducted sit-ins at lunch counters and ticket windows. In 1963, Myrna and Don Copeland, White Unitarian Universalists, joined John and Joan Cashin in an elaborate integration of the Grand Ole Opry, up the highway from Huntsville in Nashville, Tennessee. The quartet pulled up in front of the Ryman Auditorium in the Cashins's 1952 Rolls Royce. Clad in a chauffeur's uniform, Don Copeland climbed from behind the wheel to open the doors for the Cashins, who wore evening attire, while Myrna stepped out in a maid's uniform. John Cashin explained at the door that Don was his "trusted chauffeur and butler," while Joan said, "I have to have my maid."

In 1966, the Cashins were looking for a house to buy in the only school district with appropriate resources for their daughter Carroll, who was hearing impaired. For two years, they had had no success because this section of Huntsville was all White. Finally, their church friend Sas Risse bought the house in her name with their money and transferred the title to them.

In 1967, because the Alabama Democratic Party was a segregationist redoubt with the slogan "White Supremacy," John Cashin led a group of activists in founding the National Democratic Party of Alabama. The NDPA's integrated leadership, including White Unitarian Universalists such as Myrna Copeland and Rev. Jack Zylman, had Black empowerment as a prime goal. By the time he ran as NDPA candidate for governor in 1970 against George Wallace, John Cashin had joined the First Baptist Church, acknowledging, "Intellectually I'm a Unitarian, but politically I'm a Baptist."

Charles Blackburn began his ministry at the Huntsville fellowship in 1964. He arrived as well equipped as one could be to be dropped into the midst of this activity. Having grown up in tolerant Florida Methodist parsonages, Blackburn become a Unitarian in 1957 at All Souls Church in Washington, DC. He had prepared academically for Unitarian Universalist ministry at Virginia Theological Seminary, Howard University Graduate School of Religion (where he was the only White student), and Starr King School for the Ministry. In 1963, following the church bombing in Birmingham, Charles and his wife, Winona (a South Carolinian), thought they should return to the South, where they might be more effective than non-natives.

Six weeks into his Huntsville ministry, Charles Blackburn was asked by the Unitarian Universalist Regional Office to go to McComb, Mississippi, to assist in a voter registration drive. He accompanied a ninety-four-year-old Black Baptist minister and his eighty-year-old wife when they tried to register in Magnolia, Mississippi, and all three were arrested for "trespassing on the courthouse grounds." He returned home to find that a neighbor—whose father happened to be the sheriff in Magnolia—had tried to burn a cross on his lawn. A dozen members of the Huntsville congregation resigned at this point—but in the next year, seventy-five new members joined.

For a time, Blackburn was able to concentrate more on duties within the congregation and quieter forms of civil rights activity in the Human Relations Council and related organizations. Then on March 2, 1965, he was asked to gather a Huntsville contingent for an organization called Concerned White Citizens of Alabama. Selma native Joseph Ellwanger, a White Lutheran minister serving a Black congregation in Birmingham, was forming this group to protest the suppression of Black voting rights in Selma. On Saturday, March 6, Blackburn and fourteen others from Huntsville participated in a march to the county courthouse in Selma. Of the seventy-two who rallied from around the state, thirty-six were Unitarian Universalists. Later that day, in a Black church in Selma, Martin Luther King Jr.'s radical staff member James Bevel told them that when he had seen them marching to the courthouse, he had thought, "Damn, the Kingdom's coming." C. T. Vivian, also a key member of King's staff, praised them, but then posed the question, "Where have you been?"

On Sunday, March 7, the day after the Concerned White Citizens marched, Black marchers and by-standers in Selma were infamously teargassed and beaten at the Edmund Pettus Bridge. And on Tuesday, March 9, people gathered from around the country to again attempt to cross the bridge. Federal district court judge Frank Johnson had enjoined the second march, but King announced that he had to march in spite of the injunction.

Blackburn returned to Selma for that march, accompanied by men from the congregation. He writes, "There was an intense and painful consultation with the men from my church, all space-program engineers with top security clearances whose jobs might well be at stake in disobeying a federal injunction—an agoniz-

Gene Snyder to UUA official (letter, 1969)

I enjoyed very much an hour of conversation with you that eventful-unforgetable [sic] spring of 65 when the UUA board decided to adjorn[sic] and resume their board meeting in Selma, Alabama. I was proud of the UUA decision to come and take a stand and was glad that I played a small part in driving you and Ann Bowman from the Birmingham airport to Huntsville for housing over the weekend. You may have wondered why I drove my new Polara quite fast that evening and kept a continual check out the rear view mirror. Previously while on the way to Birmingham an incident occured [sic] which may have been innocent but seemed ominus [sic] at the time.

As I was doing 70, on a secondary road some young toughs started to pull up long side in a fast pickup truck. Fortunately I was driving a fast car and didn't have to stay around to see what they had in mind. There are very real risks in being an active liberal Unitarian. I could tell you a great deal about the harassment via telephone of the members of our church: immediately after Selma Rev. Blackburn had to change his telephone two different times within a month. They finally really got to him and his wife. I saw one of the men who worked under me at Chrysler, who went to Selma, literally driven from the community by harassment in part by his fellow workers to the point he found he couldn't take it. Nevertheless our church has grown, even during the year we were without a minister, and has grown significantly since Jim Anthony has been with us.

Our church provides a real haven to religious liberals both youth and adults, and the sustainence [sic] gained therefrom is quite important to its members. Much effective work in changing the stagnant attitudes that characterize the south is slowly but surely being accomplished. Real and significant progress has been made since Selma.

ing decision. Each went off alone. Each returned to say he would march—an inspiring affirmation."

Blackburn, upon hearing about the attack in Selma on James Reeb, whom he had known in Washington, went to Birmingham where Reeb was hospitalized. Later, he went to Selma for Reeb's memorial service.

When civil rights marchers from around the country finally completed the Selma-to-Montgomery march, people from Huntsville, including Blackburn, went to the final rally in Montgomery. The next day's *Huntsville Times* ran a front-page photo of Blackburn carrying the Huntsville delegation's sign in Montgomery. The church was stoned that night, with many church school windows broken. The Blackburns received 250 harassing calls before they changed to an unlisted number. After that, the family's life calmed down but they projected a sense of being under threat: mesh screens on the windows, floodlights on the house, a check every morning for bombs on the car. The church's life continued peacefully, but by early 1966 the Blackburns had moved to an exurban church in New York. After a year and a half there, Charles spent his first two post-ministry years organizing American Civil Liberties Union affiliates in ten Deep South states.

Frank Holm was one of the people who traveled to Selma with Blackburn. Holm worked for Brown Engineering and remembers a young co-worker stopping by his desk after Selma and inviting him to leave the state of Alabama. Frank established that he had lived in Huntsville and worked in Alabama longer than his young colleague and suggested that the younger man go back to Birmingham.

Tom Davis recalls that co-worker Gerald Doty, who went to Selma and had sometimes attended Unitarian Universalist services, later silently endured verbal abuse at work about going to Selma. Doty eventually left the job and Huntsville. Davis was called a "pinko" by a co-worker at NASA, but he responded immediately and forcefully, and he suffered no more harassment.

Sonnie Wellington Hereford IV provides an interesting outsider's evaluation of the Huntsville Unitarian Universalists in a 2007 article in *Notre Dame Magazine*. His physician father was a Black activist who hosted Martin Luther King Jr.'s visit to Huntsville in 1962 and the same year filed a school desegregation suit. The younger Hereford writes, "The Unitarian Church in Huntsville was the only white church that supported the civil rights movement in our area. None of the white Christian churches formally supported the movement, although I'm sure a few individuals from white Christian churches did." He recalls,

> Between the brief time of the court case decision and actually starting first grade (kindergarten was not required in those days), it was the Unitarian Church of Huntsville that put together a "playschool" for me, three other black children, and about a dozen white children. The purpose of the preschool was to enable us to get used to going to school together—to show us that children were just children.

In 1966 James Anthony was called as minister and served into the next decade.

Sources

UUA files and a February 2002 oral history interview with Tom Davis, Frank and Becky Holm, and Edna Davis provided substantial information. Charles Blackburn's February 21, 1999, sermon at the First Unitarian Church of Baltimore, "Looking Back: The Selma Period," is an unparalleled resource. Professor Sheryll Cashin of Georgetown University lovingly chronicles the life and work of her parents in *The Agitator's Daughter: A Memoir of Four Generations of One Extraordinary African American Family* (New York: Public Affairs, 2008). The article by Sonnie Hereford IV appeared in the Spring 2007 issue of *Notre Dame Magazine*.

BIRMINGHAM, ALABAMA

Birmingham was founded in 1871, after the Civil War had ended, and thus is not filled with antebellum mansions. In large measure, northern industrialists created it where coal, iron ore, and rail lines converged, offering the possibility of southern industrial development.

There was a brief effort, 1916–20, to establish Unitarianism in Birmingham. Thomas Byrnes served the congregation 1917–20, in a building at 725 N. Nineteenth Street. But it appears that when Byrnes relocated to greener pastures, the congregation disbanded.

In 1952, Unitarianism came to Birmingham permanently when a group of religious liberals gathered at the Redmont Hotel on January 18 to talk with Mary Aymer Hobart about forming a fellowship. Mrs. Hobart was a native Alabamian married to Alfred Hobart, then minister in Charleston, South Carolina, and also director of the AUA's Thomas Jefferson Conference. As the fellowship formed, Joseph Volker, dean of the University of Alabama School of Dentistry, was elected to lead.

By September 1953, Hobart left Charleston, the oldest Unitarian church in the South, and accepted a call to Birmingham, still a fellowship, not yet recognized as a church. The AUA made this possible with a subsidy to encourage emerging churches. By January 31, 1954, the Unitarian Church was chartered with 108 members from 72 families. Less than five months later, the US Supreme Court decision on school desegregation made clear that issues of race and civil rights were moving to the fore. Nowhere was this truer than in Birmingham. In a 1967 address at the Meadville

Lombard Theological School commencement, Hobart observed of the city of Birmingham, "Like a good many transplanted northerners who try to prove themselves good southerners, it has practiced the vices and ignored the virtues of the tradition it strives so mightily to emulate."

Looking back from the perspective of 2004, Rev. Ed Harris writes in *Miracle in Birmingham: A Civil Rights Memoir 1954–1965*:

> I'd found in the Birmingham Unitarian Church freedom of belief, enlarged social awareness, political consciousness and interesting people committed on the question of racial desegregation. It was a lively church pastored by the Rev. Alfred Walters Hobart. He was thoughtful, rational but sensitive and at times impassioned. The years he was minister saw bombings, riots, marches, and deaths and he maintained his little church and served the larger community.

Early in its history, the congregation met in quarters rented from the city of Mountain Brook, an affluent suburb on the southern edge of Birmingham. Charles Zukoski, a charter member of the congregation, was the mayor of Mountain Brook. By October 1958, the congregation moved into a building of its own, in the same suburb.

There are, as with all of the congregations discussed in this book, gaps in the record. Rev. Alice Syltie, once the director of religious education in the Birmingham Church, comments in a seminary paper on its social justice history, "Very little is recorded in any of the church records and the church newsletter reveals almost nothing about what was taking place. So much secrecy and fear surrounded these events that the actual facts are difficult to find." In addition, many actions were undertaken by individuals or subgroups in this and other congregations rather than by congregational vote. People were often too busy doing to sit down and document what they'd done. And they did not want a written record waiting to be found if subjected to a police raid. But in Birmingham and some other congregations, there have been efforts to collect memories, figure out what was done, and honor those who acted.

Congregational president Grady Nunn recalls two early actions in a 1985 retrospection: "In 1956 the congregation adopted a resolution condemning racial segregation. In anticipation of occupying [the church] building in 1958 it was voted that the doors would be open to all people. At that time racially integrated meetings were illegal in Birmingham."

One of the organizations to which Alfred Hobart devoted time and effort was the interracial Greater Birmingham Council on Human Relations. He was the first chairperson of the council and, for a long time, the only White minister to belong to it. For the first five years, Unitarians constituted the bulk of its White membership. In 1961, the council asked several White churches for permission to use their buildings for meetings. They all promptly declined. The board of the Unitarian Church voted in favor and took the issue to a congregational meeting, which debated for four hours and then voted seventy-one to forty-seven against approval. The illegality of interracial meetings, fear of the building being bombed, and fear of personal reprisals all played a part. Grady Nunn in 1985 notes of that 1961 meeting, "Among those indeed who spoke against granting the permit were some of the church members who were themselves members of the Council on Human Relations." Yet soon the Unitarian Church was hosting integrated gatherings.

Later in 1961, the Alabama Education Association invited and then disinvited John Ciardi, poetry editor of the *Saturday Review* magazine, to speak. The disinvitation was triggered by his column "Jim Crow Is Treason." Hobart quickly invited Ciardi to deliver his planned address at the Unitarian Church and offered for the church to pay his plane fare. Ciardi accepted, and the church was filled to overflowing with an integrated audience.

In his report to the annual meeting on the 1960–61 church year, Hobart refers to the variety of roles he had served in the local community:

Dr. Joseph F. Volker at the AUA May Meetings in 1953 (excerpt)

The Fellowship embarked on a publicity campaign that might well be the envy of a well-established church. In this we were aided and abetted by our strategically located membership. Fred Woodress, a staff columnist with the morning *Birmingham Post Herald*, saw to it that we got more than our share of newspaper space. Charles McGehee, program director of radio station WILD, talked his boss into 15 minutes of free time for Sunday morning Unitarian Sermons. Dr. Jerry Barnett promptly set about soliciting taped sermons from prominent Unitarian ministers from all over the United States. Between the two of them, they have performed the miracle of producing a continuous Sunday radio program for over a year at no cost to the membership. Emily Danton, a Fellowship member and the chief city librarian, rendered a most valuable service in making available an extensive reading list on Unitarianism. Martha Carlyle, staff member of Channel 13, one of our two local T.V. stations, managed frequent spots for us on the opening inspirational spot of "Breakfast in Birmingham."

As would be anticipated, our adherents include a significant number of professional, education, and research personnel. The University of Alabama Medical Center and the rapidly growing Southern Research Institute have contributed approximately a fourth of our membership. This is not surprising when it is remembered that in the past, four members of the Medical Center faculties have served with the Service Committee's Medical Teaching missions.

It should also be emphasized that any Fellowship in a southern city can expect that as the south develops, Unitarians will move into the area. If an active Unitarian group is functioning, they will quickly affiliate with it. The Birmingham Fellowship can attest to this from first-hand experience. In the last eighteen months we have had our ranks swelled by Unitarians from Arlington, Minneapolis, Madison, Ann Arbor, Baltimore, Miami, and Oak Ridge. Even better, we can report that we've sent off our first "home grown" Unitarian to the Nashville Fellowship.

In retrospect we can say without hesitation that we're in Birmingham to stay, and that where two years ago the local populace might have confused a Unitarian with a Martian, today it is the trademark of a liberal religion in Alabama.

Treasurer of the Jefferson County Association for Mental Health, Member of the Board of Directors of the Alabama Planned Parenthood League and of the Birmingham Civic Opera Association and secretary of the inter-racial Birmingham Brotherhood of Clergy. It may be of interest also to mention that I am a member of the Greater Birmingham Ministerial Association. I mention this because this has not been possible in other cities where I have served Unitarian churches.

In 1962, a church member formed a creative dance studio that offered classes and performances in the church building on a racially inclusive basis.

Also in 1962, as the issue of school desegregation continued to agitate people, there was political talk of closing the schools if integration was ordered. In response to a sermon by Hobart, a citizens group formed to keep the schools open under any circumstances. It organized at the Unitarian church with many church people as leaders and members.

There was a Sunday evening discussion group that offered perspectives on issues of race, among other topics, with speakers such as James Bevel (of Martin Luther King Jr.'s staff), Black Muslim leader James X, and Lucius Pitts of historically Black Miles College.

When sit-ins came to Birmingham, White allies served specific roles: to sit at the counter before the scheduled arrival of demonstrators, to show that at least some White customers would not leave when Black customers joined them, and to witness whatever might be done to the demonstrators. The Sternglanz and Fuller families sometimes involved their children, who got to drink milkshakes.

Racist bombings were so frequent in Birmingham during the 1950s and 1960s that it was sometimes called Bombingham, and a neighborhood largely populated by the Black leadership was known as Dynamite Hill. But even for Birmingham, the bombing of the Sixteenth Street Baptist Church on Sunday morning, September 15, 1963, was extreme. Four girls preparing to take part in the morning service were killed, and many other people were injured in body and/or spirit. Two of the girls killed had been attending meetings at the Unitarian Church intended to help Black and White children prepare to be part of school desegregation; indeed, the next meeting of that group had been scheduled for that Sunday afternoon.

That day, after the service at the Unitarian Church, many members donated blood. Betty Crutcher, nurse and mother of six, volunteered her services at the hospital where the injured were being treated. Peg Fuller and Ed Harris, both active in the Human Relations Council, called on the families of the girls who had been killed. Joseph Ellwanger, White pastor of the St. Paul's Lutheran Church attended by Chris McNair, father of one of the dead girls, joined in these visits. They were received in the spirit in which they came.

In his September 22 sermon "Requiem for Six Children," Hobart addressed the deaths not only of Cynthia Wesley, Carole Robertson, Denise McNair, and Addie Mae Collins, but also of Virgil Ware (shot Sunday afternoon by a White teen) and Johnnie Robinson (shot by Birmingham police). The church newsletter printed his prayer for that service, which includes the following passages:

Who can claim to love God whom he has not seen when he hates his brother whom he has seen? Can bitter cisterns give forth sweet water? Can mind jealous of privilege, place and power worship in spirit and in truth? Can hearts warped by prejudice confess a God of justice and love? Can those who harden their hearts against a brother bring acceptable gifts to the altar of their religion?

We stand now with broken hearts before the graves of six children of whose kind Jesus said: "Unless you accept the Kingdom of Heaven as a little child you shall in no wise enter therein." Six children of whose death none of us can count ourselves guiltless. For we were silent when we should have spoken, submissive when we should have rebelled, fearful when we should have been courageous.

Nothing remains now but that we should seek a renewal
of the spirit without compromise, without sophistication,
without illusion, without fear. There is no other absolution.
There is no other way. There is no other hope.

The newsletter carried Hobart's three-paragraph account of the
subsequent actions of some church members: attending the funer-
als of all six children and joining a delegation of twenty-five to
urge the mayor toward positive action, including "hiring of Negro
policemen." Members of the congregation also sent a telegram with
fifty-one signatures to Mayor Boutwell, Governor George Wallace,
and Attorney General Robert Kennedy, calling for intervention by
federal troops.

In a longer-term response to the bombing, Peggy Fuller, Sidney Fiquitte, Sandra Harris, and seven other Unitarian Universalist women formed a group they called Friendship and Action. Two
other White women and a dozen Black women joined to meet in
one another's homes, exchange ideas and information, and deepen
their connections. Ultimately, they created such unifying activities
as an interracial playgroup for sixty children.

In September 1964, Lawrence McGinty, a native of Alabama,
succeeded Alfred Hobart, who had moved to Atlanta to serve as
associate director of the Midsouth District of the UUA.

Ed Harris, who a year later would be studying for the Unitarian
Universalist ministry, was determined to offer a service of remembrance on September 15, 1964, for the four girls killed in the Sixteenth Street Church bombing and the two boys who had been
shot the same day in separate incidents. He hoped for something
big—Billy Graham coming to Legion Field—but he found no institutional support for any effort, large or small, so he rented the Unitarian church building and planned the service himself. The choir
from bombing victim Carole Robertson's school sang. The mother
of Virgil Ware attended. There was singing, sharing, remembrance,
hope, and tears. In the course of his ministerial career, Ed Harris
held to a promise he had made to himself not to let a September 15
go by unmemorialized. At one of those services, his wife, Sandra,

was asked if she had been at the 1964 service. "No," she said, "I was at home in case the church was blown up or Edward was killed, so there would be someone to raise our children."

The Concerned White Citizens of Alabama formed as an outgrowth of the Alabama Council on Human Relations. Unitarian Universalists from Birmingham and Huntsville were well represented in their ranks. In their most widely noted action, undertaken in Selma on March 6, 1965, they read a statement on the steps of the Dallas County Courthouse in support of Black voting rights. Police assistance was needed to get the seventy-two people, half of whom were Unitarian Universalists, back to their staging area in the face of threatening segregationist harassment. This event was largely overshadowed by the next day's events: the brutal beating and teargassing of marchers on the Edmund Pettus Bridge, an organized law enforcement riot known as Bloody Sunday.

The events in Selma had a major impact on the Unitarian Church of Birmingham. After James Reeb was attacked and critically injured in Selma on March 9, he was put in an ambulance to be taken to Birmingham. Phone calls to the church alerted people that the ambulance was en route. Dr. Joseph Volker, vice president for health affairs of the medical and dental colleges, and other Unitarian Universalists on the staff of University Hospital quickly prepared to give the best possible care. In his sermon "Sixteen Days of Crisis for a Group of Insiders," Larry McGinty later described in rich detail the stressors that landed one after another on the church. For two and a half weeks, the congregation dealt with the care of Jim Reeb and those around him; his death; preparation of a public statement by the board about his death; local services memorializing him; the UUA Board and many others coming through Birmingham en route to his Selma memorial service; a ten-minute board meeting that agreed to house, feed, and arrange transportation for an unknown number of Unitarian Universalists coming to join in the final day of the Selma-to-Montgomery march; and handling the arrival, feeding, housing, and dispatch of about 225 people. Church life continued in the midst of this activity. McGinty, accustomed to a carefully prepared manuscript for his sermon, had to settle for outlining it between midnight and 2:00 a.m. on March 14, knowing that the UUA Board and president would be in the congregation to hear it. March 21 was scheduled to include an after-service reception for twenty-five new members who had joined since the first of the year and an evening fellowship dinner at a restaurant to kick off the pledge drive. Police arriving to search the church for bombs shortened the after-service reception and persuaded leaders to move child care during the dinner from the church building to someone's home. But it did not keep people away from the fellowship dinner nor keep them from pledging. Pledges went up 45 percent over the previous year's drive.

On April 19, 1965, less than a month after the Selma events, the Birmingham congregation's board agreed to sponsor three centers for a new eight-week summer program for disadvantaged children called Project Head Start. A Methodist ministerial student and a Presbyterian minister, accompanied by a federal Office of Economic Opportunity staff member, reported that the Methodists and Presbyterians declined sponsorship. The program would need to be nonsegregated, nonsectarian, and backed up with social and medical services for the enrolled students and their families. The first step was writing a grant proposal to get the money, the second, getting Gov. George Wallace and the heads of city and county government to sign off on it. Church member Ethel Gorman called on the managing editor and the editor of the *Birmingham News* to encourage the political figures to do their part, and somehow it worked. With a massive input of time and energy by church members and allies they recruited from the community, a program was ready to start on July 5 for an integrated group of about a hundred children in three centers. Historically Black Miles College sponsored two additional centers that summer, and the Catholic Diocese sponsored another one in Birmingham.

Both individually and corporately, Birmingham Unitarian Universalists faced great challenges and took some significant steps forward. But the costs were sometimes high.

Hobart writes in his 1966 document, "The Unitarian Universalist Witness in the Southeast 1950–66":

The activities of members of the Birmingham congregation were not devoid of cost in terms of personal harassment at all hours of the night, some obscene, abusive, threatening and some just nuisances. Three lawyers, two teachers and a newspaper man lost their professional connections and another newspaper man was warned to stay in line or else. A high officer in one of the banks was forced to retire early. A number of others lived in fear of reprisal.

In a 1985 reflection, Ethel Gorman observes,

I was aware that many people in the community considered those of us who were native to be like the Scalawags of Reconstruction; and those from elsewhere to be like carpetbaggers. So I felt generally that I was in a sort of personal no-win situation, except that we were all doing what we thought we must as responsible Unitarians because we were in the time and place that history had thrust us. . . . Some of us who were native Alabamians were in a double bind during our church's dramatic early life. We were often regarded with sorrow and astonishment or rejected by friends and families. Some lost jobs. On the other hand, I also felt a sort of distrust and disapproval, as if I had been tarred by Bull Connor's brush, from some members of the congregation who were not native. A few of them projected an air of superiority which made me understand better how the unspoken, even unrecognized attitudes of whites affected Negroes.

As a child and teen, Carolyn Fuller grew up in the Unitarian Church and in the home of activist parents. When the schools began token desegregation, she took the radical step of talking to the Black student who had entered her high school and she suffered significant isolation as a result during the remainder of that school year. In a 2000 email, she says of the church:

It was an Oasis. Even though members/former members who attended my public school would avoid me, the only people I considered real friends came from that Church. I'm not sure I would have survived emotionally if it had not been for the Church. We were under siege which caused us to draw together very tightly. Almost all of my positive childhood memories are from the Church. The Sunday school class was the only place I felt intellectually stimulated and emotionally supported.

In 1963, Hobart had asked Ed Harris, "Why don't you consider our ministry?" Ed had considered deeply, thought about it, tested the idea and himself, and almost committed a couple of times. In his book *Miracle in Birmingham*, Harris describes his clear "call to the ministry" as a phone call on Sunday, November 14, 1964, while his family and another family were eating dinner. The caller announced, "Me and some of my good friends are coming over to blow your house up." It was not the first such threat, but something about this one told him to take it seriously. In the summer of 1965, the Harris family of five headed north, "into exile," for Ed to attend seminary at Tufts University. Rev. Larry McGinty rounded up pledges of one hundred dollars a month from twelve people to subsidize the Harris family while in Massachusetts. Harris repaid this help with a distinguished ministerial career.

Alice Syltie in a 1995 seminary essay opines,

There is a special strength and a profound connection among these people. From this experience was born a commitment and a loyalty that continues to sustain the church in times of crisis. The deeply rooted understanding of what it means to work for justice under physically demanding and emotionally challenging conditions continues to touch the life of the congregation. Their dedication and continued support of each other and the church, through the easy and the hard times, serves as an example to all.

Interview—John Fuller

John Fuller, in a 1996 piece on designing the Birmingham congregation's first building, explained that he set up his own architecture practice in late 1953, and in mid-1954 he was approached about his interest in designing a building for a new church. He was given several copies of the Unitarian Register *that had illustrations of recently built churches. He and his wife, Peggy, read the magazines, went to church the next Sunday, and didn't miss a Sunday for the next ten years. The entire family worked in various ways on issues of race and justice.*

Because we were a fairly active and outspoken family, we faced some harassment. Once a Black ambulance crew showed up at our door, saying they had been told to come by and pick up the body. We used to get harassing or threatening phone calls all night long. One night, Peg upset some poor woman who had called, saying we were promoting the annihilation of the White race. Peg got to arguing with her, something about in her Bible, it said something about being your brother's keeper. The woman informed Peg that Blacks were not her brothers; Blacks did not have souls.

I think our next door neighbor where we lived was a member of the Klan. We aren't certain. That, we think, is why we weren't bombed. It might have damaged his house too.

We used to have what we called "Sunday communion." Sunday afternoons, we'd invite people over from church to have some wine, cheese, and crackers. One Sunday, our daughter, Carolyn, had not gone to church. She'd stayed home, along with our Great Dane. A group had come in that afternoon after church. Shortly thereafter, there was a knock on the door, and it was a policeman there, and he said that they had gotten a call that a bomb had been planted in our house while we were at church. He wanted to go through the whole house. We assured him that it had not been, but the guy insisted on staying around till about 3 or 4 o'clock.

Carolyn spent her last two years of high school out of state. We put our son, Mike, in a private school. We were fighting to keep the public schools open and integrated, and we carted him off to a private school. But he wasn't getting any education. He was suffering more than anyone. He was strung upside down in a tree and the other kids dancing around him, and that sort of thing. Then the last two years, Carolyn had moved to the Boston area, and he went up and lived with her and went to school there.

The Black kids who integrated the schools and suffered all the hate and comments went home after school as heroes in their community. Whereas the White kids who supported them didn't have a support group except at the church. Our kids were very much involved with the church program, the LRY, and so on. I remember Carolyn made the comment she could almost figure out how long each of her friends would continue speaking to her.

Black civil rights figure Rev. C. H. Oliver, a president of the Greater Birmingham Human Relations Council, once observed,

For years the Unitarian Church has under the leadership of Rev. A. W. Hobart and now under the leadership of Rev. L. E. McGinty, had inter-racial meetings of various kinds in defiance of the threats of bombs. It is the only white church I know of in Birmingham which invites Negro speakers from time to time and goes out of its way to encourage Negroes to attend. I cannot say this of any other white church, regardless of how gentle or liberal the pastor may be in his own personal relations.

The church went through many moments in the cross-hairs of opponents. Longtime church administrator Eve Gerard perhaps best epitomized the church's attitude when she responded to yet another telephoned bomb threat by saying, "Get a number and get in line. There are others ahead of you."

In *Carry Me Home*, her massively detailed civil rights history of her hometown, Birmingham, Diane McWhorter correctly emphasizes such crucial actors as Fred Shuttlesworth, Bull Connor, and the Ku Klux Klan. The index includes only three entries for Unitarianism, two overlapping ones for Alfred Hobart, and two for Dr. Joseph Volker. Despite McWhorter's wry comments about "the medical center liberals' Unitarian Church," she confirms that, by the 1980s, the steel industry on which Birmingham was founded had been eclipsed as an economic engine by the University Medical Center. Volker, first president of the Unitarian Fellowship, went on to become president of the Medical College and then the University of Alabama-Birmingham. Today, the University of Alabama at Birmingham, including its medical center, is the area's largest employer, and the steel mills are shuttered reminders of a smoggy past. Forces shaping the current metropolitan area seem to have passed through "the medical center liberals' Unitarian Church."

Sources

Among the sources contributing to this account were files of the UUA and the Unitarian Universalist Church of Birmingham. General Birmingham civil rights history is covered exhaustively in Diane McWhorter's prize-winning *Carry Me Home: Birmingham, Alabama, the Climactic Battle of the Civil Rights Revolution* (New York: Simon & Schuster, 2001). Ed Harris in *Miracle in Birmingham: A Civil Rights Memoir 1954–1965* (Indianapolis: Stonework Press, 2004) tells a more personal story, including the experience of Unitarian Universalists. Alice Syltie wrote an extensive essay in 1995 for a history and polity course at Meadville Lombard Theological School. Alfred Hobart's 1966 survey, referenced in the text, offers a brief and modest review. A number of interviews provided assistance, including a group session on February 15, 2000, with Vincent and Jackie Massara, Eve Gerard, Lore and Walter Luft, Janice Williams, and Helen Sternglanz. Among others interviewed or offering tape-recorded or emailed reminiscences were Virginia Volker, Jack Zylman, Charles Zukoski, Eileen Walbert (an ally in Friendship in Action), John Fuller, and Carolyn Fuller.

MONTGOMERY, ALABAMA

In 1846 Montgomery became Alabama's capital city, and in 1861 it served briefly as the capital of the Confederate States of America.

In 1834, when Montgomery was still a small town, Universalists built a church at the corner of Perry and Alabama streets, but the congregation disbanded two years later when its minister moved away. An adventuresome beginning followed by a tenuous institutional life was a pattern among Universalist congregations in many areas, and in Montgomery, manifested itself in the efforts to organize a Unitarian fellowship.

Correspondence in the UUA files suggests a few Unitarian and Universalist attempts in the early twentieth century to gather a congregation in Montgomery. In the late 1930s and early 1940s, Unitarian efforts on at least one occasion gathered between forty and sixty people, but there is no record of a congregation.

A fellowship organized in 1953, with support from lay leaders Ray Shute of Monroe, North Carolina, and Joseph Volker of Birmingham. During its few years of existence, members debated whether it should be Unitarian or a joint Unitarian-Universalist effort. Rev. William Arms from the Universalist Church in Brewton, Alabama, and several Montgomery area residents of Universalist background wanted a joint effort, but the AUA had a policy against these unions. The fellowship met at the Montgomery YWCA in a two-story building known as the YWCA Hut. By 1956, it was meeting weekly, with Arms preaching once a month, and had purchased some religious education materials.

Munroe Husbands, fellowship director of the AUA, responded to a February 1956 letter from the fellowship seeking assistance with a building fund. His letter notes, "[W]e are growing faster in the South than in any section of the country, save California, even with the handicap that as Unitarians we pull no punches in standing for the brotherhood of all men." In his concluding paragraph, Husbands writes,

> How we wish we could meet the hundreds of requests we receive from Fellowships and churches to give financial strength to local groups. This is an impossibility. Yet we have great confidence in the growing strength of our movement, for we are attracting more people on a percentage basis than any other religious group. And then there are Fellowships such as the one at Tuscaloosa which has been taking a leading part in the Miss Lucy controversy; our Fellowship in Tampa that was integrated at the beginning of its existence; and all the other Fellowships in the South who are taking a positive stand for integration. It seems that all the groups that have a confidence in their convictions and a determination to extend the liberal religious point of view are making progress. We are glad to note that Montgomery is among this number.

It is important to remember the issues that roiled public discourse in Montgomery in 1956. In early December 1955, Rosa Parks was arrested for refusing to give up her seat on the bus so that a White passenger could sit. This latest in a long series of arrests and insults to Black passengers triggered a well-executed bus boycott by the Black community, organized by the Montgomery Improvement Association. The new young pastor of the Dexter Avenue Baptist Church, Martin Luther King Jr., was proving an effective MIA president and spokesperson. The boycott did not end until the US Supreme Court ruled against segregation of the Montgomery buses in December 1956.

A December 4, 1956, letter to Husbands from fellowship member Phyllis Fletcher lays out a sequence of events that soon led to the suspension of the fellowship's activity:

> As you have heard we had some trouble about the segregation business. Some of the older members of the group left when a resolution was passed affirming the fact that our meetings were open to anyone regardless of race or color. The members who left did so, not because they disagreed with this, but because, for economic reasons, they could not belong to such an organization.
>
> We were not openly asking for any negroes [sic] to come to our meetings just to prove they are welcome. Besides a Unitarian negro [sic] would be extremely hard to find in the South.
>
> That left the group with one Montgomery family and 3 or 4 Montgomery bachelors. The rest were and are military personnel who are never stationed here over a year. So you see one of our main problems is finding native Montgomery people to make a core group.
>
> After this we lost our meeting place, the Y.W.C.A. The reason given was that they needed the space but because of our defensive feelings we doubt that this was the real reason. We spent the summer looking for a place to meet and finally persuaded Huntingdon College to let us use a classroom on Sunday evening. We have no guarantee of how long we can stay there, it depends on how we behave. One stipulation we have is that we not advertise for negroes [sic] but we are free to state our belief. Huntingdon is a Methodist school and is not planning on integrating.

In a March 30, 1961, letter, Husbands describes a public meeting he had arranged to explore starting a new fellowship:

> Feared this place as a previous F[ellowship] was forced to quit because of race problems. Only one member of the

previous group was here. However, 19 signed out of 25. One additioan [additional] person asked to be informed of next meetings. Darn good steering Comm. It meets this Sunday with entire group week from Sunday. Getting a meeting place will be the real problem. One of Steer. Comm is a personal Friend of Martin L. King. King now lives in Atlanta, so will not be able to contact him. I was really pleased as set up for twenty, optomistically [sic]. Will have a F[ellowship] here again.

Meetings were initially at the Whitley Hotel and then once again at Huntingdon College, according to the "History of the Unitarian Universalist Fellowship of Montgomery," by Robert B. McDonald. McDonald notes, "The meetings at Huntingdon were discontinued as a result of opposition by a woman who was a substantial contributor to the Methodist Church. Her son had joined a Unitarian Universalist Church in Tennessee." From the college, the fellowship moved to Narrow Lane Inn, then the Romeo and Juliet School, and then became inactive by 1963.

That "personal Friend of Martin L. King" may have been Clifford Durr. McDonald's history lists him as an officer in the first organized group, and Clifford Durr's widow, Virginia, was on the fellowship's list of persons to receive the UUA's magazine as late as 1978. Clifford and Virginia Durr were vibrant human beings who played important background roles in American history from the 1930s to the 1960s.

A framed statement in the current Montgomery Fellowship building describes Clifford as having served as its first president. Virginia, it says, stayed with the Presbyterian Church, "refusing to be forced out." Tilla, one of the Durr daughters, joined her father in attending the fellowship, of which she says, "It was a little group of people. Basically, it was more open and liberal than any other church in Montgomery at that time."

Clifford Durr was born in Alabama in 1899. After graduating from the University of Alabama, he earned his law degree as a Rhodes Scholar at Oxford. Upon returning to Alabama, he married Virginia Foster, daughter of a Presbyterian minister. Her sister married Hugo Black, another up-and-coming Alabama lawyer. In 1933, the Durrs moved to Washington, DC, to join Franklin D. Roosevelt's New Deal. Clifford worked first with the Reconstruction Finance Corporation, then served a seven-year appointment on the Federal Communications Commission (FCC). Those years involved a circle of friends that included brother-in-law Hugo Black (a US senator before his appointment to the US Supreme Court) and Representative Lyndon Johnson of Texas. In this climate, both Durrs became increasingly and outspokenly liberal. During a 1941 filibuster of a bill against poll taxes, Virginia was called "a nigger-loving communist." Clifford opposed "loyalty" charges against government employees, whether coming from members of Congress or from the FBI. After Clifford's term on the FCC, they stayed in Washington, and Clifford practiced civil liberties law but didn't find it lucrative. For about a year and a half in 1949 and 1950, Clifford was president of the radical National Lawyers Guild. The Durrs lived in Denver briefly, where they attended the Unitarian Church, and in 1951, they moved home to Montgomery. Much of Clifford's law practice in Montgomery was for Black clients.

In 1954, the Durrs employed and befriended a talented local seamstress named Rosa Parks to alter dresses being handed down from their oldest daughter to the three younger girls. (Virginia later noted, "I couldn't call her Rosa until she could call me Virginia, and that took twenty-odd years.") In 1955, when Virginia Durr was asked to recommend a Montgomerian to attend a two-week desegregation workshop at Highlander Folk School, she recommended Parks. In December 1955, when NAACP president E. D. Nixon went to the Montgomery jail to bail out Parks after her arrest, he asked the Durrs to accompany him. When Fred Gray, a young Black attorney, began to file the legal paperwork in the cases related to the bus boycott, Clifford functioned as his assistant and law clerk. According to McDonald's history, Clifford Durr's family pressed him to return to the Presbyterian Church, but the Durrs remained friends of the Unitarian Universalist Fellowship.

In 1966, the District Extension Committee and UUA Fellowship consultant Todd Taylor instigated another attempt to organize a Montgomery fellowship. An initial meeting was held in
March, and by September, they were up and running with sixteen charter members. Almost half the members were in military
households and would be transferring within a year or less, a pattern that had contributed to the demise of earlier fellowships. This
time, Birmingham minister and District Extension Committee
member Larry McGinty helped to assess how to increase membership numbers. With funds from the district and the fellowship—a
grand total of $150—an intensive four-day field trip by McGinty
was planned. Between January 19 and 22, 1967, they carried out
an eleven-point plan involving programs, social events, and publicity. March 1–5 saw a similarly intense program with even better results. During the March event, the group agreed to a weekly
rental of meeting space at the South Montgomery YMCA. McDonald's history reports, "The South Montgomery Y was pressured to
deny meeting space to the Fellowship because it was an 'off-brand
religion.' The Fellowship overcame the objection by pointing out
that Jewish members of the Y Board were allowed to participate
and they were obviously not members of the prevailing faith in
Montgomery."

The fellowship planned a third field trip by McGinty for April
19–23, 1967. They held a brainstorming session in the Fuller and
Dees Marketing conference room, laying out a broad target audience of potential Unitarian Universalists and an ambitious program for the visit and its preparatory activities. They included a
four-to-five-thousand-letter direct mail campaign, with Morris
Dees donating four hundred dollars worth of direct mail services.
On Sunday, April 23, 108 adults attended the service, and 35 children and 7 adults participated in religious education.

With further supportive field trips by Larry McGinty and
excellent membership growth in prospect, the Montgomery Fellowship filed legal incorporation papers and bought a prospective
building lot. Beginning in May 1967, letters went out to Unitarian
Universalist congregations across the continent soliciting build-

ing loans of up to five hundred dollars. The letter from fellowship president Morris Dees notes, "If Unitarian Universalism ever had a frontier, it's in Montgomery, Alabama." The response from the UUA to this freelance fundraising was quick and discouraging. Dees was equally quick and pointed in his response:

Many Unitarian churches spent money to send marchers and demonstrators to Alabama. This was popular to do when the nation was up-in-arms over the situation in the South. These demonstrations served a purpose. Rev. Reeb is mute testimony to the part Unitarians played. But this is only a beginning for the real job that must be done. To effectively change the atmosphere, local people must be convinced by the example of other local people that we must make a change. Our group is fighting the day to day battle long after the bright light of national concern has moved on. . . . Unitarianism has remained dormant long enough. It has a message. This message must be told. There may be those who want a closed country club debate room atmosphere. If they persist, Unitarianism will die. There are at least 10 million unidentified Unitarians in America. We can have at least 4 million members and 7,000 churches by 1985 if the pessimists and fault finders will take a good look at the wonderful message Unitarians have to offer. . . . Mr. Putnam's letter sounds like the back biting attitude I'd expect from the Southern Baptist Church I just left to become a Unitarian.

With direct fundraising discouraged by the UUA, the fellowship and Dees went to work in another way to raise the funds their small group needed. Using the services of Fuller and Dees Publishing, and Morris Dees's direct mail skills, the fellowship published two cookbooks, *Unitarian Universalist Cookbook—Desserts* in 1968 and *Unitarian Universalist Cookbook—Meats* in 1969. Each included favorite recipes solicited from Unitarian Universalists around the country. Each contributor received a free copy of the book—and an opportunity to buy more copies to give to friends and family members. Congregations and women's groups could order books on credit and keep $1.00 of the $3.50 sale price as their profit. This energetic and apparently effective locally generated effort got around the UUA's dislike of appeals to sister congregations. But was it the energy of the congregation or merely of one extremely energetic and entrepreneurial member?

Construction of the new building took place 1969–70, and the congregation held its first service on Easter Sunday, March 29, 1970, with Rabbi David Baylinson speaking.

Obviously Morris Dees, whom we today think of primarily as founder and spokesperson of the Southern Poverty Law Center, was a strong motivating force in getting the 1966 iteration of the Montgomery Fellowship organized and funded. He was not on the September 18, 1966, list of charter members, but by May 1967, he was serving as congregational president. Larry McGinty's letter in the fundraising packet speaks glowingly of Dees:

> Beginning his business while a student at the University of Alabama, Dees, age 30, has built an amazingly successful business enterprise. Today, his company, Fuller and Dees Marketing Group, Inc., has offices in Chicago, Washington, Louisville and Montgomery and does business in all fifty states and over twenty foreign countries. He was honored on January 13 by the United States Junior Chamber of Commerce as one of the Ten Outstanding Young Men of America.

When asked in 2000 about how, during his years of involvement, the fellowship functioned as Montgomery moved away from strict segregation, Dees replied, "[N]othing special, except having a few Black members. Nobody seemed to care. The fellowship took no public stands that I know about. Nobody harassed us."

Taming the Storm, a 1993 biography of federal judge Frank Johnson, includes three revealing paragraphs about Dees:

Sometimes described as a direct mail merchandising and fund-raising genius, Dees developed a list of hundreds of thousands of liberal contributors while directing fund-raising for George McGovern's 1972 presidential campaign. He parlayed that list to create a multi-million dollar endowment for the Southern Poverty Law Center, which Dees and a colleague had established in Montgomery.

The center later handled a series of high-profile cases that included civil rights lawsuits stripping the Ku Klux Klan and other white supremacist groups of their operating resources. In addition, the SPLC also engaged in quiet research in its Klanwatch and other operations that included development of education materials.

Although Dees grew up on a modest farm ten miles west of Montgomery, he was already a millionaire businessman when he became involved with civil rights, with a law degree but little experience. Dees displayed an intuitive grasp of constitutional protection of civil rights and civil liberties, deep-seated feelings about injustice, and determination. Ironically, he first appeared before Judge Johnson as a twenty-five-year-old lawyer representing one of the Klansmen who had attacked the Freedom Riders.

In a further irony, Judge Johnson, often viewed as the southern federal judge friendliest to civil rights suits, was also indirectly connected to the Montgomery Fellowship. Married at nineteen, Frank Johnson worked in the New Deal's Works Progress Administration program and then went to the University of Alabama and the University of Alabama Law School. George Wallace was a law school classmate and friend. In 1956, President Eisenhower appointed Johnson as district judge, the youngest in the country at that time. In his first year on the bench, he was part of a three-judge panel that ruled Montgomery's bus segregation unconstitutional. Thereafter, he became a prime target of verbal vilification by former friend George Wallace. Johnson was involved in landmark decisions that touched on mental health treatment, school desegregation, voting rights, minimum conditions for prisons, and desegregation of the Alabama State Troopers. Following his service as district judge, he was elevated to the Fifth Circuit Court of Appeals and considered for the directorship of the FBI and service on the US Supreme Court.

Judge Frank Johnson remained a nominal member of First Baptist Church, but for many years did not attend services. His wife, Ruth, became a member of the Unitarian Fellowship. One of his closest friends for many years was Earl Pippin, a pillar of the fellowship. In 1975, Judge and Mrs. Johnson presented to the fellowship a walnut podium in memory of their son, Johnny, whose mental illness ended in suicide.

Sources

Material on the Montgomery Fellowship was drawn from files of the UUA; "History of the Unitarian Universalist Fellowship of Montgomery," by Robert B. McDonald; an interview with Bob and Patricia McDonald; an original insert from the *Unitarian Universalist Cookbook—Meats*; and correspondence with Morris Dees. Information from the framed statement about Clifford and Virginia Durr was copied on September 25, 2013. Published sources consulted include *Taming the Storm: The Life and Times of Judge Frank M. Johnson, Jr. and the South's Fight over Civil Rights*, by Jack Bass (New York: Doubleday, 1993); *Outside the Magic Circle: The Autobiography of Virginia Foster Durr*, edited by Hollinger F. Barnard (Tuscaloosa: University of Alabama Press, 1985); and *Standing Against Dragons: Three Southern Lawyers in an Era of Fear*, by Sarah Hart Brown (Baton Rouge: Louisiana State University Press, 1998).

TUSCALOOSA, ALABAMA

In 1954, the AUA organized a fellowship in Tuscaloosa, home of the University of Alabama. Early correspondence in UUA files suggests a typical program for a fellowship located in a college town. Some of the early meetings were held on Sunday evenings in a university lecture hall. Many of the presenters were faculty members, and a few spoke on clearly religious topics: the origin of man, the speeches of Paul, a comparison of the teachings of Jesus and of Paul, existentialism. A 1955 letter to Munroe Husbands reads, "The speaker for the evening is invited to base his discussion on any subject on which he has a strong conviction of truth and validity." Attendance sometimes reached seventy-five, and membership was in the mid-thirties.

Two different sources suggest that when the fellowship chartered, or within the first year or two of its existence, there were 120 to 135 members. One of those sources, a 1964 report on a visit by UUA Religious Education consultant Gene Navias, states,

This group is small, weary, and heavy-laden. After eleven years of existence, they have only twelve members. Early in their history, they mushroomed to a claimed total of 135. Then Autherine Lucy visited their Sunday service at the unauthorized invitation of their President and that ended the Fellowship. In their own descriptions, "We weren't prepared." "That was ten years ago and the community wouldn't accept what it would now." "There were riots and we were scared." . . . Civil rights issues have already burned

Homer Jack on Tuscaloosa and the South

While Homer Jack was a student at Meadville Lombard Theological School he was one of the co-founders of the Congress of Racial Equality (CORE). Later (1964–70) he was director of the UUA's Department of Social Responsibility. In early 1956 he visited Alabama to get a first-hand feel for civil rights issues there. On March 18, 1956, he preached on "Inside Alabama" at the Unitarian Church of Evanston, Illinois, where he was serving. There is no indication in the sermon that he visited local Unitarians in Birmingham, Tuscaloosa, or Montgomery during his time in those cities. He included these reflections on Tuscaloosa in his sermon:

Next day, I went the 60 miles to Tuscaloosa, to see the University of Alabama situation. We were shown the campus and the buildings where the mobs gathered when Autherine Lucy escaped with her life at the hands of a mob by a matter of seconds. A young Episcopal rector told us how he spent an entire day inside the mob and tried—unsuccessfully—to reason with some of its leaders. A professor told us how a petition originated asking the University to reinstate Miss Lucy after she was first suspended. He said they got 200 student and faculty signatures out of more than 7,000 students and faculty—but no faculty members dared make their names public when the petition was released to the press. After Miss Lucy was expelled, not a student or faculty member raised his or her voice.

This is almost a totalitarian land, the South. When I was in South Africa three years ago, I found whites there freer to speak out against apartheid than I found whites in Alabama last week free to speak out against segregation. This is a terrible indictment, and I don't want to generalize, but this was my distinct impression of Birmingham, Tuscaloosa, and Montgomery. A newspaper friend there, who recently returned from Russia, said that fear stalked Alabama just as much as Moscow, and from the hushed tones and closed doors, I can easily believe it.

this group, and the Consultant felt there was a real difference of conviction among them as evidenced by some very favorable and some very critical reactions to the recent visit of two members of our Race and Religion Commission. . . .

There were some things to praise—such as the evidence of excellent lectures . . . and there were some things difficult to talk about, and that was integration and segregation.

Autherine Lucy was the first Black student to enroll in the University of Alabama, entering under court order in early February 1956. Her enrollment lasted less than a week. University trustees expelled her because White community members rioted in response to her presence. Longtime fellowship member Charlie Wilson recalled attempting to drive through campus at the height of the riot, in which Miss Lucy was almost killed, and seeing members of the Ku Klux Klan, including one of his neighbors, running wild and attacking the car she was in.

In a 1961 report to the regional extension chairman, Evelyn Falkowski of Huntsville reports, "A fellowship folded in Tuscaloosa at the time of the Autherine Lucy incident. The new fellowship seems to be making progress. It may be mostly the original fellowship."

Sources

UUA file materials and an April 2000 interview with Charlie Wilson provided information used here. Mark Morrison-Reed located Homer Jack's sermon and provided a copy to me.

MOBILE, ALABAMA

In the nineteenth century, Unitarians expended little energy attempting to spread their faith in the South. This inaction and inattention made Unitarianism irrelevant in much of the antebellum South. Mobile was an exception.

A brief visit by James Freeman Clarke instigated the founding of a Unitarian congregation in January 1836. At that time, Clarke served the Unitarian congregation in Louisville, Kentucky. (New England Unitarians' adventurous extension efforts into "the West" included Louisville, Cincinnati, and St. Louis.) The congregation Clarke had gathered in Mobile was served by several other ministers who briefly came to the area. When Henry Whitney Bellows arrived in Mobile in 1837–38, the congregation boasted over 150 members and an attractive building.

But two factors heralded impending trouble in 1838: debt and slavery. The building had been erected in large part with borrowed money. Of the fourteen most prominent families in the congregation, eleven "owned" a total of 127 slaves.

George F. Simmons, the young minister who followed Bellows, preached on slavery on May 10, 1840, without creating much stir. His May 17 sermon on the same subject resulted in his being hauled before a grand jury and charged with inciting the slaves of Mobile to riot. Although the charge was subsequently dismissed, Simmons was advised by church members to leave the city, and he took their advice. The congregation gradually spiraled downward despite brief service by a few other ministers. It formally dissolved in 1850.

Just over a century later, there were again Unitarian stirrings in the Mobile Bay area, first in Fairhope and then in Mobile. Robert T. Weston, who had a summer cottage near Fairhope, encouraged these stirrings. Weston was at that time serving the same Louisville congregation that James Freeman Clarke had served when he visited Mobile. The Mobile Fellowship originally formed in 1954, but when it failed to come to an understanding about issues of race, it became inactive. In 1958, it organized again with more lasting results.

In 1963, a lay leader in the Mobile Fellowship noted, "The Fellowship has not yet invited a Negro speaker or visitor as far as I know; but the two key figures in race progress here, a Catholic City Commissioner and a Jesuit professor, have both spoken." At that point, approximately 15 to 20 percent of the fellowship members were involved in the local Council on Human Relations, and probably even more in a group formed to keep the public schools open. In short, the early Mobile Fellowship may not have been inclined as an organization to be on the cutting edge, but some of its members were engaged and involved in local issues.

By 1970, the membership in Mobile's fellowship included John LeFlore, who since 1925 had been a leader in Mobile's Black community. He worked early on through the NAACP, both in Mobile and along the Gulf Coast. In 1936, he had become the first chairman of the NAACP's Regional Conference of Southern Branches. When a state injunction effectively shut down the work of the NAACP in Alabama in 1956, LeFlore continued his work through the Non-Partisan Voters League. In 1973, he was the National Democratic Party of Alabama's candidate for the US Senate. That campaign was not successful, but in 1974, he was elected to the Alabama House of Representatives. He died of a heart attack in 1976. His funeral was held at the Big Zion AME Zion Church, where he continued to be a member while he was part of the Unitarian Universalist Fellowship. John Wier, a White member of the fellowship, says, "It was a great privilege to have known him. . . . I did something for him, I can't remember just what. Anyhow, he looked me squarely in the eyes and said, 'John Wier, you must have a mighty black heart.' We both laughed." In the 1980s, John LeFlore's achievements were honored by renaming a school the John L. LeFlore Magnet High School of Advanced Communication and Fine Arts.

Sources

The UUA archives, a congregational history written for a 1983 search packet, the John L. LeFlore papers at the University of South Alabama, 1984 correspondence from John Wier, and the John L. LeFlore entry for the online *Encyclopedia of Alabama* all contributed to this entry.

JACKSON, MISSISSIPPI

Until the middle of the twentieth century, it could be said that "Mississippi has two major cities: Memphis and New Orleans." Mississippi was a predominantly rural state, with small cities, towns, and minute crossroads communities scattered across its landscape. Jackson, created as the capital, sits in the middle of the state on the banks of the Pearl River but was hardly a dominating presence in its early years. Mississippi River towns Natchez, Vicksburg, and Greenville were richer due to cotton and other commerce that flowed through them. The University of Mississippi opened in the small town of Oxford rather than Jackson.

By the 1950s, growing Jackson began to achieve significance in its own right, although still overshadowed by Memphis and New Orleans. As a result of its growth, or maybe as part of it, a Unitarian fellowship began in 1951.

In November 1952, Richard Henry, minister in Knoxville, visited several cities with Unitarian groups. Of his visit to Jackson, he writes,

> What a place! Suffocating atmosphere. One hundred thousand population. Baptist headquarters for the Southeast, newspaper owned by Lay Leades [sic] of Baptist convention. Anti-immigrants (four articles today about these), anti-labor, anti-anti. No international news in a 60-page newspaper, none! Other than a passing mention of some sort of mess in Korea.

Eighteen members in this community, really valiantly struggling, though they lost by removal more members than they now have, and are losing two more of their best, one in January, one in February. Floundering some, needing some encouragement, etc. but it was thrilling to see their gallant spirit.

Race was, of course, a factor. But this was Mississippi, and if race were a complicating factor elsewhere in the South, it could be a downright convoluting factor in Mississippi. For example, an early 1956 letter to Munroe Husbands, fellowship director for the AUA, from Edith F. Ives, one of the first members of the congregation reveals,

I realize it has been a long time since I have written to you but I have tried to several times expressing indignation that you northern Unitarians should do so much to support and encourage the N.A.A.C.P. and then the letters were put in the wastebasket.

I am in a peculiar position since I am a northerner with all four grandparents abolitionists. Yet I have lived so long in the south I understand and sympathize with the southern point of view even though I know it is wrong. A personal problem is that my son-in-law is a member of the local Citizens Council.

Husbands replied to her, noting that he had missed her correspondence:

In respect to the NAACP, the Association is on record at several May Meetings as endorsing their general program. This without any opposition, and of course you must know that many of the delegates were southern Unitarians. In fact some of the Southerners were a little stronger than us conservative Northerners. But please don't get the idea that we Unitarians up here are hell-bent for immediate integration.

We, as you, know that this is a strong emotional issue rather than a rational one. The fact of the matter is that our Unitarians in the South have taken a much stronger stand than we here in the North, due undoubtedly to the fact that they are in the middle of the controversy.

After almost six years of meeting in rented spaces, the Jackson congregation moved in 1957 to buy land and erect a building. The AUA Building and Loan Fund aided with a loan of $3,000.

Six years later, the new building had not produced much—or had it? Eugene Navias of the UUA Department of Education visited Jackson on March 9 and 10, 1963. (Alice Harrison and Edna Bruner of the department had also visited during the preceding twelve months.) On Saturday, meeting with the religious education director and the president and their families over dinner, Navias initially found pessimism:

Jackson has 150,000 people and growing fast: 5 colleges; diversified industry; oil companies; medical research center; cattle; etc.

In telling the story of their Fellowship everything was problems and gloom. They sound tired, defeatist, complaining.

I said I was sorry that I was not having the opportunity to speak to the whole church; they had a twice postponed speaker scheduled who it would be awkward to postpone again since conservative members of the Fellowship had reported him to the FBI as a communist. I said I understood their problem.

They feel they haven't grown since they got their "church"—and yet they do not seem actively after members. Expect people to come to them. Get lots of visitors. Few join.

The whole solution in their thinking is a Minister for Mississippi to live in Jackson, minister to the Unitarian fellowships and Universalist churches. Cliff Hoffman, accord-

ing to their reports, assures them subsidy money is coming
—maybe $2000 a year.

Additional problems are: fear; segregation-integration;
& minority feelings.

Assets: Their own building. A lot of very talented people.

On Sunday the picture was different:

On Sunday went to attractive new church building at 10
a.m. with Bill Lynch, who realized all had been pessimism
the night before. Was astonished at the nice building and
the good group of people who assembled for 10:30 service.

Briefly greeted people at beginning of service—telling
them of our aims and asking all of them to support the
church school by their interest.

Sunday evening at a three hour long Board meeting:

They have much hope about subsidy for "Mississippi
Minister".

Hoping to grant permission for integrated Mississippi
Council on Human Relations to meet in Church. Hoping
to get good new membership and promotion chairman—
much needed. Voted money to be in hotel church directo-
ries. Board generally enthusiastic.

In May 1963, negotiations were underway with the Jackson
congregation and the UUA that would bring Donald A. Thompson to Jackson later that year to serve as the "Mississippi Minister."

Born in 1906, Donald Thompson was a son of George Linnaeus
Thompson, a minister who served both Universalist and Unitarian congregations during his career. Don earned degrees from
Tufts College, Brookwood Labor College, and Meadville Lombard
Theological School. He worked with laborers in coalfields and steel
mills. During the Great Depression and World War II, he worked
in Boston and Washington, DC, with the Works Progress Administration, the Library of Congress, and the office of the Chief of
Chaplains of the Army. In 1947–49, he was an associate professor

of religion and directed graduate studies at Florida Southern College at Lakeland. Finally, in 1950, he took up ministerial duties under Unitarian and Universalist auspices. The appeal of religiously based community organizing and extension ministry with fellowships and small churches in Illinois and Indiana distracted him from completing his doctorate in church history. Then, in 1963, he and his wife, Leila, moved to Jackson.

Looking back two years later, Don Thompson, speaking modestly of himself in the third person, reflects,

> Although the minister intended to concentrate his community action in the field of mental health and had even made arrangements with the Whitfield Hospital for regular visiting there, the needs of the reorganized Mississippi Council on Human Relations soon became paramount. This organization is designed "to carry on an educational program directed toward creating a climate of opinion favorable to an expansion of opportunity for all the people of Mississippi in economic, civic and cultural areas based on freedom from discrimination on grounds of race, religion or national origin." Not itself a civil rights organization, this Council was instrumental in sending out mailings to some 1,200 Mississippians on an average of twice a month during the time that our minister served as secretary and performed the executive functions.

The vacancy that Don Thompson filled on the Mississippi Human Relations Council board had been created by the assassination of Medgar Evers in June 1963. Don's ministry in Jackson ended in November 1965, following his being shot and critically injured. Between those two shootings, a great deal happened in Mississippi, and Don and the Jackson congregation had had small roles in much of it.

When Thompson agreed to be secretary of the Mississippi Council on Human Relations, he had assumed that meant nothing

Bill Higgs

The September 14, 1962, special issue of *Life* magazine is titled "One Hundred of the Most Important Young Men and Women in the United States." William Higgs was one of the youngest listed. The magazine describes him: "A southern maverick, he is the only white lawyer in Mississippi who actively takes civil rights segregation cases. He was the first attorney who legally challenged the powerful White Citizens Council."

The Mississippi Sovereignty Commission, a state agency to investigate and disrupt desegregation efforts, created a file on Higgs that contains a 1964 profile from the *Harvard Crimson*:

Eight years ago Mississippian Bill Higgs graduated from Harvard Law School with modest grades, unpretentious ambitions, and an unshaken faith in racism. He served an Army stint and disappeared quietly into a Jackson, Mississippi law practice. Today he is one of Washington's most militant lobbyists for integration, an attorney for SNCC, and the author of several titles of the present civil rights bill. As his close friend, Roy Wilkins, noted here last week: "When a Southerner changes, he's very thorough about it."

Higgs gave little thought to the race issue before 1959; that year, in fact, he ran for the legislature as a "staunch segregationist." However, at that time he also began accepting Negro clients "out of curiosity." "They came to me beaten, their eyes knocked out, their land stolen. I found that there was no remedy in the courts or in politics. I began to investigate my beliefs."

The step from investigation to action was a quick one. Early in 1961 Higgs was approached by a young Negro wearing a purple shirt, leather jacket, sunglasses and a determined frown. "You've spoken well of us, Mr. Higgs, but we've all heard enough talk. I plan to enter Ole Miss this year. Help me." The lawyer agreed, and eighteen months later James Meredith walked on to the Oxford campus.

Higgs soon received prestigious civil liberties awards in New York and Los Angeles—and death threats from the sheriff's office in Clarksdale, Mississippi. His parents began to receive endless insults from town folk and economic intimidation from local grocers. Finally, early last year, the Jackson District Attorney told him to expect "unlimited jailings" upon returning to the state.

Another item in the Sovereignty Commission files is a list of four people who "have expressed willingness to" collaborate with Bill Higgs. Of the four, the commission notes that Harry and Florence Newman and Sarah Davis "are members of the Unitarian Church on Ellis Ave."

The Jackson congregation's membership book shows that William L. Higgs joined on March 26, 1961. The membership book in this era had three columns: "date," "signature," and "withdrawal data." The third column next to Higgs's name displays the date February 15, 1964, with the note "barred from state."

How had Higgs been "barred" from Mississippi? For two weeks, he had befriended and taken into his house a sixteen-year-old runaway from Pennsylvania named William McKinley Daywalt. Higgs was arrested, tried in absentia (he was out of town, accepting an award, at the time his trial was called), convicted of "contributing to the delinquency of a minor" (Daywalt, with whom he was accused of having sex), and sentenced to six months in prison and a five hundred dollar fine. District Attorney William Waller promised "unlimited jailings" if Higgs ever returned to the state.

Higgs moved to Washington, DC, and provided legal services to civil rights organizations, becoming "Mississippi's lawyer-in-exile" in historian Howard Zinn's phrasing. Higgs helped draft portions of the Civil Rights Act of 1964. DA William Waller was later elected governor of Mississippi.

more than taking minutes. In reality, it meant that the files of the council took up space in the church filing cabinets, and for many months, the council's mail came to the church address. The council was highly visible in Mississippi as the only statewide organization in the 1960s that sought participation of both Black and White Mississippians. Duncan Gray Jr., a White native Mississippian and Episcopal minister who served as president of the Council, 1963–67, remembers the council's dinner meeting at the King Edward Hotel in the fall of 1964 as the first big integrated social function in the state.

Eugene Navias made another visit to Jackson on April 23–24, 1964. He notes in his report, "In the past year since the consultant visited this group, it has not grown in membership or church school registration, with newcomers equalizing those who've moved away." More dramatically, he begins the report:

> The consultant arrived in Jackson on the morning after a night of great decision in the life of the Fellowship. It would be easy for those of us who live far away to regard the debate here as a minor one, but to this small group of liberals in Mississippi, it was of paramount importance.
>
> On Easter Sunday, the Fellowship was astonished when a woman Negro college student signed the Membership Book. The fact that she had never visited the Fellowship previously and was not known by a single person in the group complicated the feelings of the membership. It is to be noted that the Fellowship has had Negro visitors for a long time.
>
> Now, however, the group reacted with understandable fear. It is no exaggeration of the facts of life in Jackson to say that having admitted a Negro to membership could plunge this group into a reign of terror involving the loss of jobs, economic and social pressures, and even the loss of life.
>
> The police, the Citizens Council and the State of Mississippi have infinite means of maintaining segregation.
>
> At the membership meeting, with the Negro member present, the group aired its fears and ideals and rose to the challenge in voting that membership be open, that such be stated openly, and that the membership book be kept out in the open.
>
> It is to be noted that the Negro member has attended regularly since joining and seems sincere in her choice of this church. It would also appear, however, that as an active member of CORE, she was making a test case.

Navias ended the report of his 1964 visit: "All in all, the group has some fine, dedicated people. There would seem to be adequate liberal potential in the community, but reaching and interesting them under present conditions is a gigantic challenge."

The 1964 Mississippi Summer Project, popularly referred to as Freedom Summer, brought hundreds of volunteers, mostly White northern college students, to the state for two or three months of organizing freedom schools, supporting voter registration, and other civil rights work. A January 1965 survey conducted by a team of four Unitarian Universalist officials found that at least twenty-eight Unitarian Universalist students participated in the Summer Project, and fourteen Unitarian Universalist clergy came to the state during and after the summer. The Jackson congregation became a touch point for many of these and other out-of-state visitors.

In response to the bombing or burning of many churches thought to be associated with the civil rights movement, a coalition of clergy and laypeople started the Committee of Concern to raise funds in Mississippi to rebuild. Don Thompson served on the executive committee of this organization and participated in other interfaith efforts.

According to the March 14 church newsletter, Thompson and Roland Toms, a church member, retired psychiatrist, and community activist, were among forty-one Unitarian Universalist ministers and thirteen laypeople who went to Selma, Alabama, on March 9, 1965, in response to Dr. King's call for religious people to join in another march after the March 7 beatings on the Edmund Pettus Bridge, called Bloody Sunday.

The May 23, 1965, church newsletter announces, "Within a few days our church is likely to be asked to cooperate with an educational program known as 'Operation Head Start.' We have already given some cooperation, and the first Jackson meeting to discuss the plan seems to have been the one held at our church." That summer, the church hosted the only integrated Head Start center in Jackson—indeed, probably in the state—and Head Start continued to use the building for several more years. Elected officials in Mississippi did not consider Head Start a benign preschool program, but rather part of a radical, federally funded assault on the southern way of life, so choosing to be a Head Start center was not a value-neutral decision by the church.

Buford Posey and Johnny Frazier

Buford Posey began as a fairly "normal" White Mississippian. A 2005 article in the *Nation* quotes Posey: "When I was coming up in Mississippi I never knew it was against the law to kill a black man. I learned that when I was in the Army. I was 17 years old. When they told me, I thought they were joking."

Buford Posey's story is continued in Seth Cagin and Philip Dray's book *We Are Not Afraid*, which chronicles the 1964 civil rights-related murders of James Chaney, Michael Schwerner, and Andrew Goodman in Neshoba County, Buford Posey's home county:

> He had been called "eccentric" practically all his adult life, since at least 1946 when, as a young man of twenty-one, he became the first white person to join the Mississippi NAACP. He later explained that he did so because he believed that black veterans of World War II deserved the right to vote in the country they had risked their lives to defend. Jack Tannehill, editor of the Neshoba Democrat, routinely referred to Posey as a "Communist" after Posey supported Truman's nomination for president in 1948 rather than the Dixiecrat ticket. In the late 1950s Posey challenged Tannehill to a duel.
>
> "I was the first man to be convicted of dueling in Mississippi in the twentieth century," Posey related proudly to a reporter some years later. "They took away my citizenship, but I didn't care to be a member of a Fascist society anyway." As a result of his conviction, Posey, like the Mississippi blacks with whom he had sided, was denied the right to vote. He was active in the NAACP Jackson demonstrations around the time of the Medgar Evers assassination.

In the wake of the June 21, 1964, murders of Chaney, Schwerner, and Goodman, Buford Posey did the utterly unpardonable in the eyes of White Neshoba County: He talked openly with FBI agents on June 23 and 27. Earlier, he had talked with Rev. Ed King, Tougaloo College chaplain and part of the leadership of Freedom Summer. Finally, on July 1, he gave a television interview to Richard Valeriani of *NBC News*, again stating his view that Sheriff Rainey and Deputy Cecil Price were deeply involved in the murders.

On July 2, the director of the Sovereignty Commission, a state agency founded in the 1950s to record and interfere with the work of civil rights organizations, sent a memo to the office of the governor. The memo reads, "If Governor Johnson wishes to send any communication to Huntley and Brinkley to discredit remarks made by Buford Posey of Philadelphia, Mississippi, on their news cast July 1, 1964, please let me know. We have a lengthy file on this subject. He at one time was a speaker for the Young Communists of America and has been an associate of several identified communists."

Apparently, the report was requested because, on the same date, the Sovereignty Commission sent a one-and-a-half-page memo to the governor. The second memo details eight facts or allegations about Posey, including the dueling conviction. Rather than casting its comments in terms of race, the report focuses on Posey's alleged Communism, as in the eighth and last item:

8. The communist activities of subject Posey were discussed on June 4, 1961, in Atlanta, Georgia, at a confidential meeting of law enforcement officers from several southern and western states. The meeting was also attended by representatives of the FBI. The Sovereignty Commission report makes this statement: "the only Mississippi communist referred to at this meeting was Buford Posey of Philadelphia, Mississippi."

Whatever the governor's office said, the national television interview was the last straw for the Ku Klux Klan. The Klan reaction rose from harassment to a determination that Posey should die. Posey wisely left town, but Cagin and Dray report that, in a parting show of his opinions, he heaved a brick through the front plate-glass window of the *Neshoba Democrat*.

The membership book of what was then called First Unitarian Church of Jackson shows that Posey signed on November 15, 1963. Typed notes in columns labeled "date of leaving" and "reason for leaving" say "7/64" and "Moved out of state."

That membership book also contains the signature of Johnny Frazier on October 18, 1964. In a March 16, 2000, interview, Frazier, a Black Unitarian Universalist minister, said that he had heard about the church through Buford Posey, whom he had met through Medgar Evers. Posey had come to Medgar Evers's office and offered to help Frazier get into the University of Southern Mississippi by providing his signature on the application (the signature of an alumnus was required). Posey, a cousin of Sheriff Rainey (with whom Posey had grown up), demonstrated remarkable courage. Frazier became intrigued by a religious tradition that could support such courage. Posey invited Frazier to attend, and Frazier did so, but only after talking with Thompson and a leading layperson, Roland Toms. After becoming a member, Frazier would stop by the church almost daily and talk with Thompson.

Regarding his attendance at services and eventual membership at First Unitarian Church of Jackson, Frazier said that it was a big deal for him, but "It was not a big deal to them." He said he attended services for about four months before filing his first application to enroll at the University of Southern Mississippi.

Frazier had worked closely with Medgar Evers, whom he saw almost daily for a while. He was president of the NAACP Youth Council for Mississippi and was the youngest member of the NAACP National Board. Early in Frazier's civil rights activities in his native Greenville, Medgar Evers would come to Greenville when Frazier was "in trouble" and Evers supported him in his college application.

The Mississippi Sovereignty Commission files—despite their frequent inaccuracies—confirm Frazier's extensive activist history. A December 7, 1962, Sovereignty Commission report notes his 1960 expulsion from high school for trying to celebrate the US Supreme Court's desegregation decision; his 1960 desegregation of a white Episcopal church in Greenville; an August 1960 arrest at the Winona, Mississippi, bus station; an August 1961 arrest and conviction for picketing Woolworths in Greenville; and his desegregation of the seating in a federal courtroom in Jackson in August 1961. The report gives his identification number at the Greenville Police Department and his fingerprint classification.

A March 2, 1964, Sovereignty Commission memorandum about "John Frazier" to W. D. McCain, the president of Mississippi Southern University (with blind copies to the governor and lieutenant governor) reads,

> Reference is made to announcement by subject that he intends to re-apply for enrollment at Mississippi Southern University.
> This memorandum is to re-affirm an oral report previously provided. You or your registrar may advise Frazier as follows:

"We have information that you are a homosexual. We also have sufficient information to prove it if necessary. If you change your mind about enrolling at an all white university we will say no more about it. If you persist in your application, we will give this information to the press and the Justice Department. We do not believe the government will back a homosexual in attempting to get admitted to a university."

Frazier confirms that something like this was said to him over the telephone. He was surprised to discover, after the release of the Sovereignty Commission files in recent years, that his situation had been addressed at such high levels of government. He, his wife, and their two adult children discussed whether to ask that the Sovereignty Commission files be sealed and not released to the public, but decided not to do so.

A May 30, 1965, article in the congregation's newsletter notes that during the summer of 1965, more out-of-state volunteers would arrive in Mississippi. The article refers to the several Mississippi congregations:

As churches or fellowships, our congregations have been neutral in regard to summer or other civil rights projects. The Jackson church, however, does have an interest in those who come here, *as persons*, and attempts to be of whatever assistance it can to visiting Unitarian Universalists especially and to all who come and can enjoy our hospitality. We are delighted when students or ministers from other states attend our services.

One of the ministers who visited that summer, Robert M. Bowman of Fort Collins, Colorado, was a longtime friend of Don Thompson, who had been a mentor to him. Bowman, in an article in the fall 1965 *Journal of the Liberal Ministry*, related that Thompson had told him "laughingly—that work with the Freedom Movement sometimes makes you want to say to your fellow worker: 'I love you; God-damn you!'" an expression he borrowed from his friend and parishioner, Roland Toms.

During the summer of 1965, Thompson and the Jackson congregation helped Ted Seaver, a volunteer from Vermont, organize what would become the Medgar Evers Neighborhood Center. This "Vermont in Mississippi" effort aimed to establish adult literacy programs, tutoring for schoolchildren, and a playground for neighborhood children.

On the evening of August 23, 1965, after a church board meeting, Don Thompson drove Johnny Frazier home. Frazier, a Black college student, had become an active member of the congregation and hoped in September to begin seminary studies in preparation for the Unitarian Universalist ministry. After dropping off Frazier, Thompson drove to the apartment building in which both the Thompsons and Roland Toms lived. As he walked toward the back door of the building, a car pulled into the parking lot, and two shots were fired at him. Thompson was not a small man; although of average height or less, he weighed well over two hundred pounds. The first shot missed him completely. The second shot hit his left shoulder with buckshot and probably would have been lethal had he been significantly thinner. He suffered at least two broken bones and considerable trauma to various body parts, but he survived and slowly recovered strength.

On September 13, the settlement director in the UUA Department of Ministry wrote to express his pleasure at Thompson's progress and the reports that he would be leaving the hospital that week. He continued, "Do you think the time is now for you to move to a more comfortable situation or a different climate. I would be pleased to assist you in whatever your plans are."

From his hospital room, Don scrawled a reply:

Thanks for your offer of assistance in placement. If any of the Miss. congregations feel that my presence is a danger to them, I'll take advantage of your offer. Otherwise, I feel that I ought to try to stay here for the next seven or eight years ("I should live so long.")

Paul and Thelma Worksman

Paul and Thelma Worksman moved to the Jackson area from the sub-
urbs of Washington, DC, in about 1966. A civilian employee of the Army
Corps of Engineers, Paul was relocated to the Waterways Experiment
Station in Vicksburg. Rather than live in Vicksburg, the Worksmans
opted to buy a house in Clinton, a suburb of Jackson that would be a
short commute via interstate to Paul's job. Clinton, home of Mississippi
College, a well-regarded Baptist school, would provide better schools for
their daughter, Lisa, and ready access to the cultural benefits that Jackson
offered, including the First Unitarian Church of Jackson.

Paul was standing in the front yard, overseeing the unloading of their
moving van, when a car pulled up. A man got out, approached Paul, shook
his hand, introduced himself as being from the Morrison Heights Baptist
Church, and invited Paul and his family to attend Morrison Heights if
they had not already found a church. Paul replied that they attended the
Unitarian Church. The man responded by turning and walking back to
his car. Before he got in, he turned back to Paul and said, "You know, they
shot the minister."

I realize that the same night riders may be out to finish
the job, but why have a successor who would also be a target.

The Klan probably is quite upset because, for once, their
execution didn't take. Maybe they'll do something about it.
Yet one cannot live on the basis of fear.

I hope that the Department of the Ministry and the Extension Department are not too disturbed about our small
membership. It takes courage in Jackson to join a liberal
church. Yet I believe that my continuing after the shooting
incident might attract some worthwhile members.

Recovering from the attack, Thompson began to get out some,
even attending a few civil rights meetings in Jackson and the UUA
Commission on Religion and Race meetings in New York. Back
home, the Thompsons received a string of threats. Then in November, a friend phoned to say that the threats should be taken seri-

ously, that Don might not be permitted to live through another night in Jackson. Reluctantly, he boarded a plane that evening, and his wife left the state the following day.

The Thompsons settled in Boston, where Don became minister of social responsibility at the Benevolent Fraternity of Unitarian Churches and minister of social concerns at Arlington Street Church. He lived an active, engaged life until his death in 1985.

The wider Unitarian Universalist community rallied to the aid of the Jackson congregation in the wake of the shooting. While Thompson was recovering from the shooting, and after he had been forced from the state, other Unitarian Universalist ministers came to Jackson to provide pulpit supply and a supportive presence. Here is where I, the author, entered the picture. I was first on the scene in late August but was followed by many others. One of those was Peter Raible of University Unitarian Church in Seattle, who arrived on January 1, 1966.

After his visit, Peter Raible prepared a four-page summary, apparently to be shared with UUA officials. Of the congregation, he writes,

> At its high point the Unitarian group had about 40 adult members and 35 children. It is almost exactly half that size at the moment. While some loss was experienced by those who moved away and were not replaced, there is no question that the major loss resulted from the civil rights identification of the church and its minister. Some quit the group because they were pro-segregationist but many more left in fear of their livelihood or even personal safety. Whether these fears were exaggerated or not, there is no question that they were truly felt by those who left the group.
>
> The group that is left is small, rather worried about its future, but strongly dedicated and committed. Virtually every member holds responsible positions of leadership; attendance is high week after week (far higher than the total membership); the group tends to seek its social outlets

among other members of the group; pledging is very high (estimated average pledge is $250 per year, but only 10 or 11 pledges). The small building is excellent for fellowship needs, though poorly located on the opposite city-side from most members. It will be fully paid for in another five years. Obviously, the group is terribly small for a city the size of Jackson and even this small group is too dependent on several older members. Nonetheless, the group shows real spirit and concern, even though there is no outstanding leadership in the entire group. . . .

The unassuming courage of our Jackson Unitarians should win the admiration of us all. Despite a decrease of half the membership and all kinds of community pressures and fears, they continue to go about their work with a great deal of zeal. Someday we will mark with great pride this small band, who without vain-seeking or grand-standing, kept alive an open membership and a courageous spirit during months and years of terror, state-wide community pressures, and religious intolerance. Such a group deserves denominational backing for its future growth.

In April 1967, District Executive Clif Hoffman reported that the congregation continued to provide "the only meeting place for the Head Start Program which permits it to be integrated." But, he added, "The group itself is becoming weaker. There is now talk of their selling the property which they occupy and purchasing property in the northeastern part of town which is the direction from which most of their growth is coming."

Eventually, the congregation did sell its property at the corner of Ellis Avenue and Lynch Street for $75,000, a sum appreciably more than they had paid just for the lots ten years earlier. Ironically, the purchaser was a restaurant owner widely known as a rabid segregationist. In a stroke of poetic justice, the location did not prove profitable for the Hayloft, the restaurant he erected there, but the $75,000 bought the congregation a house in the area they were seeking to reach and underwrote three years of ministerial services.

Meridian

During the 1950s and 1960s, there were, in addition to the Jackson congregation, three small churches with Universalist origins (two near Ellisville and one near Louisville), and a varying number of Unitarian fellowships on the Gulf Coast, in Hattiesburg, and in Meridian. Of the Meridian Fellowship, Roy Bouchillon, a birthright Universalist, reports,

In the late 1950s and 1960s we were a very small UU Fellowship in Meridian. We never had more than 12 members at any one time and they would come and go. We did not take a public stand in the Civil Rights Movement era collectively.

My wife, Emily, was director of Lauderdale Co. Public Welfare Dept. at the time. She was the first to take down "Colored" signs in the office and conferred with many civil rights workers who came into the state. She worked behind the scenes to see that everyone got a fair deal as far as regulations permitted. She feels that she did far more good in that capacity.

In early 1969, I was called as Jackson's second minister. In August 1969, my wife, Judy, our one-year-old daughter, and I moved to Jackson. Shortly after we arrived, the US Supreme Court ordered that the Jackson schools move from minimal to full integration, effective January 1970. This order spurred renewed citizen work in support of integrated public schools, and I served as the White co-chair of the biracial Community Coalition for Public Schools, funded by a federal grant. I was also active in the Jackson Area Council on Human Relations, the Jackson Clergy Alliance, and the Greater Jackson Area Committee, an organization of Whites who had worked in the civil rights movement. I served for three years as full-time minister, then resigned from that position but stayed in Jackson to work for the federal Equal Employment Opportunity Commission for seven years. I returned to serving the congregation part-time, 1978–84.

Sources

The Jackson congregation has a fairly complete file of newsletters from the Thompson years, and it was an invaluable source. The files of the UUA and the ministerial file on Thompson, at the Andover-Harvard Theological Library, were also important resources. The files of the late and lamentable Sovereignty Commission were less informative than one might have expected, reflecting either incompetence on the part of that commission (which is believable) or a cleansing of the files as it reached the end of its life (which is also believable). Peter Raible's report on his visit to Jackson came from the files of University Unitarian Church in Seattle; Mark Morrison-Reed kindly made it available when he encountered it in his own research.

Interviews with Johnny Frazier on March 16, 2000, and retired Episcopal bishop Duncan Gray Jr. on March 1, 2000, also were of use.

I tried not to rely overmuch on my fifteen years of direct experience with this congregation (briefly in 1965 and then August 1969 to December 31, 1984), but my memory provided some information for this chapter.

Published resources include the September 14, 1962, issue of *Life* magazine; *Men Like That: Southern Queer History* by John Howard (Chicago: University of Chicago Press, 2001); and *We Are Not Afraid: The Story of Goodman, Schwerner, and Chaney and the Civil Rights Campaign for Mississippi* by Seth Cagin and Philip Dray (New York: MacMillan Publishing Company, 1988). Gary Younge's article "Racism Rebooted: Philadelphia, Mississippi, Then and Now" from the July 11, 2005, issue of the *Nation*, was helpful. Robert M. Bowman's article "'Big Fella' Freedom Fighter (Donald A. Thompson)," from the fall 1965 issue (Vol. V, No. 3) of the *Journal of the Liberal Ministry* also helped. Howard Zinn's characterization of Bill Higgs appears in his *SNCC: The New Abolitionists* (Boston: Beacon Press, 1965). An August 8, 1982, letter from Roy Bouchillon provided the Meridian Fellowship information.

NEW ORLEANS, LOUISIANA

Throughout its long history, New Orleans has been a place where varying cultural currents meet, sometimes mingling and sometimes colliding. Liberal religious institutions and individuals in New Orleans have participated in both the mingling and the colliding.

The American Civil Liberties Union of Louisiana Foundation in 1988 awarded Albert D'Orlando the Benjamin Smith Civil Liberties Award. The program for that event included a description of Ben Smith:

In the early, often violent, days of the civil rights movement, Benjamin Smith, a white, Southern gentleman-lawyer, was deeply embroiled in the movement's court battles in New Orleans. Beginning with the early 1950s, Smith devoted himself to representing those whom no one else would represent. His clients were individuals and groups despised for their beliefs and scorned for the causes they espoused. Smith was motivated by a strong belief in justice, in spite of great personal and economic hardships.

The program also describes Albert D'Orlando:

The Rev. Albert D'Orlando, minister emeritus of the First Unitarian Universalist Church of New Orleans, arrived in the city in 1950. It was not long afterwards that George Dreyfous asked him to participate in the Louisiana ACLU. The chapter fell dormant in the period following George Dreyfous's death, and it was Leonard Dreyfus, Benjamin Smith, and Albert D'Orlando who reactivated and revitalized it. It was through D'Orlando's efforts that the New Orleans Unitarian church integrated all of its social activities, and he spoke from the pulpit on civil rights. As a result, some of his congregation became alienated. He organized and administered a bail/defense fund for local civil rights activists, with contributions from Unitarian and Universalist churches all over North America. This was done at a time when controversy within his congregation threatened his own livelihood. It was also during this turbulent time the Rev. D'Orlando's residence was fire-bombed and his church was dynamited, for which 3 members of the Ku Klux Klan were convicted.

Albert D'Orlando was minister and Ben Smith a member of First Unitarian Church of New Orleans. What a contrast they offer to the antebellum beginnings of that congregation.

Theodore Clapp, born in Massachusetts, educated at Yale and Andover, was called in 1822 to fill the pulpit of the First Presbyterian Church in New Orleans. In July 1834, he announced to that congregation that he could no longer avow or defend some key Presbyterian doctrines, including original sin, vicarious atonement, and endless punishment. He had embraced both universalist and unitarian theological positions. Ultimately, of course, he was charged with heresy and removed from the Presbyterian ministry, but a majority of the congregation voted to stick with their preacher and also leave Presbyterianism. By 1837, Clapp's congregation was listed by the AUA as friendly to Unitarians. When Clapp retired, the church was known as The Church of the Messiah. Its name has changed over the years and is now The First Unitarian Universalist Church of New Orleans.

Parson Clapp, as he was generally known, was one of the notable religious figures of New Orleans until his resignation for health reasons in 1856. Visitors to the city made a point of hearing him preach. During yellow fever epidemics, his pastoral presence extended far beyond his church's membership. And he became an apologist for the South and for slavery as it operated there.

The remainder of the nineteenth and the first half of the twentieth centuries saw a succession of ministers, none for very long. These included Henry Wilder Foote and Thaddeus Clark, two twentieth-century ministers who became well-known and widely respected after moving elsewhere.

Thaddeus Clark was installed in New Orleans in 1940. He came with both a Harvard Divinity School STB and a Harvard University PhD in philosophy, but he took a down-to-earth, innovative approach to the ministry in New Orleans. Clark started a radio program and initiated other outreach to revitalize a church that had been able to call him only thanks to an AUA grant of $1,000, which covered about a third of his first year's salary. During World War II, he was active in organizations offering assistance to service members and people displaced by the war. The United Service Organizations, known as the USO, sponsored social evenings for servicemen at the Unitarian Church, and Clark insisted that, contrary to local custom, these events be made open to both Black and White soldiers. In 1945, Clark was called to St. Louis, where he spent the rest of his career.

During Clark's ministry, Alfred Hobart joined the congregation. Hobart, born in Canada, had earned degrees from the University of Chicago and Meadville Lombard Theological School before serving as a Unitarian minister in St. Cloud, Minnesota, 1928–29. The combination of the Great Depression and a divorce ended that ministry, and he moved into social work in Kentucky, Alabama (where he married again), Louisiana, and Washington, DC. With the end of World War II, Hobart returned to New Orleans as director of the Veterans Information Center. When Clark moved, the ease of calling and installing one of their own members appealed to the congregation, so they offered Alfred Hobart re-entry to his ministry. In a 1959 letter to Leon Fay, Hobart writes, "You speak of my joy in the ministry. I am one of the perhaps fortunate ones who have had experience outside the ministry. It represented my first choice followed by a period of finding myself and then a considered decision to return. I have never had a moment's regret."

Ben Smith and the Testimony of Margy Hamilton

Attorney Ben Smith was an active member of the First Unitarian Church. He was one of the few White attorneys in the Deep South who took on civil rights cases, and was active throughout his career with the National Lawyers Guild, which recognized his achievements with its Franklin D. Roosevelt Award.

Smith's office had both Black and White clients. When the work became more than one secretary could handle, Smith wanted to hire a Black secretary. J. Harvey Kerns, head of the New Orleans Urban League, encouraged Margy Hamilton to apply. She interviewed and was hired. Hamilton started working for Ben Smith in 1962 and says that she was the first Black secretary in the central business district of New Orleans.

However, on the day she was supposed to begin, Smith's associate, Bruce Waltzer, called and told her not to come in. She waited a couple of days and heard nothing more. She had already been given a key to the office and decided that if they weren't hiring her, she wouldn't keep the key. She went to the office, found Smith not in, and left the key with the secretary. Then she got a call from Ben, who apologized for putting her off. He said he was trying to find another secretary. His secretary of five years' standing had announced that she would not work with Margy. Given that Margy had no experience as a legal secretary, he was looking for someone with experience to work along with her. Then he decided "the heck with it," told Margy to come in, and the White experienced legal secretary left. Margy says she "went in green as grass."

The management of the building tried to block her use of the women's restroom. They suggested that she could use a restroom in the public library across the street, or the one in the basement used by the building engineer. Smith told them he wasn't renting space in the basement or from the public library and that she would use the same restroom as other women working in the building.

The law firm had applied for some additional space, expanding his office into some recently vacated adjacent space. After Hamilton was hired, Smith received a letter saying that if he retained her, he would be denied additional space and his lease would not be renewed. He was turned down every place he looked in the central business district, including places that always advertised space available. Finally, he went to the Baronne Building at 305 Baronne Street and arranged for space on the tenth floor. Smith negotiated the square footage and the rent and then said, "I want you to know that I have a Black secretary." (In the interview, Margy commented, "Maybe we weren't Black then. I think we were still Negro.") The owner said, "I don't care what the secretary is. The rent is ____."

The office was raided in 1963. At the time of the raid, Smith and Hamilton were at an integrated meeting of lawyers he had arranged at the Hilton Hotel near the airport. It may have been the first such meeting since Reconstruction. Someone came in and whispered to Maurice Friedman, a practicing attorney who also worked as a police officer. Friedman whispered to the next person, and so on. When the whispered message reached Smith and his associate Bruce Waltzer they got up and left the meeting. When they didn't return in a few minutes, Margy Hamilton and law clerk Ardell Sherman went outside to see what was going on. They found Smith and Waltzer being frisked, handcuffed, and put in police cars. They later learned that Jim Dombrowski of the Southern Conference Education Fund (SCEF) had been arrested at the same time. Police raided and essentially ransacked both the SCEF office and the law office, removing many files that they retained for a considerable period of time. Those arrested were charged with being subversives. Hamilton noted that Smith's good relationship with Martin Luther King Jr. "proved" to Louisiana segregationists such as Leander Perez that Smith was a Communist. The state legislature's Un-American Activities Committee was behind the raid.

Thinking back on the raid, Hamilton mentioned evidence of both careful planning and considerable incompetence. The raiders left behind a file that had detailed drawings of the law office, including diagrams of who sat where. When the raiders went to Dombrowski's office, they walked past his door, open because of a problem with the air conditioning, and broke down the door of an adjacent unrelated office.

When Smith hired Hamilton, he was already litigating civil rights cases. Sometimes Smith phoned her in the middle of the night and told her to meet him at the airport because he had been called by SNCC or the Council of Federated Organizations about massive arrests and the need for legal representation. He spent as much time in Mississippi as in Louisiana. It became dangerous for him and dangerous to be with him. If he drove to Mississippi, segregationists knew him and his car. If he flew, they somehow knew that too. Once, when he tried to interview clients in jail, a deputy told him that he had no clients there and that he would be locked up if he didn't leave. Smith's life insurance was cancelled, and he couldn't get another policy. After his arrest, many "friends" around town avoided him. "He never let any of it stop him," commented Hamilton.

Nobody in the office called Ben Smith "Mr. Smith." They called him Ben. Hamilton recalls that if she called him Mr. Smith, he would say, "Oh, hell, what have I done now?"

As a result of doing so much pro bono work, Smith operated for a while on the verge of bankruptcy. There just wasn't much time to devote to paying cases.

Eventually, as a result of the stress, Smith began to drink heavily. The Smith and Waltzer firm broke up, and Smith sold his practice to his law clerk Ardell Sherman. Smith moved to Philadelphia, Pennsylvania, for a while. After a year or two, he came back to New Orleans and practiced law from his home. He died in 1976, according to Margy Hamilton.

Hobart continued many of the programs and emphases that Clark had begun, including forums and discussions on race. Hobart chaired the local Committee on Race Relations and served on the boards of the Children's Bureau, the Society for Prevention of Cruelty to Animals, and the Urban League. His son, Rev. James Hobart, recalls that one day, his father and a Black male professional left an Urban League meeting and took the same street car; the operator told them that they could not sit together, so they stood side by side at the racial dividing line in the car, continuing their conversation.

Work in religious education and conscious outreach to the broader community continued a slow but clear growth trend. From 93 members and 11 children in church school in 1939, just before Clark's arrival, the congregation had grown through the Hobart years to 181 members and 65 children in religious education. One of the new members was J. P. Bennett, a Black educator whose family had long belonged to the First Unitarian Church in Providence, Rhode Island. Hobart resigned in 1949 to go to Charleston, South Carolina, to serve the only southern Unitarian congregation older than the one in New Orleans.

Albert D'Orlando came to the New Orleans congregation from New England in 1950, fully aware that race would be an issue, but not realizing how much, how soon, and for how long. Later, in retirement, he opined that "a minister does not always choose the issues that will define his or her ministry; often he or she is pushed right into them."

J. P. Bennett, the first Black member of the church, was quite content to have a quiet seat to himself toward the back of the sanctuary and to leave once the service was over. Shortly after D'Orlando was called, two additional Black Unitarians moved to town. J. Westbrook McPherson came to New Orleans to be executive director of the Urban League, and Vernetta Hill was director of the Negro Branch YWCA. When a post-service coffee hour was introduced as a new element of Sunday programming, Hill and McPherson attended with the others. On the second Sunday of having coffee hour, members found the kitchen cabinets padlocked. The cups and saucers were the property of the Women's Alliance and were not to be available for racially mixed use. (Disposable cups saved the immediate occasion.) Then the church treasurer embarked on a personal campaign to get members to reduce their pledges in order to force D'Orlando out; fortunately for the church, his campaign actually stimulated a net increase in pledges. There was to be a Thanksgiving dinner so that church members far from their families would have a group with whom to share the holiday; the church president at the time unilaterally canceled it when he heard that Black members would be among those attending.

As these events unfolded in New Orleans, the AUA was being forced to deal with racism at the national level. They asked D'Orlando to be one of the members of the Unitarian Commission on Inter-Group Relations. Regarding the commission's work, D'Orlando said, "What we learned on the denominational level was that although our churches were not willing to have a black minister . . . many of them did have black members whose contributions on every level had added a broader dimension to denominational life." A parallel committee in New Orleans, working on the congregational level, reported that "in the time it had been studying the matter the congregation had, indeed, become fully integrated."

This degree of apparent resolution was necessary because, by the mid-1950s, issues around race were clearly coming to the forefront. In anticipation of more race-related issues arising locally and regionally, the congregation held a meeting to decide whether it could act collectively or whether the minister and individual members would each act individually. With one dissenting vote, the congregation decided to act with a single voice. D'Orlando writes of that dissenting voter, "[H]e was the person who recruited David Duke into the Ku Klux Klan, and was Duke's mentor all the time they were in the Klan together."

Issues that were racial were sometimes cloaked in political disguise. The New Orleans *Times-Picayune* 1998 obituary of D'Orlando notes, "In 1958, he was ordered to testify before the House Un-American Activities Committee after being identified as a member of the Communist Party by a New Hampshire homemaker. After the closed hearing, the Rev. D'Orlando said he had never been a member of the party."

Twice, small groups spun off from First Unitarian Church. What was originally called the Unitarian Fellowship of New Orleans was recognized by the AUA in early 1959 with fifty-two members. In due course, it became Community Church of New Orleans. The West Bank Fellowship formed in the mid-to-late 1960s. The two groups merged under the Community Church name in early 1969.

Multiple factors led to the splits and spinoffs. Some correspondence mentions a desire on the part of those departing First Unitarian to start a new congregation with a less humanistic and more traditional theology and atmosphere. One document related to the West Bank Fellowship mentions discomfort with expressing opposition to the war in Vietnam, an issue that affected many congregations. A June 1958 letter from Southern Regional Director Clif Hoffman to Fellowship Director Munroe Husbands in Boston observes,

> For four or five years there has been a group in the church which has used Al D'Orlando as a scapegoat for their discomfort in relation to the changing philosophical emphasis,

the increasing stand of the church in favor of integration, the numbers of new people who were being attracted by a more vitally liberal program in church and church school. Many of them had felt similarly toward Al Hobart.

In 1960, a federal court order began school desegregation. The New Orleans and Baton Rouge congregations placed newspaper ads advocating keeping the schools open (in opposition to legislative efforts to close the schools rather than desegregate). When the schools did minimally desegregate, members of the New Orleans church helped with driving White students to school in the face of hostile mobs. And the church appealed to Unitarians far and wide to help set up a special fund to aid integration efforts.

These special funds, sometimes doled out in small amounts, helped a variety of people. One White Methodist minister and his wife who kept their daughter in school were driven out of their parsonage for doing so, and Unitarian money helped with several months' rent for alternative housing. Other White families sticking with the public schools were also aided. The church disbursed $115.75 to house Freedom Riders before they boarded buses or trains north through Mississippi. Attorney Bill Higgs of the Jackson, Mississippi, congregation received aid when he was forced to leave that state. Some of the legal expenses while desegregating Tulane University were covered. The fund also paid for some of attorney Ben Smith's legal expenses while taking on Mississippi civil rights cases.

On November 25, 1960, Rev. Robert West of Tennessee Valley Unitarian Church in Knoxville wrote to Albert D'Orlando to inquire about Lanny Goldfinch, who was a graduate student in philosophy at Tulane: "Lanny is the son of a Baptist missionary who attended Carson-Newman College and joined our church while a student there. He commuted quite frequently the considerable distance from his school in order to attend our morning services and was an enthusiastic member of our group while he lived in this area." In New Orleans, Goldfinch had participated in a sit-in and had been charged with criminal anarchy (later reduced to criminal mischief). The church's special fund helped during the successful appeal of this case all the way to the US Supreme Court, and Goldfinch did not have to serve the ten-year sentence the trial court had imposed.

Not all of the considerable attention that D'Orlando received for his and his church's work was welcome. Speaking to the Unitarian Universalist Ministers Association in 1970, he admitted,

> Living with threats could fill hours of stories of unheroic fear and disillusionment, but also some of macabre humor. Such as the phone call that came at three in the morning, after a long series of such calls, warning, "If you don't get out in three minutes, your home will be blown up." You never know whether this is it. Well, this time my terrified wife woke up to search my face for the meaning of the call. I covered the phone to tell her, in a reassuring voice, "It's all right dear, you can go back to sleep; it's only a suicide." She did put her head down for a few seconds before bolting upright again: "Only a suicide!"

More ominous were the events on the night of Saturday, March 13, 1965. D'Orlando was preparing a sermon memorializing his colleague James Reeb, who had just died of injuries inflicted in Selma, when a firebomb exploded outside his parsonage. He extinguished the fire with a garden hose before it could ignite a 250-gallon oil tank under his study. Then, on May 11, 1965, the New Orleans church was bombed and damaged. The 1968 conviction of three Klan members in the parsonage bombing was a first in such matters in Louisiana.

The UUA awarded Albert D'Orlando its annual Holmes-Weatherly Award in 1966, recognizing "life-long commitment to faith-based social justice."

In 1996, well into his retirement, D'Orlando indicated that his ministry in New Orleans had been its own reward. Asking himself (as others had asked him) if he would do it all over again, he responded, "Yes, of course I would, for I cannot imagine another calling through which I could have given emphasis to human worth and dignity and which, in doing so, would have opened the way for me to give meaning to my own life."

Sources

Especially useful in looking at New Orleans developments were the excellent files that Albert D'Orlando maintained; his widow, Dr. Catherine Cohen, was extremely gracious and helpful in making them available. As always, the files of the UUA and the material on file at the Andover-Harvard Theological Library on deceased Unitarian Universalist ministers were consulted. A church history by Meg Dachowski provided some of the material on the Thaddeus Clark and Alfred Hobart years. James Hobart, Alfred Hobart's son, took time in 2000 to write illuminating emails about his father's career. Parson Clapp wrote an engaging memoir, *Autobiographical Sketches and Recollections, During a Thirty-five Years' Residence in New Orleans* (Boston: Phillips, Sampson & Company, 1857). *Standing Against Dragons: Three Southern Lawyers in an Era of Fear* by Sarah Hart Brown (Baton Rouge: Louisiana State University Press, 1998) provided valuable data on Ben Smith and his courageous practice of law. An interview with Margy Hamilton was held on February 24, 2000, in her home.

BATON ROUGE, LOUISIANA

Baton Rouge, the home of state government in Louisiana, has also been home to a Unitarian (and then Unitarian Universalist) congregation since 1951. What might be called "the usual ingredients" were present at its creation: a hotel function room, Munroe Husbands from the Fellowship office in Boston, and a group of interested individuals who numbered in the teens. An extra ingredient in this instance was Albert D'Orlando, minister of the First Unitarian Church of New Orleans, who provided guidance, encouragement, and occasional ministerial services over eighteen years before the first settled minister was called to serve in Baton Rouge.

The nomadic phase of the congregation's existence included a variety of interesting meeting places. A room in the basement of the Old State Capitol worked until veterans of the Spanish American War objected to sharing "their" space with "subversives." The YWCA rented space to the congregation until 1955, when it said it needed the space for its own programs—but church members thought that their Sunday program on the murder of Emmett Till, which drew a visit by nine or ten "Southern gentlemen" wearing dark suits and dark hats in the style of mobsters, was a more likely reason for the invitation to leave the space. The shop area of the Baton Rouge Trade School worked for a while; a member of the congregation taught there. Eventually, the congregation purchased a house and lot on Government Street that had been used as a United Methodist parsonage. Fortuitously, this property turned out to be in the path of Baton Rouge's first interstate highway.

Rebecca Cureau

Rebecca Cureau became a member of the congregation after moving to Baton Rouge from New Orleans. She had been raised Methodist and married a Catholic but had discovered Unitarianism in New Orleans in the 1950s. The Unitarian Church of Baton Rouge became her spiritual home during the years she taught at historically Black Southern University as well as after her retirement.

She grew up in New Orleans but enrolled in Bennett College, a historically Black college in Greensboro, North Carolina, a generation before the sit-ins in that community. She and many other women in the Bennett student body were discouraged from endangering themselves but did push boundaries when they went into Greensboro stores. They tried on hats, drank from the water fountains labeled "White," used the "wrong" dressing rooms, and requested service at Woolworths. Cureau spent her junior year as an exchange student at predominantly White Heidelberg College in Tiffin, Ohio. The president of the Greensboro Branch of the NAACP asked if on her way to Tiffin, she would test the practice of segregation in interstate commerce, which had already—on paper—been ruled illegal. Consequently, everyone gave her a big send-off at the Greensboro railroad station, and she was put on a coach designated for White passengers. This small woman—at the time 110 pounds and not quite five feet tall— was visited by multiple White conductors, and solicitously cared for by a Black porter. The conductors told her she must move, and they moved her luggage, piece by piece, to the coach for Black passengers. Finally, the porter pleaded with her to move before they stopped the train and put her off. She could feel the train slowing down, so moved to the coach for the sake of the Black passengers; the reception there upset her, because many apparently regarded her as a troublemaker. There were three other Black students at Heidelberg that year, and one Black family living in Tiffin, although protests had postponed their moving in.

A few years later, riding north from Cincinnati, Cureau again tested segregated seating on a passenger train and had a "good dialogue" with a conductor who seemed to be trying to fathom her intent. She also remembered that, while she and other Black students were riding from New Orleans to North Carolina, they would sometimes all go to the dining car at the same time in a concerted effort to overwhelm the number of curtained-off tables allocated for serving Black passengers.

Later, after she was back in New Orleans at Dillard University, she declined to use the small, ill-lit fitting room that the Gus Mayer store had set aside for Black women. She handed six dresses back to the clerk and announced that she would tell all the women at Dillard not to shop there. As president of the Women's Club on campus, she did just that.

Cureau first encountered a Unitarian church while she was in Chicago working toward a master's degree at Northwestern University. She was staying with her brother in the Hyde Park neighborhood, and a friend of his attended First Unitarian Church of Chicago and arranged for her to practice on the organ there.

In the late 1950s, she was invited to become the organist at First Unitarian Church of New Orleans. She recalled that, shortly after she began her duties, Albert D'Orlando used a reading from Martin Luther King Jr. She appreciated hearing King's words in a service, used because they were appropriate to the topic at hand. Becky and her husband became friends with Albert and Pauly D'Orlando; Mrs. D'Orlando and Mr. Cureau were both artists.

The Cureau family's experience moving from New Orleans to Baton Rouge included encountering physicians' offices with segregated waiting rooms well into the 1960s. Once Becky took their very young son to a new doctor, entering through the front door and taking a seat in that waiting room; they were soon taken past the "colored" waiting room and left to wait a long time in an examining room.

The Unitarian Church of Baton Rouge was important to her, not for taking overt public stands on issues, but for providing a place with positive experiences to offset or contrast with still-segregated waiting rooms and other demeaning experiences.

Becky Cureau sought to find ways to be involved and connected with efforts to change society, but she never chose to march. She felt anger about segregation and discrimination but avoided angered approaches. She also drew on positive experiences with White colleagues, such as a faculty member at Dillard; when they rode the bus together to the music store, they would both stand in the aisle, side by side, one in the White section and one in the Black, and continue their conversation, much to the annoyance of the drivers.

Describing herself as "a proud Black woman," Cureau didn't want to be recognized first by her race. She preferred to be seen as herself, with race as one aspect of that self.

Over the years she had connections with Bernice Johnson Reagon, Vernon Johns and Altona Trent Johns, Martin Luther King Jr., and Coretta Scott King. Cureau and Reagon shared research interests in the role of music, especially music from the Black church, in inspiring and powering civil rights work. Vernon Johns, pastor of the Dexter Avenue Baptist Church in Montgomery immediately preceding King, was notable for what Cureau described as "fearless, agitational, and iconoclastic behavior." She met Johns during her student days and heard him speak both then and later. After his death in 1964, his widow, Altona Trent Johns, moved to Baton Rouge and became a friend. Becky met King when he came to Dillard University to speak at the chapel. As the speaker, he sat right next to Becky, who was the organist. King spoke to her about her playing as he was being introduced. Many years later, Cureau did some work at the King Center, and met and worked with Coretta Scott King and Yolanda King.

When the government took the land for that purpose, it provided the congregation with a nice nest egg for the purchase of a more suitable lot, which is still in use today. The initial building on that lot was dedicated in 1965.

A draft of a church history notes that, for the building fund, the congregation wrote to every Unitarian Universalist church

asking for $10 and promising to return the favor, if needed. Not all the responses were profitable—a New York church wrote such a nasty letter that our Board of Trustees voted to send *them* $10.00. An Ohio church wrote saying, "We've never heard of you. Are you integrated?" Baton Rouge answered, "Yes, are you?" To date, there has been no answer from Ohio.

Arthur Olsen, made available through the UUA's minister-at-large program, served the congregation during 1969, building its membership and its financial capacity. Edgar T. Van Buren, known to all as Toby, was called in November 1969.

Several people whose membership in the congregation dates back to the early years describe a pattern of less concerted congregational action and more encouraging and supporting members in addressing social justice issues, including those of race.

With the threat of local public schools closing rather than desegregating in September 1961, members of the congregation were among those who demonstrated and organized to keep schools open. They also pondered a contingency plan of using the congregation's building as the site for a parent-run school, should that become necessary. Fortunately, the situation never got bad enough to put the plan into action.

Larry Hamby, then minister of the Community Church (Unitarian Universalist) in New Orleans, in a December 1962 report to the UUA, writes,

> These people have been very courageous in meeting community hostility about the integration issue, and at present look on it with some amusement. They have had their rough moments in the past, with members of the local Citizen's Council coming to heckle their meetings, etc. . . . Practically every person in this group is doing something; this speaks well of the leadership they have had in the past and are getting at present. Morale and spirits are high. One gets the feeling that this fellowship is very significant in these peoples [sic] lives. It is healthy, moving and meaningful!

Longtime members Mel Dakin and Roger Manghan recall collaborating with an effort funded by Quakers to support and aid the half dozen or so Black students integrating the high schools. Members of the fellowship hosted some meetings called Institutes of Religion "to give the kids a chance to see a White face that wasn't snarling at them." The sessions drew the attention of the district attorney, who sent his staff to record license plate numbers and once sent a photographer to take pictures of a session. Dakin and Manghan were not aware of any other White church in that area open to Black attendance and membership.

Dr. Page Acree, a member since moving to Baton Rouge from New Orleans in 1957, said that with only about thirty pledging units, the congregation then was loathe to take on major issues, but that individually people could and did act. "We had a group to come back to and nurse our wounds. We had a place to come back to and talk to each other," he said. The petitions he signed would often list his name first alphabetically when they were published. If the presence of his name offended anyone, to the extent that they did not want his services, they were out of luck—he was the only heart surgeon in town. His wife was more likely to receive negative phone calls or to be the subject of remarks at a PTA meeting. Their three children also played roles as the high schools desegregated, and their daughter helped integrate a high school dance.

Sources

UUA files and the local church files offered some material. Interviews with Margie Belk, Mel Dakin, and Roger Manghan on February 17, 2000, and with Page Acree and Rebecca Cureau on February 18, 2000, were invaluable in filling out the story of the Baton Rouge congregation. The draft of a Baton Rouge church history was found in the ministerial files of Albert D'Orlando.

LITTLE ROCK, ARKANSAS

Representing liberal religion in Arkansas fell strictly to Universalism in the nineteenth and early twentieth centuries. The *Universalist Register* for 1893 notes of Arkansas, "Rev. S. M. Simons, residing at Ramsey, itinerates over a large territory." Starting in at least 1914, the small Universalist congregation in Little Rock had a running dialogue via correspondence with the Universalist General Convention about trading or selling its less-than-adequate building. They sold the building and dissolved the congregation in 1920.

And yet, energy persisted even in the midst of what sounds like a slow downward spiral. Henry Clay Ledyard served the Universalists of Little Rock in 1914 and 1915. He had been born in Michigan, called to the ministry by Congregationalists in Louisiana, and educated for the ministry by Universalists at St. Lawrence University, from which he graduated in 1912. Of Ledyard's Little Rock ministry, Rev. James D. Hunt writes,

The church was ridiculously small: 15 resident members and a parish list of 30 names, yet he gave himself to his work with vigor and in the first year added 33 new members and increased the parish list to 64. In March, the Mayor sent him to represent Little Rock at a child labor convention in New Orleans, and in November the Universalists began Sunday evening services in a downtown theater, where his vigorous and dramatic preaching could be displayed to advantage to a wider audience. In December he began a campaign against capital punishment in Arkansas, collecting over 5,000 signatures on a petition, and the names of over 100 leading Little Rock citizens on his letterhead. His sermons in Little Rock were characterized by a sense of urgency. They are a succession of forceful appeals to be active, to be of service, to see religion as a program of work. The church must do useful work to justify itself. They are energetic, eager, full of a sense of crisis.

But in October 1915, Ledyard announced that he was resigning due to "ill health" and would take some time off before taking on the work of the Universalist congregation in Cortland, New York. In reality, his time off barely gave him enough time to get him to Cortland.

In 1930, John Petrie, minister of the Memphis congregation, apparently explored prospects for Unitarianism in Arkansas. He found in Little Rock that Hay Watson Smith, the pastor of Second Presbyterian Church, was so liberal that he was being investigated for heresy. Smith welcomed Unitarians as members of his congregation. Mr. L. W. Lowry, who held a lay license from the Universalists, thought that a middle-class liberal church in the city was out of the question, but that there were prospects among the organized workers of Little Rock, most of whom were unchurched. Newspaper announcements of a meeting with Petrie to talk about Unitarianism and Universalism brought out three people who had been members of the now-defunct Universalist church. Petrie notes that three names furnished to him, apparently from records in Boston, represented "very old people at the Confederate veterans' home and a dead man." In Conway, Arkansas, Petrie found two faculty members at the State Teachers College who identified as Unitarian; Dr. McBrien headed the History Department and Mr. Cordrey chaired Physical Sciences and taught "evolution openly in defiance of the Arkansas law."

Finally in 1950, Felix Arnold took the lead in starting a fellowship in Little Rock. He had experience with a fellowship start-up in Albuquerque. E. E. Cordrey, professor emeritus at Arkansas State

Teachers College, spoke at the first public meeting, which drew forty-two adults. By December 15, 1950, Felix Arnold could report that the "Jewish congregation has befriended us by giving us a meeting place; the president of the Little Rock Ministerial Alliance has set an encouraging precedent by serving us, on November 19, as guest preacher; the *Arkansas Gazette* has given us a good press, publishing a feature article concerning our president, Dr. E. E. Cordrey, as well as news from time to time about our speakers and meetings."

The fellowship under the leadership of Arnold quickly staked out a social and ethical position by having "a Negro minister as guest speaker" on February 18, 1951, Brotherhood Sunday. The congregation held a fairly tense meeting early in February to discuss Arnold's inviting the minister without consulting anyone else, but they voted ten to zero, with three abstentions, to affirm the invitation.

Even before then, an interracial connection had come their way. In a December 5, 1950, letter to Munroe Husbands, Arnold writes,

The attached ad [no longer attached to the letter in UUA files] was printed gratuitously in *The Arkansas World*, leading Negro newspaper in Arkansas. It came about this wise. In a traffic jam one day, I was inching along going over the Arkansas River Bridge just behind a Negro driving a fine Lincoln automobile. He unintentionally backed into me and broke off my fender guard. I set my brake, got out, picked up the broken part, saying no word to him. He then told me to follow him and he would repair the damage. Doing so, I wound up in a 9th Street Negro garage, having my car fixed at the colored man's expense. We got into a conversation, and I learned that I was making the acquaintance of the editor and publisher of two Negro newspapers, one published here and one in Memphis. So I told him about the Unitarian group and invited him to come and talk at one of our meetings, later sent him pamphlets and all the dope. This ad is his reply, so far.

Arnold's October 2, 1951, letter to Husbands reports his continuing efforts on racial issues:

> George [sic] and Wilma Iggers and I, with John Lofton from the editorial staff of *The Arkansas Gazette*, with four Negro members of the faculty of Philander Smith College, have started an informal inter-racial discussion group. We're going to meet every week, at least bi-weekly, to talk books and just shoot the breeze. Have had two meetings already.
>
> The second meeting was to be at my "house" but as my landlady refused her consent for Negro Ph.D's and their wives to come here, we've met both times at the Iggers. They're white, Jewish members of Philander Smith's faculty. And I'm looking for another rooming place.

In the letter, Arnold also reports that the fellowship was thinking of moving its meetings to the Sam Peck Hotel, although he worried that they might not be open to interracial meetings. Worried about the move from the Jewish Temple, known to be open to all people, he pushed for a clear statement by the fellowship of racial inclusion but found some resistance to a clear, binding statement.

In February 1953, a Little Rock Unitarian Fellowship for Social Justice (UFSJ) formed, with Georg Iggers, now a member of the Little Rock Unitarian Fellowship, as president. Accounts differ as to whether it formed with the blessing of the Little Rock Fellowship or independently of it, and whether or not it was to be the social action committee of the fellowship. In July, newly elected fellowship president Joe Bill Hocott wrote to Munroe Husbands in the Fellowship Office in Boston asking for assistance and clarity. Husbands replied,

> When, O when will we get a stable Unitarian group in Little Rock? With each change of officers I hope that the problems and misunderstandings between various members have been ironed out and from that time on there will be

smooth sailing. Unfortunately this has not been the case. To date there have been four or five different sets of officers, representing what I am afraid are different factions within the Fellowship. Although Unitarianism could, I believe, be a strong and growing concern in Little Rock, it seems to have preferred to expend its energy in jockeying for the leadership position. . . . We have organized at least 125 groups, and I think without exception none has gone through the turmoil Little Rock has.

In November 1953, Philip Schug, newly appointed Assistant Regional Director in Charge of Fellowships, visited Little Rock. The second paragraph of his written report reads,

The Fellowship at Little Rock has apparently gone through many struggles which have resulted in the breaking away of a substantial portion of the people who should now be in the Fellowship. I discovered a good bit of bewilderment and not a little rancor among those who met with me. The main problem as I see it is the problem of central purpose. The question that has to be solved in their thinking is the question of whether they want to be primarily a religious organization giving place to people of many opinions in the area of social conflict or whether they want to be a social action group. Apparently there are some within the Fellowship, including Felix Arnold who is looked up to by all that I met as the founder and most dynamic person within the Fellowship, who feel that no group such as this should exist without a definite social action purpose at all times. This has, in my estimation, been the chief reason for the splitting of the group. As I worked over the problem with the people who attended the first meeting and those who met individually with me in my hotel room, I came to the conclusion that only as this organization concentrated upon the religious purposes would they be able to maintain themselves. I suggested to them individually and collectively that the concentration upon a church school, upon matters of a Sunday morning service and upon the social programs that go with religious organizations should receive their attention. I expressed my opinion to the effect that inasmuch as they had been divided often on social action programs it would seem wise to simply drop that side of their work at the present.

Not insensitive to social issues or the need of a religious institution to be able to speak to them, Schug adds, "I also suggested that any social action programs that might be carried out in the future might better be carried out by small committees working under the general direction of the Executive Committee and with no attempt to involve the entire membership of the Fellowship."

At this juncture, some of those most deeply involved in the now-disbanded Little Rock Unitarian Fellowship for Social Justice, including Georg and Wilma Iggers and Felix Arnold, formed a nonsectarian Little Rock Film Society to continue the UFSJ project of showing movies of artistic and general cultural significance. Notice of the films was given in both White and Black communities, and attendance included people of both races.

During the summer of 1954, the Little Rock Fellowship arranged through the AUA Fellowship Office to have a student minister. Carl Whittier, then a student at Harvard Divinity School, gave the congregation a steady diet of "uniformly good" sermons, which afforded the group some cohesiveness and pulled people in from the periphery to greater involvement. His presence also provided a sense that having a settled minister would be empowering rather than disempowering and reassured a majority of members that they should move in that direction.

Subsequently, the fellowship hoped for the services of an AUA minister-at-large to spend a few months in Little Rock and move them solidly into a membership and financial situation to call a minister. One 1957 letter from fellowship member Neil Bratt to the president of the AUA opines,

From the viewpoint of Unitarians everywhere, indeed from
the viewpoint of our national welfare, strong Unitarian
churches in this part of the Country are socially very de-
sirable. Sane and level reasoning backed by the strength of
an organization is needed in solving the problems generally
associated with this part of our country. I am not thinking
only of the problem of integration although this does immediately and exemplarily come to mind.

Issues of segregation and integration indeed were present, and
although most of the people who had pushed hardest for the fellowship to act on those issues were former members, some action
was taken. In a June 1956 congregational meeting, the Social Service Committee proposed a statement on segregation. Ultimately,
only one paragraph of the full statement was adopted:

Unitarians are on record as desirous of facilitating the process to non-segregation in our American public schools
and the full recognition of the rights of all minority groups
in our democracy. Therefore the Little Rock Unitarian Fellowship wishes to state that as concerned citizens of Arkansas we accept the decree of the Supreme Court regarding
segregation in the public schools.

Of course, in September 1957, Little Rock and its Central High
School became a temporary ground zero in America's attempt to
end school segregation.

In early 1958, Charles Wing finally arrived at Little Rock to
serve as minister-at-large. He encountered intense religious con-
servatism in the area. Noting that a majority of fellowship members had come to Little Rock from elsewhere, he reports that "they
eventually discover that the only spot where they can feel reason-
ably comfortable is the Unitarian Fellowship." Wing encouraged
them to canvass for pledges so they could afford to call a minister,
and he set up a task group of a dozen to follow up on visitors. He
commented that he had never met a nicer group of people, but

that they were not aggressive in moving toward their goals. His concluding observation touches on the issue of integration: "In the Fellowship, I was unable to discover a single member who was opposed to what is now the law of the land. All of which means that there is no controversy whatever in the group over that issue."

In September 1958, after the US Supreme Court in *Cooper v. Aaron* had ordered that desegregation of the Little Rock high schools should proceed, Arkansas govenor Orval Faubus closed all four. In response, the Women's Emergency Committee to Open Our Schools formed "to inform the people of Little Rock and the state of the necessity of maintaining public schools and the economic consequences if the schools remain closed." In 2013, the interim minister at the Unitarian Universalist Church of Little Rock reported that the congregation remembers having more members of the Women's Emergency Committee than any other congregation in Little Rock except possibly the Jewish congregation.

In November 1958, journalist Ben Bagdikian wrote an article in the *Unitarian Register* about the fellowship in Little Rock, a city still a center of conflict over ending segregation. The article spotlights the fellowship's need for a minister and for a building of its own. From Yonkers, New York, Rev. J. Robert Smudski wrote to Richard Gibbs of the AUA Extension Department, suggesting a national drive among Unitarians, perhaps on Brotherhood Sunday in February, to raise a building fund. Gibbs responded,

> The thing I am always concerned about is that we don't put the people there on a spot. If our Unitarian group was singled out for national publicity, it is possible that they could be the target for all the crackpots in the community, including bombs tossed their way. The decision as to how much spotlighting they wanted should come from them. . . . We at "25" are taking the position that our Southern brethren must tell us what form and when assistance should be given. Otherwise, we might blunderingly make local situations worse.

The fellowship voted to call as minister Richard W. Kelley, who was then serving the Newburgh, New York, congregation, in March 1959. Within a few weeks of accepting the call, Kelley pointed out to Gibbs the possibility that in the legal battling between Governor Orval Faubus and the NAACP, all the public schools of Arkansas might be closed in the fall, with devastating results for the fellowship. He wrote, "Should such happen, you can probably expect to lose at least half the fellowship members, since they'll seek jobs elsewhere, rather than sacrifice their children's educations and futures."

The school situation did result in fallout for fellowship members, but it was more personal and less global. In a November 18, 1959, letter to Munroe Husbands, Kelley reports,

> Our current president, Neil Bratt, and his wife were both much too active in the STOP campaign which unseated the segregationist members of the school board, and in other activities aimed at furthering integration. In September, the insurance company of which Neil was vice-president and soon-to-be executive director, was purchased *in toto* by the Stephens Brothers, prominent backers of Governor Faubus. So now, Neil has been "frozen out" and has taken a job with a company in Fort Worth, to "start over again," as he puts it. To my knowledge, he has no regrets, for which I am very pleased. (I mention this, of course, because what he lost in terms of his professional career, he may never be able to replace; if things had been different, he'd have run the entire insurance company for the rest of his life.)

During 1960–61, the whole issue of a meeting place again became critical, then subsided, but remained troubling. In March 1960, Kelley preached about the sit-ins that were then happening across the South. He applauded the essentially "religious, Christian basis for the students' actions—which is pretty conservative for an old non-Christian." Local radio, TV, and newspapers picked up on his sermon. The following Friday, the rental agent for the American Legion post where they had been renting meeting space told them to vacate. After a couple of more days to think about it, the Legion apparently decided that the $65 monthly rent (which covered their mortgage costs) was too valuable to forgo. Still, the fellowship was meeting in a space that they had agreed to leave if they got "any Negro members, or if Negroes should even attend services." Kelley had been invited into the pulpit of the only Congregational church in the state, an all-Black congregation, but he realized that if he accepted that invitation, he could not invite his Black Congregational colleague into his pulpit. A commitment to build or buy space of their own came out of this conundrum, but that was more easily said than done. By November 1961, they had purchased a two-and-a-half acre building site. But Kelley noted in a letter to Boston, "So far, our American Legion land-lord has been quiet. But since one Negro lady has been attending regularly the last 3 or 4 Sundays, I expect the axe to fall at any time."

A self-survey of the Little Rock membership in early 1961, as it moved from fellowship to church status, suggests that it included a healthy share of "homegrown" people. Some 47 percent of the families were native to Arkansas, and another 7 percent hailed from elsewhere south of the Mason-Dixon line.

The Unitarian Universalist Church of Little Rock finally moved into its own building on its own land in January 1965. Dana McLean Greeley, president of the UUA, attended the building dedication.

Fred Campbell served as the second called minister in Little Rock, 1967–75.

Sources

The files of the UUA provided most of the material for this chapter. An article by James D. Hunt in the 1964–65 volume of the *Annual Journal of the Universalist Historical Society* provided supplementary material on Henry Clay Ledyard. The *Universalist Register: Giving Statistics of the Universalist Church and Other Denominational Information, Etc. for 1893* also provided some information. In 2013, Jennie Barrington emailed information describing congregational memories of the civil rights era.

A SUMMARY OF DISPARATE GIFTS

Before 1945, when World War II ended and much of American society began to change, Unitarianism was not an essential factor in the religious life of the South. The churches founded in Charleston, New Orleans, and Memphis in the eighteenth and nineteenth centuries were lonely outposts.

Universalism had a greater presence in the South, but most Universalist congregations of record in 1945 were located in rural areas or in small towns.

The fellowship movement changed the nature and extent of liberal religion in the South. That change coincided with seismic forces realigning southern folkways, mores, and laws. Unitarian Universalism had its own small impact on those changes in the larger society, and that process of change also challenged and changed Unitarian Universalism.

A 1944 summation of Unitarian principles enumerated:

1. Individual freedom of belief
2. Discipleship to advancing truth
3. The democratic process in human relations
4. Universal brotherhood, undivided by nation, race, or creed
5. Allegiance to the cause of a united world community

Whether in this or another formulation, or in one less articulate, such values collided with patterns long dictated by southern White culture, at least in its worst manifestations. Out of that collision, a remarkable and constructive southern Unitarian Universalist sensibility was born and flourished for a time. People practiced an individual freedom of belief in contradiction to a standard of social conformity. Advancing truth bumped headlong into "what we all know to have always been right." Democratic process in human relations lived unhappily in a society arranged to honor hierarchies of worth and respectability. Universal brotherhood was severely divided in the minds of some White southerners, with some brothers and sisters not even treated as members of the human family. And the world community of southern White culture was most definitely divided into "us" and a number of "thems."

As Alfred W. Hobart, himself a key actor in this drama on several different stages, wrote in 1966,

> Unitarians in the Southeast were probably earlier and more actively concerned with racial injustice than were their fellows in the rest of the country. General interest was generated following the Supreme Court decision of May 1954 but for at least a decade prior to that Unitarians in southern churches and fellowships were actively associated with committees, councils, and various associations whose concern was to break down segregation, bring about equal justice, and develop opportunities economically and socially for Negroes.

Clif Hoffman, district executive in the southeast in the early years of the UUA, looking back in 1982, writes,

> In large part, . . . we saw ourselves as part of a liberating tradition. This had been the framework within which our "great ones" had functioned, often at considerable sacrifice. It was the quality and the spirit to which those of us who had anything to say at all persistently pointed. What impresses me still so deeply is that the new societies emerging in our movement for the most part took this liberating tradition as theirs. They often represented UUism in their respective communities as part of such a tradition and sometimes suffered persecution for doing it.

Suddenly—more suddenly than we were prepared to handle the ramifications of broad social dynamics at work in the country—we were making tradition ourselves. It was no longer adequate as a response *and* a responsibility to laud the liberating tradition of the past in a museum-like atmosphere that paraded this very spirit.

In my opinion, the fellowship movement fostered this response. So did the tone of those seed churches founded under the aegis of Lon Ray Call. Then, when at lunch counters, public schools, state universities, and many other places black people refused to be cowed by authority, we had a momentum and direction that carried us into the forefront of supportive protest.

Or, as Unitarian Universalist layperson Virginia Volker of Birmingham observed in 1982, it may have been that Unitarian Universalist rhetoric made Unitarian Universalist involvement inescapable.

In short, the core message was crucially important. That message included individual responsibility and supportive community, intellectual belief and principled living, freedom and responsibility, and a valuing of each and every human being. The crucible of rapid, challenging social change in the South clarified the tenets of Unitarian Universalism, both religiously and socially, to most of its adherents.

Along with the core message, its institutional embodiment in fellowships played an important role, combining strengths from the Universalist and the Unitarian traditions—strengths that were uniquely important in the South as these congregations faced more than just the challenge of newness. The fellowship form also overcame weaknesses that each tradition had experienced previously.

Those strengths and weaknesses become clear in light of one writer's typology of religious institutions in the South. He identifies two basic modes of denominational expansion, which he referred to as the Presbyterian and the Baptist.

"Presbyterians" would study and pray over the matter, carefully determine where they should establish a new congregation, and then dispatch a minister to gather people and found a church. This is very much what Unitarians in Boston did when they decided in the first third of the nineteenth century to send a few missionaries to the West: Cincinnati, Louisville, and St. Louis. No comparable Unitarian effort was ever made in the South. In Charleston and New Orleans, strong congregations emerged in other traditions and later identified as Unitarian. When, in the first half of the nineteenth century, Unitarian congregations spontaneously arose in such cities as Savannah, Augusta, and Mobile, either good ministers such as Henry W. Bellows and James Freeman Clarke went there for short-term service, or someone in Boston would recommend a minister who was ailing, inappropriate, or marginal who eventually failed.

In contrast, "Baptists" would do no planning. Baptist congregations appeared wherever someone became inspired, started preaching, and got up a following. There was no process of denominational planning or supervision. New churches just happened. In similar mode, Universalist churches grew up wherever someone lived who embraced the good news of universal salvation. In the often inspiring and sometimes amusing accounts of people reading or reasoning their way to the conviction that God would not condemn people eternally to hell, we see, organizationally, a Baptist story. Itinerating Universalist ministers and missionaries also played a role but seldom stayed in one place for more than a few days, hardly long enough to leave a durable structure in place. As a result, the 1881 Universalist directory shows forty-one congregations in eight Deep South states, while it took Unitarians until 1959 to plant a similar number of congregations there. The problem for Universalism was that the forty-one were not strong, growing congregations in promising locations. They were generally small congregations in or near small towns. One family often served as the dominating and driving force in a given congregation. They were served, often sporadically, by a handful of Universalist circuit-riding ministers.

An organizational key to Unitarian Universalist success in the South in the 1950s and 1960s was a melding in the fellowship movement of the strengths of the Baptist and Presbyterian models. Fellowships were radically democratic and depended on local enthusiasm and skill for ultimate success, much as the small, scattered Universalist groups across the South had for 150 years. But the fellowships had something more going for them, something new and positive: They had a broader connectedness, some foresight in their founding, the support of a continental movement that provided resources and checked on their well-being—an affirming form of the Unitarian style that had previously ignored the South or failed in it. And in the midst of an essentially closed society, these southern fellowships believed in and modeled an openness that in most places was expressed not only theologically but also in saying, no matter the cost, "everyone welcome."

Clearly, the southern growth of the 1950s and 1960s was due to the fellowship movement. The forty-one Unitarian groups in 1958–59 had only eleven ministers among them. Of course, some dedicated, brilliant ministers greatly strengthened what was happening in the congregations: Alfred Hobart, Don Thompson, Albert D'Orlando, Ed Cahill, Charles McGehee, Bob Palmer, Dick Henry, Clif Hoffman, Bob West, and Gene Pickett, among others. But a much longer list of laypeople thought and acted in ways that breached boundaries, challenged shibboleths, and traversed minefields. And those laypeople, a few of whom are named in this narrative, are too little known today, even in the congregations that they animated, served, and challenged in the middle of the last century.

We can also see a theological component to the vitality of these southern congregations. Their values and beliefs were not measurably different from Unitarian Universalists elsewhere in North America. But in the South, living out those beliefs in the larger society was more challenging. Southern Unitarian Universalists were practicing a kind of liberation theology, even though this had not yet been fully formulated in Central and South America, where it developed. The challenges posed to liberal religion by southern society forced southern Unitarian Universalists to move from reflection on and articulation of their beliefs into practical application of them. After this praxis, they had to cycle back to deeper, newly informed reflection on what their beliefs meant in their individual lives and the life of their congregation. Southern society, by opposing many central Unitarian Universalist values, forced southern Unitarian Universalists into a deeper understanding, a clearer formulation, a more passionate embrace of those values—often leading to an active practical expression or embodiment of those values.

And, because fellowships represented the dominant mode of Unitarian Universalist organization in the South in this era, both the praxis and the reflection were practiced predominantly by the laity. When similar pressures were felt in congregations elsewhere on the continent, usually the minister guided or verbalized the praxis-reflection cycle.

Both in southern fellowships and in southern congregations that had ministers, a minority of the members carried out much of the praxis. Many people lacked the inclination, the freedom in their family or work situations, or the considerable courage necessary to speak or act publicly on issues of race and justice. Yet as part of the congregation where the minority who did act could reflect on the praxis, they were part of the praxis-reflection cycle. The congregation provided an accepting context and a supportive framework in which both the activists and those who simply helped them reflect on their actions were part of a process that critiqued and challenged "the way things had always been."

In Central and South America, the primary context for the application of liberation theology has been the base Christian community: a small, lay-led, church-supported, socially involved group of believers gathered for study, worship, and social service. In both the organizational structure and the engaged style of doing theology, we see notable similarities between those base Christian communities and the southern Unitarian Universalist congregations of the 1950s and 1960s.

• • •

The scores of fellowships and the smaller number of church plantings in the South in the 1950s and 1960s were not universally successful. Fellowships sometimes died, as in Hattiesburg and Meridian, Mississippi, never quite achieving critical mass. Some that survived failed to thrive. In Montgomery, Alabama, it took several attempts before a fellowship with staying power was established. But once established, fellowships did seem to have a capacity to identify more with the emerging southern culture than with the old reactionary one.

Longer-established churches, on the other hand, seemed to struggle with adaptation to the changing South. The long-established Unitarian congregations in New Orleans and Charleston suffered agonies as socially conservative members actively resisted change. In Memphis, the newer Unitarian congregation—dating only to the late nineteenth century—experienced strong resistance. Alfred Hobart, who had served in New Orleans and Charleston, writes in a 1959 letter while serving in Birmingham, "All of my churches have been interesting and challenging, but of course this one is very special. Everyone should have the experience of starting a new congregation. These people are really wonderful. They respond to every occasion, and somehow, having served 'old' congregations, it never ceases to surprise and delight me."

As with all generalizations, there are exceptions. In Shreveport, Louisiana, a fellowship organized in 1950 experienced internal struggles between those who wanted to remain a lay-led fellowship and those who wanted to grow to be a church with a minister. To some extent, this fault line also separated those satisfied with the racial status quo from those who wanted to be involved in changing society for the better. When the UUA asked congregations what they had done following the killing of Jim Reeb, Helen Pease, vice chair of the fellowship, sent a copy of the newsletter article she had written. But she also noted that, while she was out of town, another member "preached one of the all-time hateful messages from our pulpit including running down James Reeb."

She opined that due to the "lack of feeling for humanity in our fellowship," she and her husband planned to become inactive in the
next year. Her son reports that his parents did just that, dropping
out for five years or so until an influx of new members changed
congregational dynamics.

• • •

Universalists are not well represented in this story for a variety of
reasons, but perhaps primarily because almost all of their congregations were older, dating from no later than the early twentieth
century. Most were also small, of the scale known as a family-sized
church, and in some instances, members of a single extended family held key offices or had authority even if they held no office. Furthermore, a majority of the southern Universalist congregations
were in rural areas or small towns, which were even less likely than
urban areas to harbor, welcome, or be challenged to face progressive ideas. For example, in 1961 Georgia had four churches of solely
Universalist origin, located in Canon, Senoia, Winder, and Windsor; they reported memberships between twenty and forty-six.

Northern urban Unitarians sometimes were inclined to dismiss
southern Universalists as socially and perhaps religiously conservative or even reactionary. I cannot accept any such blanket categorization, but I concur that some southern Universalists claimed
to be conservative in many respects. The Colemans were one of the
families involved in founding Liberty Universalist Church near
Louisville, Mississippi, in about 1846. A descendent of those early
Universalists was J. P. Coleman, governor of Mississippi, 1956–60,
subsequently a judge on the US Fifth Circuit Court of Appeals,
and undeniably a conservative segregationist. Coleman, although
no longer claiming Universalist membership, was in line with the
state Universalist conventions in the South that supported slavery
prior to the Civil War.

At the same time, there were other, different Universalists.
During the Civil War, Hope Bain was known in North Carolina
to support the Union but was so respected for his integrity that he
continued his Universalist ministry to both Union and Confed-

erate sympathizers. Henry Clay Ledyard was a strong and vigorous progressive voice during and after his Little Rock ministry. In 1944, *Life* magazine devoted a four-page spread to the North Carolina ministry of Gustav Ulrich, described as a "practical idealist who works hard." A photo caption reads, "Though Negroes do not attend his church, Ulrich likes to help them." Emily Bouchillon, a layperson with a Universalist background, bravely removed signs designating race in the waiting areas in the Meridian, Mississippi, welfare office.

The Wrong Side of Murder Creek: A White Southerner in the Freedom Movement, by Bob Zellner, again illustrates the progressive side. Zellner, who grew up in Methodist parsonages in Alabama, was SNCC's first White field secretary. In this memoir, he relates that he began to think consciously about race and class after being hired, at fourteen, to help out in a country store in East Brewton, Alabama. One day, the owner overheard Zellner's interaction with a Black couple and warned him about the practical limits of politeness. He said, "I'm sorry to have to teach you this, but you can get in trouble saying yes sir and no sir to a colored person, and I can get in trouble too. They all know I'm a Unitarian, so I'm in enough trouble already." Actually, there was no Unitarian congregation within eighty miles, so the owner was probably a member of the Brewton Universalist Church, founded in 1883. He continued the conversation, deploring the exploitation of the poor by the rich and the use of racism to divide Black and White and disempower both. He was far from the only Universalist to hold such views, but not all did.

There are many more examples of people who took such actions, just as there are many more examples of segregationists among Universalists.

Universalist churches are underrepresented in these stories. Long-established churches of Unitarian or Universalist background sometimes seemed more in need of being transformed than of being transformative. But these new creatures called fellowships (and the handful of Unitarian or Unitarian/Universalist church plantings started off with ministers) often rose well to the challenges of time and place. Several factors led not only to their survival, but also their success, and sometimes their impact on the wider communities.

When they succeeded, it was often their very newness that helped them to be both religiously and socially relevant. A relatively new congregation could approach issues unburdened by extensive prior institutional accommodation to "the southern way of life." Many of these new congregations consisted of a mix of those brought to the area by job opportunities and southern-born people who had been liberated from a constricted vision of religion and society. Some congregations were mostly "Yankee" and some mostly home grown, but virtually all were blended. And the congregations themselves were new institutions.

These new institutions, as noted earlier, operated in a new format that emphasized personal participation and democratic process. At their best, both the civil rights movement and Unitarian Universalist fellowships were radically democratic, providing them some kinship and perhaps facilitating the participation of some people in both simultaneously. Certainly the emphasis on open, democratic participation contrasted strongly with the values and practices of the "closed society."

The fellowships and churches described here were all predominantly White organizations. The Tampa, Florida, fellowship started in 1955–56 with a significant proportion of Black members, but in subsequent years, moved closer to the usual pattern. Most or all of the other fellowships started with all-White memberships. But those congregations that succeeded in speaking of racial justice as *the* issue of the day in the South either had Black members or had White members who were actively involved in the work of the local Black community. These congregations could not be monolithically White and hope to relate to the Black-led Movement. Many, as a first step, had welcomed Black speakers to their pulpits or forums, at least opening the possibility of an honest dialogue of equals. There were White people in the South who made significant and sacrificial contributions to the movement, but they were followers and supporters in a Black-led cause that sought to liberate all of society from the bonds of oppression. Frequently, these kinds of people could find a spiritually comfortable home in a Unitarian Universalist congregation.

Unitarian Universalist congregations, laypeople, and clergy tend to act as bridges. Our openness to "truth, known or to be known" and to varied expressions of faith and belief predisposes us to converse and work across lines that others find forbidding. In the South of the 1950s and 1960s, this predisposition put Unitarian Universalism at odds with a carefully segmented and segregated society, and put us in service of the civil rights movement and its White allies. It sometimes meant providing a meeting place where both Black and White people knew they were welcome. Over and over, it expressed itself as being the first local White congregation open to Black members, or the location and organizing force of a pioneering interracial preschool. Where clergy were involved, the bridging involved mutually supportive relations among a wondrous array of rabbis, ministers, and priests.

How lovely for the reputation of Unitarian Universalism if we could cite social and ecclesiological analysis on our part in the 1930s and 1940s that foresaw the coming seismic changes in southern society and carefully devised appropriate messages and institutional forms to address those changes constructively and prophetically. But this would be a charming fiction. Our theology was what it had evolved to be. The fellowship format was what Unitarianism and Universalism could afford to do coming out of the Great Depression and World War II. Yet, the ideas and tools of these religious liberals helped advance freedom, justice, openness, and human dignity in southern society. Even though Unitarian Universalists were a tiny fraction of the southern population, they played a much larger role than their numbers would suggest in offering a prophetic witness to the South.

REVELATION: WHAT WE CAN LEARN
FROM WHAT WE DID

One function Unitarian Universalist congregations provided in the South of the civil rights era was to provide a safe place to decompress and to process. The reflection phase of praxis-reflection could be far more than an intellectual exercise. It could be an emotional necessity. If you were a housewife who had just taken part in a sit-in, or a high school student ostracized at school for supporting desegregation, or a businessperson suddenly fired or demoted because of speaking publicly for civil rights, where could you go for support? Certainly not to the circles of "friends" who now avoided you, and perhaps not even to many family members. Emotionally, you would need to feel accepted, and, ideally, affirmed and embraced. While some Black civil rights participants were called troublemakers and got the cold shoulder from a few neighbors and co-workers, many others close to them honored their courage and accomplishments. White civil rights participants, on the other hand, could feel uniquely isolated unless they lived within a context like a Unitarian Universalist congregation.

Extreme stress, especially when it cannot be openly admitted and discussed, can result in post-traumatic stress disorder (PTSD). Particularly harmful is the stress that some people might say "you brought on yourself." Today, we mostly hear about PTSD regarding military veterans. Participants in the movement are veterans of a different type—veterans with no Veterans Administration to care for them, to help them deal with the emotional and sometimes physical violence they witnessed and perhaps endured.

They too can be affected by PTSD. However, I have observed that when people openly discuss stressful incidents and receive support in response, they sometimes experience not PTSD but PTSG: post-traumatic stress growth. Within a generally supportive context, such as a Unitarian Universalist congregation may provide, the strains and stresses imposed by a repressive social system may be reinterpreted and understood in a way that brings personal growth rather than disorder and dysfunction.

Looking back at the stories shared here, we see over and over again that the local congregation provided a context of support for those who acted. In Birmingham and Charlotte, in Jackson and Huntsville, in cities all across the South, terms such as *a safe place*, *a refuge*, and *an oasis* describe the role a Unitarian Universalist congregation could play, even if imperfectly.

This congregational role was perhaps uniquely urgent in the South in the 1950s and 1960s, but it remains important widely today and in days to come. Everyone, especially those who are idealistic and socially engaged, will inevitably encounter stressful situations. If their religious home affirms their ideals and willingly hears their stories of confronting injustice, they will have a context in which to constructively identify and process their stressors. They will be able to learn from those stressors and will be less likely to succumb to them. They will be able to reflect on and learn from their attempts to live out their ideals. And as they share with others, those others will also be able to learn from their praxis and their reflection.

On the other hand, a religious community that does not encourage its members to act on the basis of their beliefs will have fewer people bringing back experiences that engender deep reflection. In addition, a religious community that offers few contexts for deep sharing and reflection is not likely to meet the needs of some of its most vital members.

Healthy, engaged, constructive religious communities come in a variety of sizes. Size can matter; congregations so small that they constantly teeter on the edge of dissolution are unlikely to have the capacity to do much or to facilitate their members being socially engaged. But many of the religious communities whose stories we have visited were not large. Even in congregations with membership numbers in the hundreds, a great portion of the most engaged social justice work was carried out by a relatively small subset. And sometimes large membership numbers can diminish rather than increase social engagement, either by focusing narrowly inward on congregational issues, or by delegating social engagement to church staff rather than involving members.

The size of the religious community mattered less than its essence. If the congregation understood itself as a religious community existing and working in a societal context, its members actively noticed what was going on in the wider community and found places to live out their values. We have explored stories of both institutions and individuals because both are important. The institution set a tone, established an outlook and a range of expectations. Often, individuals responded to those messages by taking action, empowered and enabled by the institution.

It was not only the congregations that were small. The Unitarian Universalist population in the South overall was relatively minuscule. Still, this did not prevent this group from contributing to the changes of the civil rights era. A civil rights historian and I once agreed that one could write a history of the civil rights movement without using the words *Unitarian Universalist*. And yet, one could not write a detailed history that excluded individuals who identified as Unitarian Universalist. Furthermore, to get the full texture of that era, one would have to concede that Unitarian Universalist institutions often played a role, even if one somehow tiptoed around naming those institutions. Unitarian Universalists and their institutions functioned primarily as adjuncts to the Black-led freedom struggle, but few if any other majority-White religious institutions were as deeply involved in and affected by that struggle.

• • •

We may devoutly hope and should doggedly work to avoid a return to the repressive social conditions of the South in the 1950s and 1960s. We should praise the notable gifts of the Unitarian Universalist fellowship movement, while noting its accompanying weaknesses and dysfunctions. We cannot re-create or re-live the era in which witness, in the form of Unitarian Universalist belief and practice (among other forms), was provided in the South. Instead, we can learn from the Unitarian Universalist experience of that era. We can learn the value of articulating and applying our values. We can strive for a praxis that can inform our reflection, and reflection that may goad us into praxis. We can learn that an informed and empowered laity is an awesome force. We can learn that having a racially inclusive constituency is important to the health, well-being, and relevance of a congregation. We can learn that we need not only to build bridges, but also to *be* a bridging institution, wherever we exist. We can learn that it is healthy to keep ourselves fresh and new, rather than to unconsciously accommodate the environing society. We can learn that it matters what we believe and how we organize ourselves.

We need to learn to hold up as exemplars not only the White male Universalist and Unitarian pulpit giants of the nineteenth century. We need to remember the small acts of great courage that came from women, men, and children all across the South in outposts of liberal religion in the middle of the twentieth century. They are closer to us in time and in situation than Channing and Parker, Murray and Ballou.

Our day, no less than the civil rights era of the 1950s and 1960s, contains challenges to core Unitarian Universalist values and beliefs. Today's challenges may be less clear-cut, more multi-faceted, but they are no less real. Can we, laypeople and clergy, be as effective today at carrying our faith into society for service and action? Can we today bring our experiences back into our sanctuaries for reflection and deepening? If not, what must we do to change ourselves and our institutions?

One thing we must not do is to reflect on these stories with pride that we have done so much. Rather, these stories must lead us to understand that we have so much to do.

ABBREVIATIONS

AUA—American Unitarian Association

BAC—Black Affairs Council

COFO—Council of Federated Organizations

CORE—Congress of Racial Equality

NAACP—National Association for the Advancement of Colored People

NDPA—National Democratic Party of Alabama

SCEF—Southern Conference Education Fund

SNCC—Student Nonviolent Coordinating Committee

UCA—Universalist Church of America

USC—Unitarian Service Committee

UUA—Unitarian Universalist Association

UUSC—Unitarian Universalist Service Committee

ACKNOWLEDGMENTS

This book could not have been written without the support, advice, and cooperation of many people. Most of those who granted interviews are named in the text and their words quoted or paraphrased. In the course of conducting research, especially on my sabbatical in 2000, my way was made easier by many generous hosts and hostesses.

It could go without saying, but it won't, that family support has been crucial. My late parents laid much of the groundwork for my interests and commitments. My wife, Judy, has been supportive, encouraging, and tolerant of my foibles, as have our daughters.

It has been a delight to have the intellectual companionship of Mark Morrison-Reed as he worked on *The Selma Awakening* while I worked on this book. Mark specializes in asking good questions, and so I was always pleased when one of his emails arrived.

Three institutions should be mentioned. The Unitarian Universalist Fellowship of Elkhart, Indiana, provided two sabbaticals which afforded me time for historical research, including significant parts of the work reflected here. Board meetings of the Unitarian Universalist Historical Society (now the Unitarian Universalist History and Heritage Society) gave me opportunities to be in the Boston area where I could delve into the Unitarian Universalist Association records overseen by John Hurley and his staff. My colleagues in the Living Legacy Project have deepened my feeling that these stories are among those that are important opportunities for learning about justice, beloved community, and the potential of Unitarian Universalism.

Finally, it is vital to acknowledge that there are individuals and institutions whose stories are not here. If we had started actively collecting these stories decades earlier, we would have avoided the perils of mortality and fading memories. But there are still people out there to talk with, and files to be located and read. May those pursuits, and correcting errors that crept into this narrative, be your work.

INDEX

Please note that the book is organized by city and state. This index does not duplicate information provided in the table of contents indicating the pages that address the cities that are the topics of their respective chapters.